WebRTC Integrator's Guide

Successfully build your very own scalable WebRTC infrastructure quickly and efficiently

Altanai

BIRMINGHAM - MUMBAI

WebRTC Integrator's Guide

First published: October 2014

Production reference: 1251014

Published by Packt Publishing Ltd.
Livery Place
35 Livery Street
Birmingham B3 2PB, UK.

ISBN 978-1-78398-126-7

www.packtpub.com

Cover image by Gagandeep Sharma (er.gagansharma@gmail.com)

Credits

Author
Altanai

Reviewers
Alessandro Arrichiello
Pasquale Boemio
Antón Román Portabales
Andrii Sergiienko

Commissioning Editor
Usha Iyer

Acquisition Editor
Llewellyn Rozario

Content Development Editor
Akashdeep Kundu

Technical Editor
Menza Mathew

Copy Editors
Karuna Narayanan
Laxmi Subramanian

Project Coordinator
Neha Thakur

Proofreaders
Jenny Blake
Stephen Copestake
Maria Gould
Joel T. Johnson

Indexers
Hemangini Bari
Mariammal Chettiyar
Rekha Nair

Graphics
Ronak Dhruv
Valentina D'silva
Disha Haria
Abhinash Sahu

Production Coordinators
Adonia Jones
Nitesh Thakur

Cover Work
Nitesh Thakur

About the Author

Altanai, born into an Indian army family, is a bubbly, vivacious, intelligent computer geek. She is an avid blogger and writes on Research and Development of evolving technologies in Telecom (http://altanaitelecom.wordpress.com).

She holds a Bachelor's degree in Information Technology from Anna University, Chennai. She has worked on many Telecom projects worldwide, specifically in the development and deployment of IMS services. She firmly believes in contributing to the Open Source community and is currently working on building a WebRTC-based JS library with books for more applications.

Her hobbies include photography, martial arts, oil canvas painting, river rafting, horse riding, and trekking, to name a few.

This is her first book, and it contains useful insight into WebRTC for beginners and integrator in this field. The book has definitions and explanations that will cover many interesting concepts in a clear manner.

Altanai can be contacted at tara181989@gmail.com.

About the Reviewers

Alessandro Arrichiello is a computer enthusiast. He graduated in Computer Engineering from the University of Naples Federico II, Italy.

He has a passion for and knowledge of GNU/Linux systems that began at age of 14 and continues today. He is an independent Android developer, who develops apps for Google Play Store, and has strong knowledge of C++, Java, and other derivatives. He also has experience with many other interpreted languages such as Perl, PHP, and Python.

Alessandro is a proud open source supporter and has given his contribution to many collaborative projects developed for academic purposes.

Recently, he enriched his knowledge on Network Monitoring, focusing on Penetration Testing and Network Security in general.

At the moment, Alessandro is working as a software engineer in the Communications and Media Solution group of Hewlett Packard in Milan, Italy. He's involved in many business projects as a developer and technology consultant.

Alessandro has worked as a reviewer and author for Packt Publishing. He has technically reviewed the book, *WebRTC Blueprints*, and now, he's working on a video course on developing an application using the WebRTC technology.

Pasquale Boemio fell in love with Linux and the open source philosophy at the age of 12. He has a Master's degree in Computer Engineering, and he works as a researcher at the Computer Engineering department of the University of Naples Federico II, Italy. At the same time, he collaborates with Meetecho (`www.meetecho.com`), experimenting with a large number of innovative technologies such as WebRTC, Docker, and Node.js.

Even though Pasquale is involved in such activities, he still releases free software on GitHub (`www.github.com/helloIAmPau`).

Antón Román Portabales is the CTO of Quobis. After graduating as a telecommunications engineer, he began working in Motorola as an IMS developer. In 2008, he left Motorola to join Quobis, a Spanish company focused on SIP interconnection. It works for major operators and companies in Europe and South America. In 2010, he finished a Pre-PhD program in Telematics Engineering as the main author of a paper about the use of IMS networks to transmit real-time data from the electrical grid; he presented this paper in an IEEE conference in 2011.

He has been actively working on WebRTC since 2012, when Quobis decided to focus on this technology. He has recently got involved in the activities of IETF, along with other colleagues from Quobis. He also frequently participates in VoIP-related open source events.

Andrii Sergiienko is an entrepreneur who's passionate about IT and also about travelling. He has lived in different places, such as Ukraine, Russia, Belarus, Mongolia, Buryatia, and Siberia, spending a considerable number of years in every place. He also likes to travel by an auto rickshaw.

From his early childhood, Andrii was interested in computer programming and hardware. He took the first steps in this field more than 20 years ago. Andrii has experience in a wide set of languages and technologies, including C, C++, Java, Assembler, Erlang, JavaScript, PHP, Riak, shell scripting, computer networks, security, and so on.

During his career, Andrii has worked for both small, local companies, such as domestic ISP; and large world corporations, such as Hewlett Packard. He also started his own companies; some of them were relatively successful, while others were a total failure.

Today, Andrii is working on growing Oslikas, his company, headquartered in Estonia. The company is focused on modern IT technologies and solutions. They also develop a full-stack framework to create rich media WebRTC applications and services. You can find them at `http://www.oslikas.com`.

www.PacktPub.com

Support files, eBooks, discount offers, and more

You might want to visit www.PacktPub.com for support files and downloads related to your book.

Did you know that Packt offers eBook versions of every book published, with PDF and ePub files available? You can upgrade to the eBook version at www.PacktPub.com and as a print book customer, you are entitled to a discount on the eBook copy. Get in touch with us at service@packtpub.com for more details.

At www.PacktPub.com, you can also read a collection of free technical articles, sign up for a range of free newsletters and receive exclusive discounts and offers on Packt books and eBooks.

http://PacktLib.PacktPub.com

Do you need instant solutions to your IT questions? PacktLib is Packt's online digital book library. Here, you can access, read and search across Packt's entire library of books.

Why subscribe?

- Fully searchable across every book published by Packt
- Copy and paste, print and bookmark content
- On demand and accessible via web browser

Free access for Packt account holders

If you have an account with Packt at www.PacktPub.com, you can use this to access PacktLib today and view nine entirely free books. Simply use your login credentials for immediate access.

Table of Contents

Preface

WebRTC Integrator's Guide is a deep dive into the world of real-time telecommunication and its integration with the telecom network. This book covers a wide range of WebRTC solutions, such as GSM, PSTN, and IMS, designed for specific network requirement. It also addresses the implementation woes by describing every minute detail of the WebRTC platform setup from the APIs to the architecture, code-to-server installations, RCS-to-Codec interoperability, and much more. It also describes various enterprise-based use cases that can be built around WebRTC.

What this book covers

Chapter 1, Running WebRTC with and without SIP, is a quick brush-up of WebRTC basics such as Media APIs. It also describes the use of plain WebSocket signaling to deliver WebRTC-based browser-to-browser communication.

Chapter 2, Making a Standalone WebRTC Communication Client, talks about the use of the Session Initiation Protocol (SIP) as the signaling mechanism for WebRTC. It describes the setup of the SIP server for this purpose.

Chapter 3, WebRTC with SIP and IMS, outlines the interaction of a SIP-based WebRTC client with the IP Multimedia Subsystem (IMS).

Chapter 4, WebRTC Integration with Intelligent Network, describes the ways in which WebRTC can be made interoperable with mobile phones, as the majority of mobile communications today are still on GSM under the IN model.

Chapter 5, WebRTC Integration with PSTN, describes the backward compatibility of the WebRTC technology to the old, fixed-line telephones.

Chapter 6, Basic Features of WebRTC over SIP, describes the basic WebRTC SIP services such as audio/video call, messaging, call transfer, call hold/resume, and others.

Chapter 7, WebRTC with Industry Standard Frameworks, discusses the development of the WebRTC client over the industry-adopted framework (that is, Model-View-Controller).

Chapter 8, WebRTC and Rich Communication Services, discusses how RCS enriches the communication technology with features such as file transfer, Presence, phonebook, and others.

Chapter 9, Native SIP Application and Interaction with WebRTC Clients, addresses a very important concern, that is, the WebRTC interoperability with other SIP endpoints such as desktop clients, SIP hardphones, and mobile-based SIP applications.

Chapter 10, Other WebRTC Use Cases, presents an interesting array of WebRTC use cases that are both innovative and practical with the current WebRTC standards.

What you need for this book

A brief understanding of SIP is required to set up the operation environment. It is recommended that you use Linux, as it supports the installation of many open source components described in the book. Web development skills are required to make the WebRTC web-based application using HTML and browser APIs. It is recommended that you use the Eclipse IDE for client-side development, as depicted in many screenshots provided in the book. To host the applications, any web server, such as Apache, will do.

Who this book is for

Web developers, SIP application developers, and IMS experts can use this book to develop and deploy a customized, readily deployable WebRTC platform. The use cases described in the book cater to WebRTC integration in any industry segment. Therefore, anyone with basic knowledge of HTML and JavaScript can develop a WebRTC client after referring to this book.

Conventions

In this book, you will find a number of styles of text that distinguish between different kinds of information. Here are some examples of these styles, and an explanation of their meaning.

Code words in text, database table names, folder names, filenames, file extensions, pathnames, dummy URLs, user input, and Twitter handles are shown as follows: "We saw how to program the three basic APIs of WebRTC media stack namely, `getUserMedia`, `RTCPeerConnection`, and `DataChannel`."

A block of code is set as follows:

```
public class loginServlet extends HttpServlet {
  public loginServlet() {
    super();
  }
  ...
```

Any command-line input or output is written as follows:

```
ws://ns313841.ovh.net:10060/
Request Method:
GET
Status Code:
101 Switching Protocols
```

New terms and **important words** are shown in bold. Words that you see on the screen, in menus or dialog boxes for example, appear in the text like this: "As peer 1 keys in the message and hits the **Send** button, the message is passed on to peer 2."

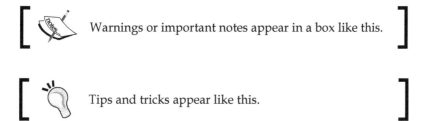

Warnings or important notes appear in a box like this.

Tips and tricks appear like this.

Reader feedback

Feedback from our readers is always welcome. Let us know what you think about this book—what you liked or may have disliked. Reader feedback is important for us to develop titles that you really get the most out of.

To send us general feedback, simply send an e-mail to `feedback@packtpub.com`, and mention the book title via the subject of your message.

If there is a topic that you have expertise in and you are interested in either writing or contributing to a book, see our author guide on `www.packtpub.com/authors`.

Customer support

Now that you are the proud owner of a Packt book, we have a number of things to help you to get the most from your purchase.

Downloading the example code

You can download the example code files for all Packt books you have purchased from your account at `http://www.packtpub.com`. If you purchased this book elsewhere, you can visit `http://www.packtpub.com/support` and register to have the files e-mailed directly to you.

Downloading the color images of this book

We also provide you a PDF file that has color images of the screenshots/diagrams used in this book. The color images will help you better understand the changes in the output. You can download this file from: `https://www.packtpub.com/sites/default/files/downloads/12670S_ColoredImages.pdf`.

Errata

Although we have taken every care to ensure the accuracy of our content, mistakes do happen. If you find a mistake in one of our books—maybe a mistake in the text or the code—we would be grateful if you would report this to us. By doing so, you can save other readers from frustration and help us improve subsequent versions of this book. If you find any errata, please report them by visiting `http://www.packtpub.com/submit-errata`, selecting your book, clicking on the **errata submission form** link, and entering the details of your errata. Once your errata are verified, your submission will be accepted and the errata will be uploaded on our website, or added to any list of existing errata, under the Errata section of that title. Any existing errata can be viewed by selecting your title from `http://www.packtpub.com/support`.

Piracy

Piracy of copyright material on the Internet is an ongoing problem across all media. At Packt, we take the protection of our copyright and licenses very seriously. If you come across any illegal copies of our works, in any form, on the Internet, please provide us with the location address or website name immediately so that we can pursue a remedy.

Please contact us at `copyright@packtpub.com` with a link to the suspected pirated material.

We appreciate your help in protecting our authors, and our ability to bring you valuable content.

Questions

You can contact us at `questions@packtpub.com` if you are having a problem with any aspect of the book, and we will do our best to address it.

1
Running WebRTC with and without SIP

WebRTC lets us make calls right from a web page without any plugin. This was made possible using media APIs of the browser to fetch user media, WebSocket for transportation, and HTML5 to render the media on the web page. Thus, WebRTC is an evolved form of WebSocket communication. WebSocket is a Transport Layer protocol that carries data. The WebSocket API is an **Application Programming Interface (API)** that enables web pages to use the WebSocket protocol for (duplex) communication with a remote host.

In this chapter, we will study how WebRTC really works. We will also demonstrate the use of WebRTC media APIs to capture and render input from a user's microphone and camera onto a web page. In the later part of chapter, we will find out how to build a simple standalone WebRTC client using the plain WebSocket protocol as the signaling mechanism.

JavaScript Session Establishment Protocol (JSEP)

The communication model between a client and remote host is based on the JSEP architecture, which differentiates the signaling and media transaction into different layers.

The differentiation is shown in the following figure:

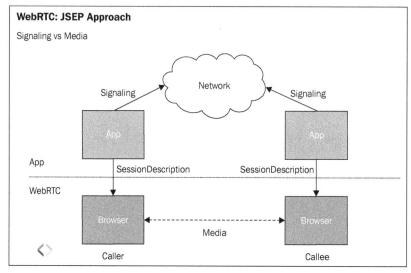

JSEP signaling and media

As an example, let's consider two peers, A and B, where A initiates communication with B. Initially, in the first case, A being the offerer will have to call the `createOffer` function to begin a session. A also mentions details such as codecs through a `setLocalDescription` function, which sets up its local config. The remote party, B, reads the offer and stores it using the `setRemoteDescription` function. The remote party, B, calls the `createAnswer` function to generate an appropriate answer, applies it using the `setLocalDescription` function, and sends the answer back to the initiator over the signaling channel. When A gets the answer, it also stores it using the `setRemoteDescription` function, and the initial setup is complete. This is repeated for multiple offers and answers. The latest on JSEP specifications can be read from the **Internet Engineering Task Force (IETF)** site at `http://datatracker. ietf.org/doc/draft-ietf-rtcweb-jsep/`.

Signal and media flows

The differentiation between signal and media flows is an important aspect of the WebRTC call setup.

The signaling mechanism can be any among HTTP/REST, **JavaScript Object Notation (JSON)** via **XMLHttpRequest (XHR)**, **Session Initiation Protocol (SIP)** over websockets, XMPP, or any custom or proprietary protocol. The media (audio/video) is defined through the **Session Description Protocol (SDP)** and flows from peer to peer.

A few instances of end-to-end signaling and media flow variants are shown in the following screenshot:

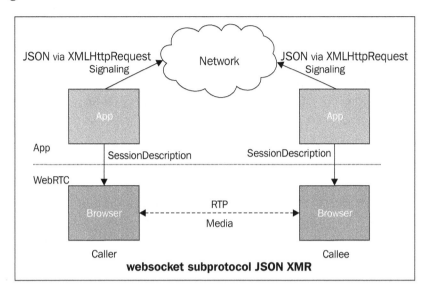

The preceding figure depicts signaling over the WebRTC API in the JSON format via XHR.

Now, the following figure depicts signaling over the WebRTC API in **eXtensible Messaging and Presence Protocol (XMPP)**:

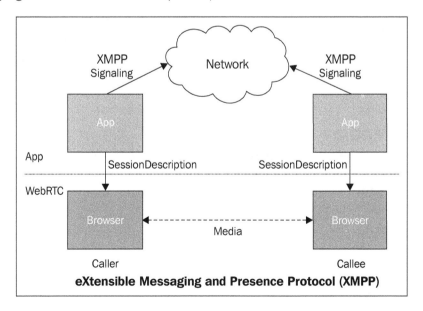

While it's very popular to use the WebRTC API with SIP support through JavaScript libraries such as JSSIP, SIPML5, PJSIP, and so on, these libraries cater to the SIP/IMS (IP Multimedia Subsystem) world and are not mandatory for setting up enterprise-level WebRTC Infrastructure. In fact, it is a misconception that WebRTC is coupled with SIP in itself; it isn't.

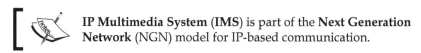 **IP Multimedia System (IMS)** is part of the **Next Generation Network** (NGN) model for IP-based communication.

Running WebRTC without SIP

HTML5 websockets can be defined by `ws://` followed by the URL in the server field while readying a WebRTC client for registration. This enables bidirectional, duplex communications with server-side processes, that is, server-side push events to the client. It also enables the handshake after sharing media metadata such as ports, codecs, and so on.

It should be noted that WebRTC works in an offer/answer mode and has ways of traversing the **Network Address Translation (NAT)** and firewalls by means of **Interactive Connectivity Establishment (ICE)**. ICE makes use of the **Session Traversal Utilities for NAT (STUN)** protocol and its extension, **Traversal Using Relay NAT (TURN)**. This is covered later in the chapter.

Sending media over WebSockets

WebRTC mainly comprises three operations: fetching user media from a camera/microphone, transmitting media over a channel, and sending messages over the channel. Now, let's take a look at the summarized description of every operation type.

getUserMedia

The JavaScript `getUserMedia` function (also known as `MediaStream`) is used to allow the web page to access users' media devices such as camera and microphone using the browser's native API, without the need of any other third-party plugins such as Adobe Flash and Microsoft Silverlight.

For simple demos of these methods, download the WebRTC read-only by executing the following command:

```
svn checkout http://webrtc.googlecode.com/svn/trunk/
webrtc-read-only
```

The following is the code to access the IP camera in the Google Chrome browser and display the local video in a `<video/>` element:

```
/*The HTML to define a button to begin the capture and HTML5 video
element on web page body */
<video id="vid" autoplay="true"></video>
<button id="btn" onclick="start()">Start</button>


/*The JavaScript block contains the following function call to start
the media capture using Chrome browser's getUserMedia function*/
video = document.getElementById("vid");
function start() {
  navigator.webkitGetUserMedia({video:true}, gotStream,
    function() {});
  btn.disabled = true;
}


/*The function to add the media stream to a video element on a page*/
  function gotStream(stream) {
  video.src = webkitURL.createObjectURL(stream);
}
```

 When the browser tries to access media devices such as a camera and mic from users, there is always a browser notification that asks for the user's permission.

 Downloading the example code

You can download the example code files for all Packt books you have purchased from your account at http://www.packtpub.com. If you purchased this book elsewhere, you can visit http://www.packtpub.com/support and register to have the files e-mailed directly to you

The following screenshot depicts the user notification for granting permission to access the camera in Google Chrome:

The following screenshot depicts the user notification for granting permission to access the camera in Mozilla Firefox:

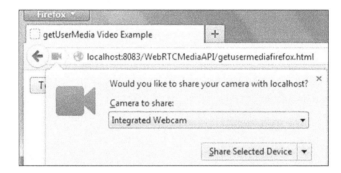

The following screenshot depicts the user notification for granting permission to access the camera in Opera:

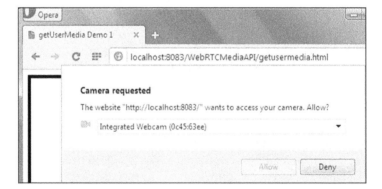

RTCPeerConnection

In WebRTC, media traverses in a peer-to-peer fashion and is necessary to exchange information prior to setting up a communication path such as public IP and open ports. It is also necessary to know about the peer's codecs, their settings, bandwidth, and media types.

To make the peer connection, we will need a function to populate the values of the RTCPeerConnection, getUserMedia, attachMediaStream, and reattachMediaStream parameters. Due to the fact that the WebRTC standard is currently under development, the JavaScript API can change from one implementation to another. So, a web developer has to configure the RTCPeerConnection, getUserMedia, attachMediaStream, and reattachMediaStream variables in accordance to the browser on which we are running the HTML content.

 It is noted that WebRTC standards are in rapid evolution. The API that was used for the first version of WebRTC was the PeerConnection API, which had distinct methods for media transmission. As of now, the old PeerConnection API has been deprecated and a new enhanced version is under process. The new Media API has replaced the media streams handling in the old PeerConnection API.

The browser APIs of different browsers have different names. The criterion is to determine the browser on which the web page is opened and then call the appropriate function for the WebRTC operation. The identity of the browser can be determined by extracting a friendly name or checking for a match with a specific library name of the different browser. For example, when navigator.webkitGetUserMedia is true, then WebRTCDetectedBrowser = "chrome", and when navigator.mozGetUserMedia is true, then WebRTCDetectedBrowser = "firefox". The following table shows the W3C standard elements in Google Chrome and Mozilla Firefox:

W3C Standard	Chrome	Firefox
getUserMedia	webkitGetUserMedia	mozGetUserMedia
RTCPeerConnection	webkitRTCPeerConnection	mozRTCPeerConnection
RTCSessionDescription	RTCSessionDescription	mozRTCSessionDescription
RTCIceCandidate	RTCIceCandidate	mozRTCIceCandidate

Such methods also exist for Opera, which is a new addition to the WebRTC suite. Hopefully, Internet Explorer, in the future, would have native support for WebRTC standards. For other browsers such as Safari that don't support WebRTC as yet, there are temporary plugins that help capture and display the media elements, which can be used until these browsers release their own enhanced WebRTC supported versions. Creating WebRTC-compatible clients in Internet Explorer and Safari is discussed in *Chapter 9, Native SIP Application and Interaction with WebRTC Clients.*

The following code snippet is used to make an RTC peer connection and render videos from one HTML video frame to another on the same web page. The library file, `adapter.js`, is used, which renders the polyfill functionality to different browsers such as Mozilla Firefox and Google Chrome.

The HTML body content that includes two video elements for the local and remote videos, the text status area, and three buttons to start capturing, sending, and stop receiving the stream are given as follows:

```
<video id="vid1" autoplay="true" muted="true"></video>
<video id="vid2" autoplay></video>
<button id="btn1" onclick="start()">Start</button>
<button id="btn2" onclick="call()">Call</button>
<button id="btn3" onclick="hangup()">Hang Up</button>
<xtextarea id="ta1"></textarea>
<xtextarea id="ta2"></textarea>
```

The JavaScript program to transmit media from the video element to another at the click of the **Start** button, using the WebRTC API is given as follows:

```
/* setting the value of start, call and hangup to false initially*/
btn1.disabled = false;
btn2.disabled = true;
btn3.disabled = true;

/* declaration of global variables for peerconecection 1 and 2, local
streams, sdp constrains */
var pc1, pc2;
var localstream;
var sdpConstraints = {'mandatory': {
                        'OfferToReceiveAudio':true,
                        'OfferToReceiveVideo':true }};
```

The following code snippet is the definition of the function that will get the user media for the camera and microphone input from the user:

```
function start() {
  btn1.disabled = true;
  getUserMedia({audio:true, video:true},
  /* get audio and video capture */
  gotStream, function() {});
}
```

The following code snippet is the definition of the function that will attach an input stream to the local video section and enable the call button:

```
function gotStream(stream){
   attachMediaStream(vid1, stream);
   localstream = stream;/* ready to call the peer*/
btn2.disabled = false;
}
```

The following code snippet is the function call to stream the video and audio content to the peer using RTCPeerConnection:

```
function call() {
   btn2.disabled = true;
   btn3.disabled = false;
   videoTracks = localstream.getVideoTracks();
   audioTracks = localstream.getAudioTracks();
   var servers = null;

   pc1 = new RTCPeerConnection(servers);/* peer1 connection to server
*/
   pc1.onicecandidate = iceCallback1;
   pc2 = new RTCPeerConnection(servers);/* peer2 connection to server
*/

   pc2.onicecandidate = iceCallback2;
   pc2.onaddstream = gotRemoteStream;
   pc1.addStream(localstream);
   pc1.createOffer(gotDescription1);
}

function gotDescription1(desc){/* getting SDP from offer by peer2 */
pc1.setLocalDescription(desc);
pc2.setRemoteDescription(desc);
pc2.createAnswer(gotDescription2, null, sdpConstraints);
}

function gotDescription2(desc){/* getting SDP from answer by peer1 */
pc2.setLocalDescription(desc);
pc1.setRemoteDescription(desc);
}
```

On clicking the **Hang Up** button, the following function closes both of the peer connections:

```
function hangup() {
  pc1.close();
  pc2.close();
  pc1 = null; /* peer1 connection to server closed */
  pc2 = null; /* peer2 connection to server closed */
  btn3.disabled = true; /* disables the Hang Up button */
  btn2.disabled = false; /*enables the Call button */
}
function gotRemoteStream(e){
  vid2.src = webkitURL.createObjectURL(e.stream);
}
function iceCallback1(event){
  if (event.candidate) {
    pc2.addIceCandidate(new RTCIceCandidate(event.candidate));
  }
}
function iceCallback2(event){
  if (event.candidate) {
    pc1.addIceCandidate(new RTCIceCandidate(event.candidate));
  }
}
```

In the preceding example, JSON/XHR (XMLHttpRequest) is the signaling mechanism. Both the peers, that is, the sender and receiver, are present on the same web page; this is represented by the two video elements shown in the following screenshot. They are currently in the noncommunicating state.

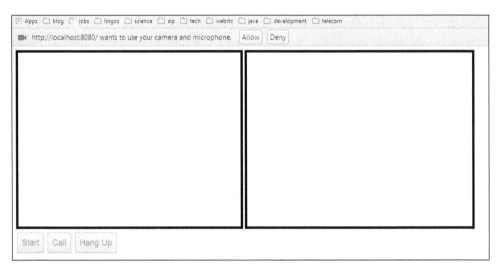

As soon as the **Start** button is hit, the user's microphone and camera begin to capture. The first peer is presented with the browser request to use their camera and microphone. After allowing the browser request, the first peer's media is successfully captured from their system and displayed on the screen. This is demonstrated in the following screenshot:

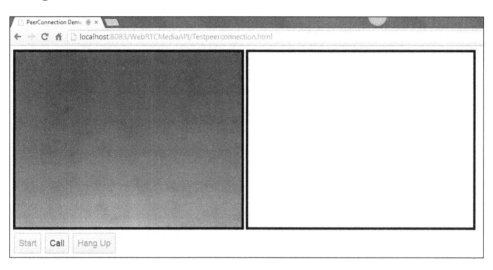

As soon as the user hits the **Call** button, the captured media stream is shared in the session with the second peer, who can view it on their own video element. The following screenshot depicts the two peers sharing a video stream:

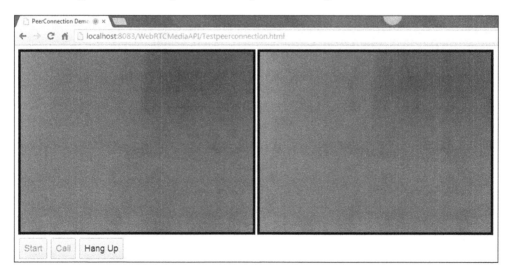

The session can be discontinued by clicking on the **Hang Up** button.

RTCDataChannel

The DataChannel function is used to exchange text messages by creating a bidirectional data channel between two peers. The following is the code to demonstrate the working of RTCDataChannel.

The following code snippet is the HTML body of the code for the DataChannel function. It consists of a text area for the two peers to view the messages and three buttons to start the session, send the message, and stop receiving messages.

```
<div id="left">
<br>
<h2>Send data</h2>
<textarea id="dataChannelSend" rows="5" cols="15"
  disabled="true">
</textarea>
<br>
<button id="startButton" onclick="createConnection()">
  Start</button>
<button id="sendButton" onclick="sendData()">Send Data</button>
<button id="closeButton" onclick="closeDataChannels()">
  Stop Send Data
</button>
<br>
</div>
<div id="right">
<br>
<h2>Received Data</h2>
<textarea id="dataChannelReceive" rows="5" cols="15"
  disabled="true">
</textarea><br>
</div>
```

The style script for the text area is given as follows; to differentiate between the two peers, we place one text area aligned to the right and another to the left:

```
#left { position: absolute; left: 0; top: 0; width: 50%; }
#right { position: absolute; right: 0; top: 0; width: 50%; }
```

The JavaScript block that contains the functions to make the session and transmit the data is given as follows:

```
/*Declaring global parameters for both sides' peerconnection, sender,
and receiver channel*/
var pc1, pc2, sendChannel, receiveChannel;
```

```
/*Only enable the Start button, keep the send data and stop send data
button off*/
startButton.disabled = false;
sendButton.disabled = true;
closeButton.disabled = true;
```

The following code snippet is the script to create `PeerConnection` in Google
Chrome, that is, `webkitRTCPeerConnection` that was seen in the previous table.
It is noted that a user needs to have Google Chrome Version 25 or higher to test
this code. Some old Chrome versions are also required to set the `--enable-data-
channels` flag to the enabled state before using the `DataChannel` functions.

```
function createConnection() {
  var servers = null;
  pc1 = new webkitRTCPeerConnection(servers,{
    optional: [{RtpDataChannels: true}]});
    try {
      sendChannel = pc1.createDataChannel("sendDataChannel", {
        reliable: false});
    } catch (e) {
      alert('Failed to create data channel.' +
        'You need Chrome M25 or later with
          --enable-data-channels flag'););
    }

  pc1.onicecandidate = iceCallback1;
  sendChannel.onopen = onSendChannelStateChange;
  sendChannel.onclose = onSendChannelStateChange;
  pc2 = new webkitRTCPeerConnection(servers,{
    optional: [{RtpDataChannels: true}]});

  pc2.onicecandidate = iceCallback2;
  pc2.ondatachannel = receiveChannelCallback;

  pc1.createOffer(gotDescription1);
  startButton.disabled = true; /*since session is up,
    disable start button */
  closeButton.disabled = false;  /*enable close button */
}
```

The following function is used to invoke the `sendChannel.send` function along with
user text to send data across the data channel:

```
function sendData() {
  var data = document.getElementById("dataChannelSend").value;
  sendChannel.send(data);
}
```

The following function calls the `sendChannel.close()` and `receiveChannel.close()` functions to terminate the data channel connection:

```
function closeDataChannels() {
sendChannel.close();
receiveChannel.close();
pc1.close();        /* peer1 connection to server closed */
pc2.close();        /* peer2 connection to server closed */

  pc1 = null;
  pc2 = null;
startButton.disabled = false;
sendButton.disabled = true;
closeButton.disabled = true;
document.getElementById("dataChannelSend").value = "";
document.getElementById("dataChannelReceive").value = "";
document.getElementById("dataChannelSend").disabled = true;
}
```

Peer connection 1 sets the local description, and peer connection 2 sets the remote description from the SDP exchanged, and the answer is created:

```
function gotDescription1(desc) {
  pc1.setLocalDescription(desc);
  pc2.setRemoteDescription(desc);
  pc2.createAnswer(gotDescription2);
}

function gotDescription2(desc) {
  pc2.setLocalDescription(desc);
  trace('Answer from pc2 \n' + desc.sdp);
  pc1.setRemoteDescription(desc);
}
```

The following is the function to get the local ICE call back:

```
function iceCallback1(event) {
  if (event.candidate) {
    pc2.addIceCandidate(event.candidate);
  }
}
```

The following is the function for the remote ICE call back:

```
function iceCallback2(event) {
  if (event.candidate) {
    pc1.addIceCandidate(event.candidate);
  }
}
```

The function that receives the control when a message is passed back to the user is as follows:

```
function receiveChannelCallback(event) {
  receiveChannel = event.channel;
  receiveChannel.onmessage = onReceiveMessageCallback;
  receiveChannel.onopen = onReceiveChannelStateChange;
  receiveChannel.onclose = onReceiveChannelStateChange;
}

function onReceiveMessageCallback(event) {
  document.getElementById("dataChannelReceive").value =
    event.data;
}

function onReceiveChannelStateChange() {
  var readyState = receiveChannel.readyState;
}

function onSendChannelStateChange() {
  var readyState = sendChannel.readyState;
  if (readyState == "open") {
    document.getElementById("dataChannelSend").disabled = false;
    sendButton.disabled = false;
    closeButton.disabled = false;
  } else {
    document.getElementById("dataChannelSend").disabled = true;
    sendButton.disabled = true;
    closeButton.disabled = true;
  }
}
```

The following screenshot shows that Peer 1 is prepared to send text to Peer 2 using the `DataChannel` API of WebRTC:

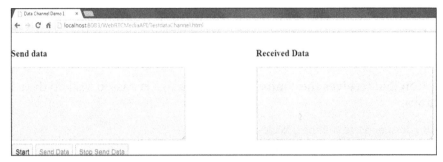

Empty text areas before beginning the exchange of text

On clicking on the **Start** button, as shown in the following screenshot, a session is established between the peers and the server:

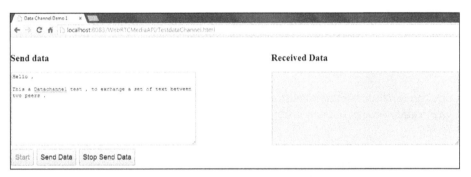

Putting in text from one's peers after hitting the Start button

As Peer 1 keys in the message and hits the **Send** button, the message is passed on to Peer 2. The preceding snapshot is taken before sending the message, and the following picture is taken after sending the message:

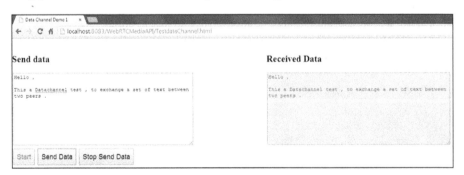

Text is exchanged on DataChannel on the click of the Send button

However, right now, you are only sending data from one localhost to another. This is because the system doesn't know any other peer IP or port. This is where socket-based servers such as Node.js come into the picture.

Media traversal in WebRTC clients

Real-time Transport Protocol (RTP) is the way for media to flow between end points. Media could be audio and/or video based.

 Media stream uses SRTP and DTLS protocols.

RTP in WebRTC is by default peer-to-peer as enforced by the **Interactive Connectivity Establishment (ICE)** protocol candidates, which could be either STUN or TURN. ICE is required to establish that firewalls are not blocking any of the UDP or TCP ports. The peer-to-peer link is established with the help of the ICE protocol. Using the STUN and TURN protocols, ICE finds out the network architecture and provides some transport addresses (ICE candidates) on which the peer can be contacted.

An `RTCPeerConnection` object has an associated ICE, comprising the `RTCPeerConnection` signaling state, the ICE gathering state, and the ICE connection state. These are initialized when an object is first created. The flow of signals through these nodes is depicted in the following call flow diagram:

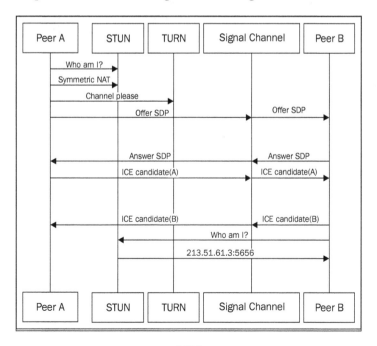

ICE, STUN, and TURN are defined as follows:

- **ICE**: This is the framework to allow your web browser to connect with peers. ICE uses STUN or TURN to achieve this.

- **STUN**: This is the protocol to discover your public address and determine any restrictions in your router that would prevent a direct connection with a peer. It presents the outside world with a public IP to the WebRTC client that can be used by the peers to communicate to it.

- **TURN**: This is meant to bypass the Symmetric NAT restriction by opening a connection with a TURN server and relaying all information through this server.

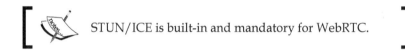 STUN/ICE is built-in and mandatory for WebRTC.

WebRTC through WebSocket signaling servers

Signaling is a crucial activity to establish any kind of network-based communication. It lets the endpoints share the session description and media information before setting up the path to actually exchange media. For a simple WebRTC client, there are JavaScript-based WebSocket servers that can provide such signaling in a permanent, full duplex, real-time manner. Node.js is one such server.

Node.js

Node.js is an asynchronous, server-side JavaScript server powered by Chrome's V8 JS engine. There are many WebSocket libraries, such as Socket.io and SockJS, that can run over it. Why are they used? They are used because the WebSocket server will do the WebSocket signaling between WebRTC clients and the server without using other protocols such as XMPP or SIP.

Let's see how we can use Node.js signaling server through the following simple steps:

1. On a Windows machine, install `nodejs.exe` from the official download site, `http://www.nodejs.org`.

2. To check whether Node.js is properly installed and working, check the version using the following command lines

   ```
   node -v
   ```

   The output in my case is `v0.10.26`.

3. Open the command prompt, and type `node <name of the JS file>` in the window. Consider the following command line as an example:

   ```
   node signaler.js
   ```

To write and run a simple server-side program, open Notepad, make a sample JS file with a name, say, `console`, and add some content to the `console.log('node.js running fine')` file. Run this file using the following Node.js command from the command prompt:

```
node console.js
```

The following screenshot shows the output of the preceding command line:

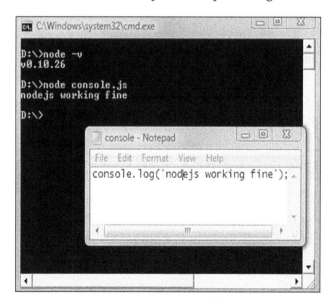

Let's now look at the overview of steps using Node.js to set up the signaling environment for a WebRTC client.

1. First, we need a JavaScript library to support WebRTC signaling operations. We can use `signaller.js` for this. Download `signaller.js` from `https://github.com/muaz-khan/WebRTC-Experiment/blob/master/websocket-over-nodejs/signaler.js`.

2. Next, we should run the JavaScript library using the Node.js server. We can do so by executing the following command in the terminal window:

   `node signaler.js`

3. Specify the address of the Node.js server machine in the WebRTC client.

   Now, we can make inter-browser WebRTC audio/video calls, where the signaling is handled by the Node.js WebSocket signaling server. The following diagram depicts how Node.js is used as a signaling server:

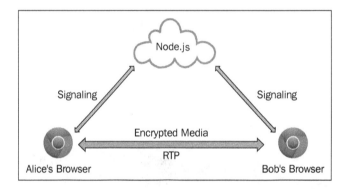

The preceding diagram denotes signaling across WebRTC clients over the Node.js WebSocket-based server. The media flows from peer to peer.

Making a peer-to-peer audio call using Node.js for signaling

We have seen how a JavaScript program is hosted on a Node.js signaling server. Now, let's study the process of making an audio/video call using this setup. The following code references Muaz Khan WebRTC experiments, which is under the MIT license. The library used is `PeerConnection.js`. The following are the CSS descriptions for the audio and video content on a page:

```
audio, video {
  vertical-align: top;
```

```css
}
.setup {
  border-bottom-left-radius: 0;
  border-top-left-radius: 0;
  margin-left: -9px;
  margin-top: 8px;
  position: absolute;
}
.highlight { color: rgb(0, 8, 189); }
```

Next, we will look at the JavaScript functions that define the behavior of the WebRTC client. This is a modified version of code from one-to-one-peerconnection.html under the WebRTC experiments master from Muaz Khan. For better clarity and easy understanding, I have removed the functions of unique ID, rotate video, and scale video, and have minimal CSS styling.

The following code defines the websocket.onopen and websocket.send operations:

```javascript
var channel = location.href.replace( /\/|:|#|%|\.|\[|\]/g, '');
var websocket = new WebSocket('ws://' + document.domain +
  ':12034');
websocket.onopen = function() {
  websocket.push(JSON.stringify({
    open: true, channel: channel
  }));
};
websocket.push = websocket.send;
websocket.send = function(data) {
  websocket.push(JSON.stringify({
    data: data, channel: channel
  }));
};
```

The following code is for the creation of a new peer connection and for every user who joins a session:

```javascript
var peer = new PeerConnection(websocket);
peer.onUserFound = function(userid) {

  if (document.getElementById(userid)) return;

  /* adding the name of room to room list */
  var tr = document.createElement('tr');
  var td1 = document.createElement('td');
  var td2 = document.createElement('td');
```

```
td1.innerHTML = userid + ' video call';

/* creating element button to room list */
var button = document.createElement('button');
button.innerHTML = 'Join';
button.id = userid;
button.style.float = 'right';

/* add the user to session on button click */
button.onclick = function() {
  button = this;
  getUserMedia(function(stream) {
  // get user media
  peer.addStream(stream);
  // add the stream

  peer.sendParticipationRequest(button.id);
  });
  button.disabled = true;
};

td2.appendChild(button);
tr.appendChild(td1);
tr.appendChild(td2);
roomsList.appendChild(tr);
};
```

The following code adds streaming to the video element of HTML and sets its characteristics:

```
peer.onStreamAdded = function(e) {
  if (e.type == 'local')
    document.querySelector('#start-broadcasting').disabled =
  false;
  var video = e.mediaElement;
  video.setAttribute('width', 400);
  video.setAttribute('height', 400);
  video.setAttribute('controls', true);
  videosContainer.insertBefore(video,
    videosContainer.firstChild);
  video.play();
};
```

The following code is to close the streaming session:

```
peer.onStreamEnded = function(e) {
var video = e.mediaElement;
if (video) {
  video.style.opacity = 0;
  setTimeout(function() {
    video.parentNode.removeChild(video);
    scaleVideos();
  }, 1000);
}
};

document.querySelector('#start-broadcasting').onclick =
  function() {
  this.disabled = true;
  getUserMedia(function(stream) {
  peer.addStream(stream);
  peer.startBroadcasting();
  });
};
document.querySelector('#your-name').onchange = function() {
  peer.userid = this.value;
};

var videosContainer = document.getElementById(
  'videos-container') || document.body;
var btnSetupNewRoom = document.getElementById('setup-new-room');
var roomsList = document.getElementById('rooms-list');

if (btnSetupNewRoom) btnSetupNewRoom.onclick =
  setupNewRoomButtonClickHandler;
```

The following code is to capture the user media:

```
function getUserMedia(callback) {
  var hints = {
    audio: true,
    video: {
      optional: [],
      mandatory: {
        minWidth: 200, minHeight:200, maxWidth: 400,
          maxHeight: 400, minAspectRatio: 1.77
      }
    }
  };
```

```
navigator.getUserMedia(hints, function(stream) {
  var video = document.createElement('video');
  video.src = URL.createObjectURL(stream);
  video.controls = true;
  video.muted = true;
  peer.onStreamAdded({
    mediaElement: video,
    userid: 'self',
    stream: stream
  });
  callback(stream);
});
}
```

The following is the web page's HTML content to add a button to start transmitting the media, a video element to display the media, a text field to add a user's name, and a table to list the existing available sessions:

```
<input type="text" id="your-name" placeholder="your-name">
<button id="start-broadcasting" class="setup">
Start Transmitting Yourself!</button>

<!-- list of all available conferencing rooms -->
<table id="rooms-list" style="width: 100%;"></table>

<!-- local/remote videos container -->
<div id="videos-container"></div>
```

The following screenshot depicts a user, Alice, creating a new session named `alice`. Here, the user Alice creates a session for broadcasting video, which will be added to the room list.

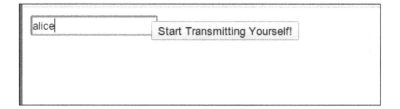

Alice's media is streamed on the session space, as shown in the next screenshot:

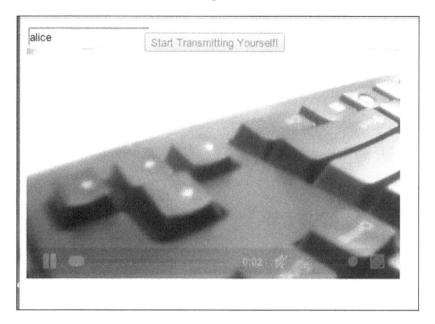

A new user, Bob, views the list of ongoing sessions from his remote computer, and clicks on the **Join** button, as shown in the following screenshot, to join Alice's session:

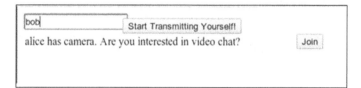

The following screenshot displays a two-way audio and video session in progress between Bob and Alice:

Bob and Alice are in an audio/video sharing session. Using other WebRTC APIs, we can also add file sharing, text chat, screen sharing capabilities, and so on to this simple demonstration to turn it into a multifeatured communication tool.

Running WebRTC with SIP

This section introduces the approach to use the SIP signaling mechanism with WebRTC. Like any other VoIP protocol, SIP also provides the signaling framework before setting up an actual media path. However, the foundation of open standard and industry-adopted signaling protocol such as SIP is recommended, as it provides the first and most crucial step to a strong, scalable architecture.

Session Initiation Protocol (SIP)

As we already know, SIP is a signaling protocol that is used to establish an RTP between two endpoints.

 As per the official document, *RFC 3261*, SIP is an application-layer control protocol that can establish, modify, and terminate multimedia sessions (conferences) such as Internet telephony calls.

The SIP stack defines the Request and Response methods. These methods are used to gather the information about endpoints that wish to participate in a communication so that the device-specific information such as IP, port, availability, media understanding, and audio-video device compatibility can be sorted out before establishing a flowing media connection.

However, it should be noted that traditional SIP is a bit different from **SIP over WebSocket (SIPWS)**, which is used in case of WebRTC with SIP signaling. It is not by default that every SIP server would understand SIPWS. Only those SIP servers that have WebSocket support, or state that they are WebRTC compliant, will be able to proxy or understand the SIP messages sent from a WebRTC client.

Why do we use SIPWS? This protocol allows the development of **Convergent applications**, that is, applications that support SIP for communication, HTTP for web components, and WebRTC for media. SIPWS can be transformed into plain SIP signal through a gateway, which can then interact with the IMS network. Also, SIP can be used to integrate application logic such as call screening and call rerouting, with the help of SIP Servlets or other kinds of SIP programming. More of this is given in *Chapter 3, WebRTC with SIP and IMS*.

SIPWS is explained in detail in the IETF draft, *The WebSocket Protocol as a Transport for the Session Initiation Protocol (SIP) draft-ietf-sipcore-sip-websocket-10* and can be found at `http://tools.ietf.org/html/draft-ietf-sipcore-sip-websocket-10`.

The following figure depicts the use of SIPWS signaling plane with WebRTC media plane:

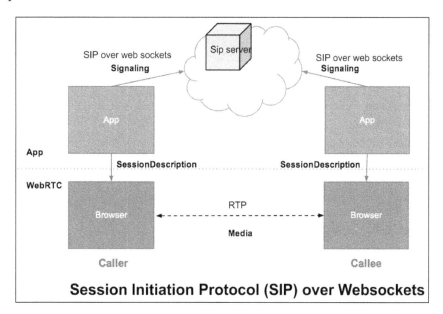

The following figure provides the call flow of the SIPWS signaling mechanism. Any SIP request is preceded by a one-time WebSocket handshake.

```
Alice      (SIP WSS)      proxy.example.com
|                          |
|HTTP GET (WS handshake) F1 |
|------------------------->|
|101 Switching Protocols F2 |
|<-------------------------|
|                          |
|REGISTER F3               |
|------------------------->|
|200 OK F4                 |
|<-------------------------|
|                          |
```

Alice loads a web page using her web browser and retrieves the JavaScript code that implements the SIP WebSocket subprotocol. The JavaScript code (SIP WebSocket Client) establishes a secure WebSocket connection with a SIP proxy/registrar (SIP WebSocket Server) at `proxy.example.com`.

The following is an example of a WebSocket handshake in which the Client requests the WebSocket SIP subprotocol support from the Server:

`ws://ns313841.ovh.net:10060/`

Request Method:
GET
Status Code:
101 Switching Protocols

Request Headers:
Provisional headers are shown.
Cache-Control:no-cache
Connection:Upgrade
Host:ns313841.ovh.net:10060
Origin:http://sipml5.org
Pragma:no-cache
Sec-WebSocket-Extensions:permessage-deflate; client_max_window_bits,
x-webkit-deflate-frame
Sec-WebSocket-Key:4aUpDOwtSWPaLmXKzQefJQ==
Sec-WebSocket-Protocol:sip
Sec-WebSocket-Version:13
Upgrade:websocket

```
User-Agent:Mozilla/5.0 (X11; Linux i686 (x86_64)) AppleWebKit/537.36
(KHTML, like Gecko) Chrome/32.0.1700.102 Safari/537.36
```

Response Headersview source

```
Connection:Upgrade
```

```
Content-Length:0
```

```
Sec-WebSocket-Accept:516iqk2+moekkwZsqlXo4cewzcw=
```

```
Sec-WebSocket-Protocol:sip
```

```
Sec-WebSocket-Version:13
```

```
Upgrade:websocket
```

The following diagram shows the call between Alice and Bob through the SIP proxy server over WebSocket signaling:

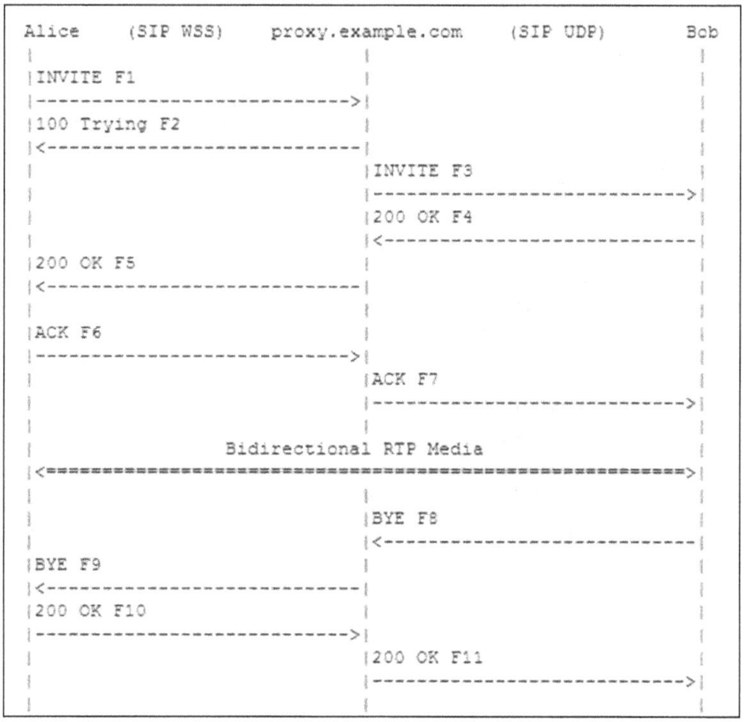

```
Alice     (SIP WSS)     proxy.example.com     (SIP UDP)     Bob
|                            |                                |
|INVITE F1                   |                                |
|--------------------------->|                                |
|100 Trying F2               |                                |
|<---------------------------|                                |
|                            |INVITE F3                       |
|                            |------------------------------->|
|                            |200 OK F4                       |
|                            |<-------------------------------|
|200 OK F5                   |                                |
|<---------------------------|                                |
|                            |                                |
|ACK F6                      |                                |
|--------------------------->|                                |
|                            |ACK F7                          |
|                            |------------------------------->|
|                            |                                |
|          Bidirectional RTP Media                            |
|<===========================================================>|
|                            |                                |
|                            |BYE F8                          |
|                            |<-------------------------------|
|BYE F9                      |                                |
|<---------------------------|                                |
|200 OK F10                  |                                |
|--------------------------->|                                |
|                            |200 OK F11                      |
|                            |------------------------------->|
|                            |                                |
```

Every SIP endpoint is registered with the SIP Server by a unique callable ID. This is referred to as the SIP URI and is denoted by the sip:<username>@<domainname> format. When a user, Alice, calls another user, Bob, through Bob's SIP URI, then the SIP WebSocket Server at proxy.example.com acts as a SIP proxy node and routes the INVITE call to Bob's contact. Bob answers the call to start a conversation and then terminates it with a BYE request when the communication is over.

JavaScript-based SIP libraries

There are many popular JavaScript libraries that offer easy-to-integrate support for WebRTC communication using SIP signaling:

- **SIPJS**: This is an SIP stack in JavaScript to implement SIP-based audio and video user agents in the browser. You can find a running demo at `http://theintencity.com/sip-js/phone.html?network_type=WebRTC`. The demo application has the option to switch between WebRTC capabilities and Flash for browsers that support and do not support WebRTC.

- **JSSIP**: This is an SIP over WebSocket transport API for audio/video calls and instant messaging. It works with all SIPWS-compatible SIP servers such as OverSIP, Kamailio, and Asterisk servers. You can find a running demo at `http://tryit.jssip.net/`.

- **sipML5**: This is an open source JavaScript library with a provision for RTCWeb Breaker (audio and video transcoding when the endpoints do not support the same codecs or the remote server is not RTCWeb compliant). For example, features such as audio/video call, instant messaging, presence, call hold/resume, explicit call transfer, and **Dual-tone multi-frequency (DTMF)** signaling using SIP INFO are present. You can find a running example at `http://sipml5.org/call.htm`.

- **QuoffeSIP**: This is another WebRTC SIP library to establish real-time communication between browsers. This is developed in CoffeeScript (simple syntax). It features video/audio call capabilities using SIP over the Websockets protocol and also uses the SIP Outbound and GRUU protocols. You can find a running example at `http://talksetup.quobis.com/`.

The implementation of the sipML5 and JSSIP libraries to constitute a simple WebRTC browser client that is able to communicate to a similar peer in any WebRTC-supported browser is covered in the next chapter.

Summary

In this chapter, we learned that a WebRTC communication process is divided into two parts: signaling, where the session setup and teardown is agreed to, and media transactions, which deals with the actual RTP streams that contain voice/video/data that the user has sent. We saw how to program the three basic APIs of WebRTC media stack, namely, `getUserMedia`, `RTCPeerConnection`, and `DataChannel`. The *Running WebRTC without SIP* section described signaling done over JSON via XMLHttpRequest using Node.js as the intermediately signaling server to connect the peers and prepare for the media flow. The next section, *Running WebRTC with SIP*, listed the libraries or WebRTC clients that use SIP over WebSocket to take care of the signaling between WebRTC peers. In the following chapters, we will see how to use WebRTC media APIs over the SIP WebSocket protocol in detail.

2
Making a Standalone WebRTC Communication Client

The objective of this chapter is to make a simple WebRTC client and server module that bypasses a centralized server and, instead, makes a direct peer-to-peer connection between browsers through a **Session Initiation Protocol** (**SIP**) proxy server. The aim is to connect a WebRTC client to another WebRTC client using SIP over WebSocket as the signaling protocol. In this chapter, we will study the following three prime ways of making SIP WebRTC calls:

- WebRTC to WebRTC call through a public cloud-hosted, WebRTC-capable SIP server, such as SIP2SIP

- WebRTC to WebRTC call through a locally hosted, WebRTC-capable SIP server, such as OfficeSIP

- WebRTC call to SIP phone through a WebSocket gateway and SIP server, such as Kamailio

We will begin the chapter by describing a simple WebRTC client-server model.

Description of the WebRTC client-server model

The components of a typical WebRTC SIP-based client include the following:

- SIP stack, in the form of a JavaScript library, to perform signaling
- **Cascading Style Sheets (CSS)** to style a page
- WebRTC media API to render a peer-to-peer connection between the audio-video components of a page
- An HTML5-based graphical interface to provide inputs such as registration parameters, self-URI (short for Uniform Resource Identifier), URI of the party to be called, and so on

The following diagram depicts the important components to set up a WebRTC infrastructure:

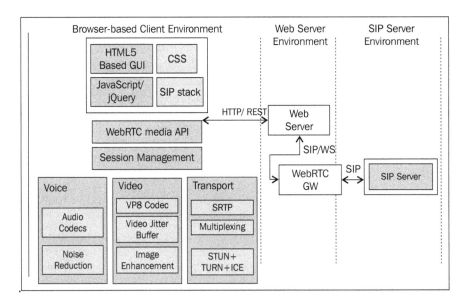

The client side must be linked to a server that runs on the network side to complete the signal flow. The components that must be deployed on the network side are as follows:

- The WebRTC gateway to connect to the native SIP world
- The SIP server to embed the SIP application/proxy logic

The web browser is the key component in WebRTC transactions. It is the client-side environment that pulls out the HTML content from a web server, interprets the HTML tags, and displays the web page to the user. A WebRTC-capable browser has the additional ability to access the user's input media devices, such as microphones and camera, and stream them across the network. In the preceding diagram, there are some key functions of WebRTC media API that are embedded in the browser. These include codecs for audio and video, noise reduction, image enhancements, jitter buffer, multiplexing, SRTP, ICE in STUN /TURN, and so on. The gateway is the internetworking node between WebRTC's SIP over WebSocket side and traditional SIP/IMS side. The traditional SIP-based network is depicted by the SIP server in the preceding diagram.

The parts for media handling between WebRTC and non-WebRTC clients, such as relay and transcoding, will be explained in depth in later chapters. Here, we shall look at an infrastructure compromising of only SIP and WebRTC. For now, consider a simple WebRTC client trying to communicate with another WebRTC client through the browser interface. There are many SIP and WebRTC implementations available today; we will consider sipML5 and jsSIP among these to make a simple WebRTC client, which will communicate via an SIP server.

The sipML5 WebRTC client

The sipML5 client is a library of SIP and **Session Description Protocol (SDP)** stacks written in JavaScript, using WebSocket as the network transport mechanism. It supports TCP, UDP, and TLS transports. It is provided under the BSD license. There are three ways of using SipML5 WebRTC client:

- The first option is to use the online demo version available at `http://sipml5.org/call.htm`
- The second option is to make use of the minified version of the JavaScript API and code that can be imported and loaded directly using the web server
- The third option (recommended for integrators) is to get the developers' version of the sipML5 master that can be checked out from GitHub and used for development and debugging for enhanced operations

Let's begin the exercise using only the primitive and necessary sipML5 functions to make a call successfully from a web page without the need of backbone components such as `web.xml` and the Java source. To simplify things, we will not look into the enhanced features such as Presence (Subscribe, Notify), DTMF, and speed dialing at this point. These topics will be covered in *Chapter 6, Basic Features of WebRTC over SIP*.

Developing a minified webphone application using Tomcat

The steps to set up a Tomcat web server are described in this section.

1. First is the installation of a web application server to host the web archive (`war`) that contains the WebRTC call page. We are using Apache Tomcat Version 7.0.50 here. It can be downloaded from `https://tomcat.apache.org/`.

2. We must ensure that `JAVA_HOME` is set as an environmental variable for Tomcat in Windows (refer to the following screenshot).

3. Start the Tomcat batch script after the preceding two steps. You will see the following output in the console:

```
D:\workspacenativewebrtc\apache-tomcat-7.0.50\bin>set JAVA_HOME=C:\Program Files
\Java\jdk1.6.0_06

D:\workspacenativewebrtc\apache-tomcat-7.0.50\bin>startup.bat
Using CATALINA_BASE:   "D:\workspacenativewebrtc\apache-tomcat-7.0.50"
Using CATALINA_HOME:   "D:\workspacenativewebrtc\apache-tomcat-7.0.50"
Using CATALINA_TMPDIR: "D:\workspacenativewebrtc\apache-tomcat-7.0.50\temp"
Using JRE_HOME:        "C:\Program Files\Java\jdk1.6.0_06"
Using CLASSPATH:       "D:\workspacenativewebrtc\apache-tomcat-7.0.50\bin\bootst
rap.jar;D:\workspacenativewebrtc\apache-tomcat-7.0.50\bin\tomcat-juli.jar"
D:\workspacenativewebrtc\apache-tomcat-7.0.50\bin>
```

The code for the web page that acts like a web-based phone using WebRTC calls (along with the explanation of various code snippets) is given as follows:

1. Start the process by making a local copy of the SIP-signaling JavaScript file. Open an empty text file and import the `sipml5-api` JS library file from `http://sipml5.googlecode.com/svn/trunk/release/SIPml-api.js`.

2. Write the following JavaScript functions to initialize the engine:

    ```javascript
    var readyCallback = function(e){
      createSipStack();      // see next section
    };
    ```

```
var errorCallback = function(e){    // stack failed to initialize
    console.error('Failed to initialize the engine:' + e.message);
}
SIPml.init(readyCallback, errorCallback);
```

3. The following function shows how to define event reactions when the client has started and when a call arrives:

```
var eventsListener = function(e){
  if(e.type == 'started'){
    login();
  }

  else if(e.type == 'i_new_call'){
 // incoming audio/video call acceptCall(e);
  }
}
```

4. The following is the JavaScript code to start an SIP stack with parameters in SIPml:

```
var sipStack;
function createSipStack(){
  sipStack = new SIPml.Stack({
    realm: 'sip2sip.info',    // mandatory : domain name
    impi: 'altanai',          // mandatory : IMS Private Identity
    impu: 'SIP:altanai@sip2sip.info',
    // mandatory  : IMS Public Identity

    password: '/*enter sip2sip.info account password*/',
    display_name: 'altanai',
    websocket_proxy_url: 'wss://sipml5.org:10062',
    outbound_proxy_url: 'udp://example.org:5060',
    enable_rtcweb_breaker: false,
    events_listener: { events: '*', listener: eventsListener },
    //optional: '*' means all events
  });
}
sipStack.start();
```

5. The declaration of the elements to make and receive a call is given as follows:

```
var callSession;
var makeCall = function(){
  callSession = sipStack.newSession('call-audiovideo', {
    video_local: document.getElementById('video-local'),
```

```
        video_remote: document.getElementById('video-remote'),
        audio_remote: document.getElementById('audio-remote'),
        events_listener: { events: '*', listener: eventsListener }


    });
    callSession.call('johndoe');
}
```

6. The function definition to accept an incoming call using the sipML5 library is given as follows:

```
var acceptCall = function(e){
    e.newSession.accept();
    // e.newSession.reject() to reject the call
}
```

7. Add HTML containers for local and remote videos as shown in the following lines of code:

```
<video width="100%" height="100%" id="video_remote"
autoplay="autoplay"></video>

<video class="video" width="88px" height="72px" id="video_local"
autoplay="autoplay" muted="true">
```

8. Make a folder under the `webapps` folder within the `Tomcat` folder. Name it `miniSipml5phone`, place the `SIPml5-API.js` file, and rename the file we created as `index.html`.

9. Open `http://<ip>:<port>/<foldername>` in a browser to load the web page. To test whether this code is working on the machine or not, add `http://localhost:8080/miniSipml5phone` in the address bar to load the call page.

After developing the WebRTC client and deploying it over the Application Server, it's time to test its functions. The best way to do this is by inspecting the traces. Use the console screen of Chrome or Firefox to see the traces of SIP requests. The trace for an SIP stack initialization should be of the following structure.

```
SIPML5 API version = 1.3.214

User-Agent=Mozilla/5.0 (Windows NT 6.0) AppleWebKit/537.36 (KHTML, like
Gecko) Chrome/34.0.1847.116 Safari/537.36

WebSocket supported = yes

SIP stack start: proxy='ns313841.ovh.net:12060', realm='<SIP:sip2sip.
info>', impi='altanai', impu='<SIP:altanai@sip2sip.info>'
```

```
Connecting to 'WS://ns313841.ovh.net:12060'
```

```
__tsip_transport_WS_onopen
```

```
State machine: c0000_Started_2_Outgoing_X_oINVITE PeerConnectionClass =
function RTCPeerConnection() { [native code] } SessionDescriptionClass
= function RTCSessionDescription() { [native code] } IceCandidateClass =
function RTCIceCandidate() { [native code] }
```

```
Video Constraints:{ /* video constrains added to WebRTC client appear
here */}
```

```
ICE servers:[/* list of stun servers added to WebRTC client appear here
*/]
```

```
onGetUserMediaSuccess
```

```
createOffer
```

If an exception occurs for a missing resource such as an audio, a JavaScript, or an image file, the browser console depicts a notification for it. The following statement is a "GIF file not found" notification:

```
GET http://144.55.64.89:8080/WebRTCphone/images/.gif 404 (Not Found)
```

We must make amendments to the HTML content that points to the correct resource path so as to run the WebRTC client code unobstructed. In case the JavaScript file for SIP functions is not loaded properly, the web handshake and the subsequent communication operation will not take place.

The SIP requests and SDP can be viewed here; this can help in solving errors. The trace for the SIP INVITE request from the WebRTC client is of the following structure. The ICE candidates come in to play first. After this, the SIP INVITE request for a call is generated and sent to the other user along with SDP.

```
ICE GATHERING COMPLETED!
```

```
onIceGatheringCompleted
```

```
SEND: INVITE SIP:testagent@sip2sip.info SIP/2.0
```

```
Via: SIP/2.0/WS df7jal231s0d.invalid;branch=z9hG4bKSM7tGLdSUy3DpGehaPa78H
Hpvmir89Uh;rport
```

```
From: <SIP:altanai@sip2sip.info>;tag=2CEhe0X78NxVm7aRCaBa
```

```
To: <SIP:testagent@sip2sip.info>
```

```
Contact: "undefined"<SIP:altanai@df7jal231s0d.invalid;rtcweb-breaker=no;c
lick2call=no;transport=WS>
```

```
Call-ID: 16a15a79-e4a6-78a1-2310-1243ebafe826
```

```
CSeq: 59935 INVITE

Content-Type: application/sdp

Content-Length: 3984

Max-Forwards: 70


v=0

o=- 6574822970880695000 2 IN IP4 127.0.0.1

s=Doubango Telecom - chrome

t=0 0

a=group:BUNDLE audio video

m=audio 15856 RTP/SAVPF 111 103 104 0 8 106 105 13 126

c=IN IP4 103.253.172.143

a=ice-options:google-ice

a=mid:audio

a=sendrecv

a=ice-options:google-ice

a=mid:video

a=sendrecv

a=rtcp-mux
```

The SDP and SIP traces shown here are modified to depict only the important headers. Many other headers have been removed from traces for clarity.

Now that we have gained a bit of insight into WebRTC code components, let's use this to develop the complete JavaScript of the sipML5 library and constitute a dynamic web project, which will be later used to embed the logic of other features such as phonebook, call logs, voicemail, and user profile.

Developing our customized version of the sipML5 client

This section describes the process of building our own customized WebRTC client. It is built over the SIP library, WebRTC API, and the web-based **Graphical User Interface (GUI)** to enable the user to make and receive calls. The following steps outline the process of creating a customized WebRTC client using Dynamic Project wizard of Eclipse. This differs from the earlier approach, in which we were using the web-deployed sipML5 WebRTC web page.

Once we set up our own sipML5 web project, it is easy to make changes in the configurations and user interface.

1. Download sipML5-master from GitHub (refer to `https://github.com/sipml5`). Unzip and extract the folder.

2. Make an empty, dynamic, web project in Eclipse. Let's assume that the name of the project is `WebRTCSimpl5`.

3. Copy the files under the release folder into the `WebContent` folder of Eclipse. Now, the project explorer should look like the following screenshot:

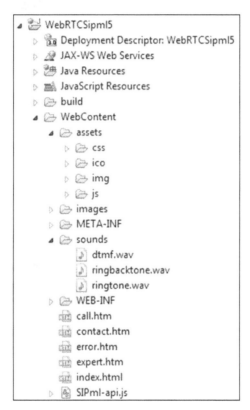

4. Run `call.htm` on any web server such as Tomcat. Tomcatv7.0 is used on the localhost.

5. Open the web page in a web browser that supports WebRTC. We must add our SIP credentials on this page for the server to register the WebRTC SIP client. An SIP client registration requires the authentication name, SIP URI, password, and domain name fields to be specified at the time of registration. The following screenshot shows the call.htm page that runs from the local Tomcat web server:

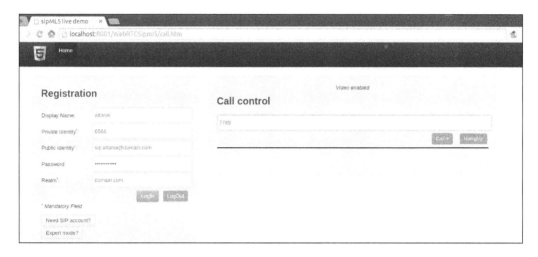

6. Open the expert.htm page by clicking on the **Expert mode?** button. When using a public server such as iptel or SIP2SIP, the domain name entered in the registration section is enough to locate the server and connect the client with it. However, for self-configured servers, the server address of the WebSocket server must be entered in the **WebSocket server URL** field. For example, if the WebSocket SIP server is installed on the machine with IP 97.54.67.12 and the ws port is 443, then the ws URL will be ws://97.54.67.12:443. The following screenshot shows the Expert.htm page, where the server parameters are entered when the page is run from the local Tomcat web server:

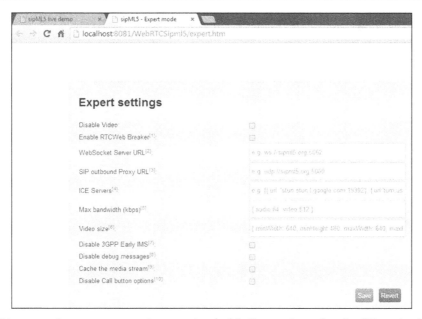

Expert.htm page, where server parameters are entered while the page is run from local Tomcat web server

7. Register the client with the SIP server by clicking on the **Register** button. The browser console can be monitored at this stage; the console depicts the registration SIP request being generated and sent to the SIP server.

   Check browser console traces to find out any server errors of components and missing exceptions on the web page.

Similarly, a jsSIP WebRTC client can also be configured to use a WebRTC-supported SIP server.

The jsSIP WebRTC client

The jsSIP client is a JavaScript library of the SIP stack and SDP, much similar to sipML5.It can also be used in the following three ways:

- The first option is to use the online demo of the jsSIP WebRTC client that can be found at http://tryit.jssip.net/.

- The second option is to use the minified version of the jsSIP JavaScript API, and the code.

- The third option is to get the developer's version of the jsSIP master from GitHub and use it for development and debugging.

Developing our version of the jsSIP client

To integrate the SIP WebRTC functionality into an existing web application, it is required that you develop the WebRTC client from basic components so that it can be customized later. We can perform the following steps to make a Dynamic Web Project of the jsSIP WebRTC client using Eclipse Wizard, similar to the sipML5 project:

1. Download `jsSIP-demo-master` from GitHub (`http://jssip.net/download/`) and unzip it.

2. Make an empty dynamic web project in Eclipse. Let's assume that we name it `WebRTCJssip`.

3. Copy the files into `WebContent` of the project in Eclipse. The project explorer should look like the following screenshot:

4. Open the `index.html` file to add the reference to the latest `jssip-0.3.0.js` library file using the following line of code:

```
<script src="http://jssip.net/download/jssip-0.3.0.js" type="text/javascript"></script>
```

5. Instantiate the following config parameters now or add them later:

```
$(document).ready(function(){

  // Default settings.
  var default_SIP_uri = "jmillan@jssip.net";
  var default_SIP_password = '';
  var outbound_proxy_set = {
    host: "tryit.jssip.net:10080",
WS_path:'WS',
WS_query: 'wwdf'
  };
JSsipPhone = new JsSIP.UA(configuration);
```

6. Use the existing event definition or add your own under the existing function's body. The event definition is as follows:

```
//WebSocket connection events
JSsipphone.on('connected', function(e){ });
JSsipphone.on('disconnected', function(e){ });

//New incoming or outgoing call event
JSsipphone.on('newRTCSession', function(e){ });

//New incoming or outgoing IM message event
JSsipphone.on('newMessage', function(e){ });

//SIP registration events
JSsipphone.on('registered', function(e){ });
JSsipphone.on('unregistered', function(e){ });
JSsipphone.on('registrationFailed', function(e){ });
```

7. The following functions describe how to make an outgoing or receive an incoming audio/video call. Use the existing function calls to add your **Graphical User Interface (GUI)** response with the help of CSS and jQuery, such as show remote and local video captured in the video div and print console info traces for tracing.

8. The following are the HTML5 `<video>` elements in which local and remote videos will be shown:

```
var selfView = document.getElementById('my-video');
var remoteView = document.getElementById('peer-video');
```

9. Register callbacks to the desired call events using the following lines of code:

```
var eventHandlers = {
  'progress':   function(e){ },
  'failed':     function(e){ },
  'started':    function(e){
    var rtcSession = e.sender;
```

10. Attach local stream to `selfView` using the following lines of code:

```
if (rtcSession.getLocalStreams().length > 0) {
  selfView.src = window.URL.createObjectURL(
    rtcSession.getLocalStreams()[0]);
}
```

11. Attach remote stream to `remoteView` using the following lines of code:

```
if (rtcSession.getRemoteStreams().length > 0) {
  remoteView.src = window.URL.createObjectURL(
    rtcSession.getRemoteStreams()[0]);
}},
  'ended': function(e){ /* Your code here */ }
};

var options = {
  'eventHandlers': eventHandlers,
  'extraHeaders': [ 'X-Foo: foo', 'X-Bar: bar' ],
  'mediaConstraints': {'audio': true, 'video': true}
};
JSsipPhone.call('SIP:bob@somedomain.com', options);
```

12. The event handlers for messages are similar to the event handlers for a call. To send or receive messages, use the existing function calls to add your GUI responses, such as open a new window or show an alert on successful sending of messages using the following lines of code:

```
var text = 'Hello';

// Register callbacks to desired message events
var eventHandlers = {
  'succeeded': function(e){ },
  'failed': function(e){ };
};

var options = {
  'eventHandlers': eventHandlers
};

JSsipPhone.sendMessage('SIP:bob@somedomain.com', text, options);
```

13. Run `index.html` that contains the phone elements and uses the jsSIP call functions on any web server, such as JBoss or Apache.

14. Open the web page in the Google Chrome or Firefox web browser.

15. Register the client with SIP server-supporting WebSockets, such as Kamailio, or use a WebSocket gateway as OverSIP.

16. Monitor the WebRTC client traces on Wireshark.

In a similar fashion, other SIP stacks can also be integrated with WebRTC media APIs to make a ready script to make and receive WebRTC calls over SIP.

 The SIP stack can also be a proprietary C code or adopted from freely available version of the Internet. JavaScript will aim to invoke the functions from an HTML-based web page. WebRTC browser media APIs will provide a way to capture and route the media.

SIP servers

The WebRTC client with an SIP stack can be registered and can send an invitation or give answers through an SIP server. The SIP server might or might not have the support for WebSocket. This categorization can be understood in two parts:

• This part consists of a WebRTC-compliant SIP server, and the caller and receiver are both on SIP over WebSocket (SIP WS to SIP WS). The WebRTC-compliant SIP server can belong to one of the following two categories:

    ◦ Using open public domains (such as SIP2SIP, JSSIP Tryit Server, or sipML5.org). This is demonstrated in the following diagram:

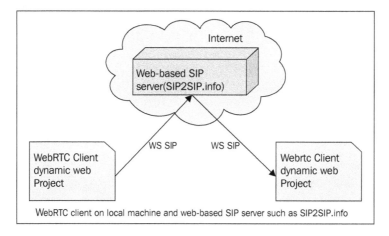

WebRTC client on local machine and web-based SIP server such as SIP2SIP.info

    °   Using locally hosted WebRTC-compatible SIP server (OfficeSIP). This is demonstrated in the following diagram:

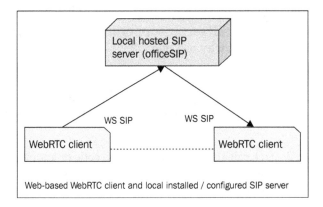

Web-based WebRTC client and local installed / configured SIP server

- This part consists of a simple SIP server that does not respond to SIP over WebSocket, but only to SIP (Sip WS to Sip). This server can belong to one of the following two categories:

    °   Using the WebRTC2sip gateway as an inter-conversion node between SIPWS and SIP. This enables the WebRTC client to connect with a legacy SIP server (such as Bea WebLogic, Rhino Telecom Application Server, and Brekeke), which does not have support for WebSocket yet. The OverSIP gateway also achieves the same goal. This architecture is diagrammatically represented as follows:

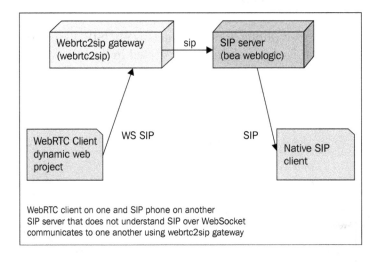

WebRTC client on one and SIP phone on another
SIP server that does not understand SIP over WebSocket
communicates to one another using webrtc2sip gateway

    °   If we implement a Telecom Server with both WebSocket and SIP support, then the traditional SIP clients and WebRTC clients can connect to each other without the use of any external gateway. This is due the fact that the server itself does the conversion between the SIPWS and SIP protocols as and when a request arrives. Kamailio, FreeSwitch, and Mobicents are some of the open source SIP servers of this nature. This architecture is diagrammatically represented as follows:

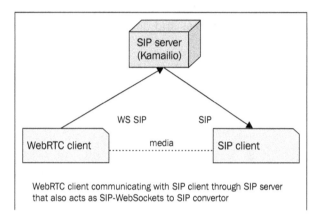

WebRTC client communicating with SIP client through SIP server
that also acts as SIP-WebSockets to SIP convertor

SIP-WS to SIP-WS

This section describes a SIP-WS to SIP-WS call, which involves making a call from the WebRTC client to another WebRTC client using SIP over WebSocket as the signaling protocol. To begin this task, we can use either the online-hosted demo WebRTC-enabled projects of sipML5/jsSIP, or the self-compiled source code on the local machine, as seen in the first part of this chapter. In addition to this, we must set up a WebRTC server to provide signaling. The signaling can be in any of the following ways:

- Publicly hosted SIP server with WebRTC support as SIP2SIP

- SIP servers' executables hosted in our servers, such as the OfficeSIP server

- SIP servers built from source and hosted in our servers, such as Kamailio

SIP2SIP

To test the functionality of our customized WebRTC client, let's register it with the SIP2SIP server.

The steps to register the client with the SIP2SIP server are as follows:

1. To register the client with the SIP2SIP SIP server, make an account at `https://mdns.sipthor.net/register_sip_account.phtml`

2. Log in with the credentials. On the home page, click on the **Identity** tab to view your public address and outbound proxy, as shown in the following screenshot:

The SIP2SIP Internet-based account page

3. Go to our WebRTC client, leave the `expert.htm` page empty, and enter values into the `call.htm` page directly. The following screenshot shows the registration fields of the `call.htm` page to be registered with SIP2SIP:

4. Click on the **Login** button to register with the server. Successful registration will be indicated by the connected status on the web page.

OfficeSIP

OfficeSIP is the Window's version of an SIP server. It is free for academic and personal use. To use the OfficeSIP server to register the clients we made, we will first have to install and configure it by performing the following steps:

1. Download the OfficeSIP server msi file from `http://www.officesip.com`. It is free for academic use. Click on the **Next** button on successive windows to proceed with the installation of the OfficeSIP software.

2. Start the admin console `.exe` file from the installation directory or the shortcut icon that gets created during the installation or can be seen on the Windows start menu. Alternatively, go to `http://localhost:5060/admin/`.

3. Add **Domain Name** from the **Domain** tab. Add users to the domain from the **.csv File** tab under **USERS**, as shown in the following screenshot:

4. Register the WebRTC clients with the OfficeSIP server and make calls.

5. In the earlier example, we made use of a simple browser console debug logfile to see the SIP transaction. The following screenshot shows Wireshark traces for the OfficeSIP server. This is used to view the incoming and outgoing data packets:

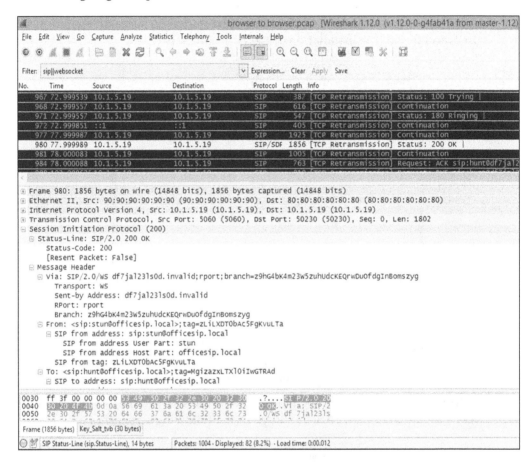

SIP WS to SIP and vice-versa

The task of connecting a WebRTC client to a native SIP client such as X-Lite, Twinkle, and SIP phone is dealt with in two ways:

Through a WebRTC to SIP gateway, use a gateway that does the SIPWS to SIP conversion so that the traditional SIP server in the SIP legacy network can understand the SIP request originating from WebRTC clients. To understand this better, we can consider any native SIP server such as the Brekeke SIP proxy registrar server or Bea WebLogic Sip Application server. These do not understand the WebSocket protocol in their default behavior.

The hosted server supports SIP over WebSocket. In this case, the WebRTC client does not need a gateway to pass its SIP messages, as the SIP server itself understands WebSocket with SIP protocol. There are some popular servers that understand WebSocket, such as Kamailio, Asterisk, and FreeSWITCH. It is, however, required that you customize the default behavior of these servers, and add the WebSocket module to the configuration file before usage. We shall cover both of these approaches in the sections that follow.

The gateway to convert SIP over WebSocket to native SIP

There can be custom-built or open source SIPWS to SIP gateways. To be able to communicate with these SIP servers, we need to first use a WebRTC to SIP gateway, such as WebRTC2sip or OverSIP.

The WebRTC2SIP gateway

WebRTC2Sip is a gateway that uses RTCWeb Breaker and SIP. It allows calls from the SIP legacy network to operate with calls from the SIP-based WebRTC client. It primarily has the following three modules:

- SIP proxy is used to convert the SIP transport from WebSocket protocol to UDP, TCP, or TLS; these are supported by all legacy networks

- RTCWeb Breaker is used to negotiate and convert the media stream to allow SIP legacy endpoints and WebRTC clients to interoperate

- Media coder is for interoperability between different codecs supported by different endpoints

The following diagram shows the overall functioning of the WebRTC to SIP gateway:

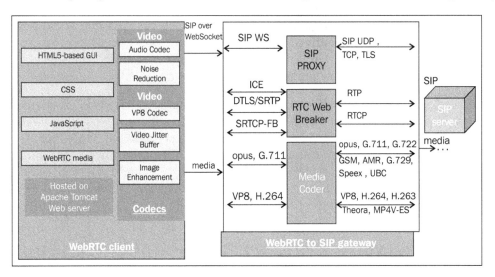

The call flow of the SIPWS request from the WebRTC client, conversion to a simple SIP request, and the passage from the SIP legacy network to reach the SIP legacy endpoint via the WebRTC2sip gateway is shown in the following figure:

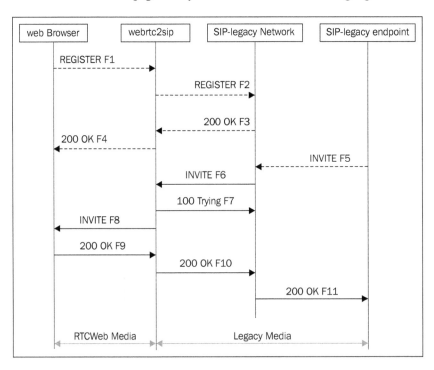

The steps for the installation of the WebRTC2sip gateway are described as follows:

1. The source code for webrtc2sip can be downloaded from `http://WebRTC2sip.org/` or by executing the following `svn checkout` statement from the terminal window:

   ```
   svn checkout http://WebRTC2sip.googlecode.com/svn/trunk/
   WebRTC2sip-read-only
   ```

   After this, follow the technical guide in the document folder.

2. The WebRTC2sip gateway depends on Doubango IMS Framework v2.0. Therefore, to configure the WebRTC2sipgateway, we first need to install the Doubango IMS framework by running the following command line in the command prompt:

   ```
   svn checkout http://doubango.googlecode.com/svn/branches/2.0/
   doubango doubango
   ```

3. Also, we need to install some mandatory and optional libraries such as the following ones:
   - libsrtp for SRTP
   - openSSL for WSS
   - libspeex and libspeexdsp (these are audio codecs)
   - YASM to enable VPX (VP8 video codec) or x264 (H.264 codec)
   - libvpx ,libyuv provide support for video calls
   - libopus for Opus audio codec
   - libgsm for GSM based audio codecs
   - g729, iLBC for G.729, and iLBC audio codecs
   - x264, FFmpeg for H.263, H.264, and MP4V-ES video codecs

4. Build and install Dubango using the following command lines:

   ```
   cd doubango && ./autogen.sh && ./configure --with-ssl --with-srtp
   --with-vpx --with-yuv

   --with-amr --with-speex --with-speexdsp --with-gsm --with-ilbc
   --with-g729 --with-ffm

   --with- ffm-peg

   make && make install
   ```

The following screenshot shows how Dubango IMS is installed to support libraries for the WebRTC2sip gateway:

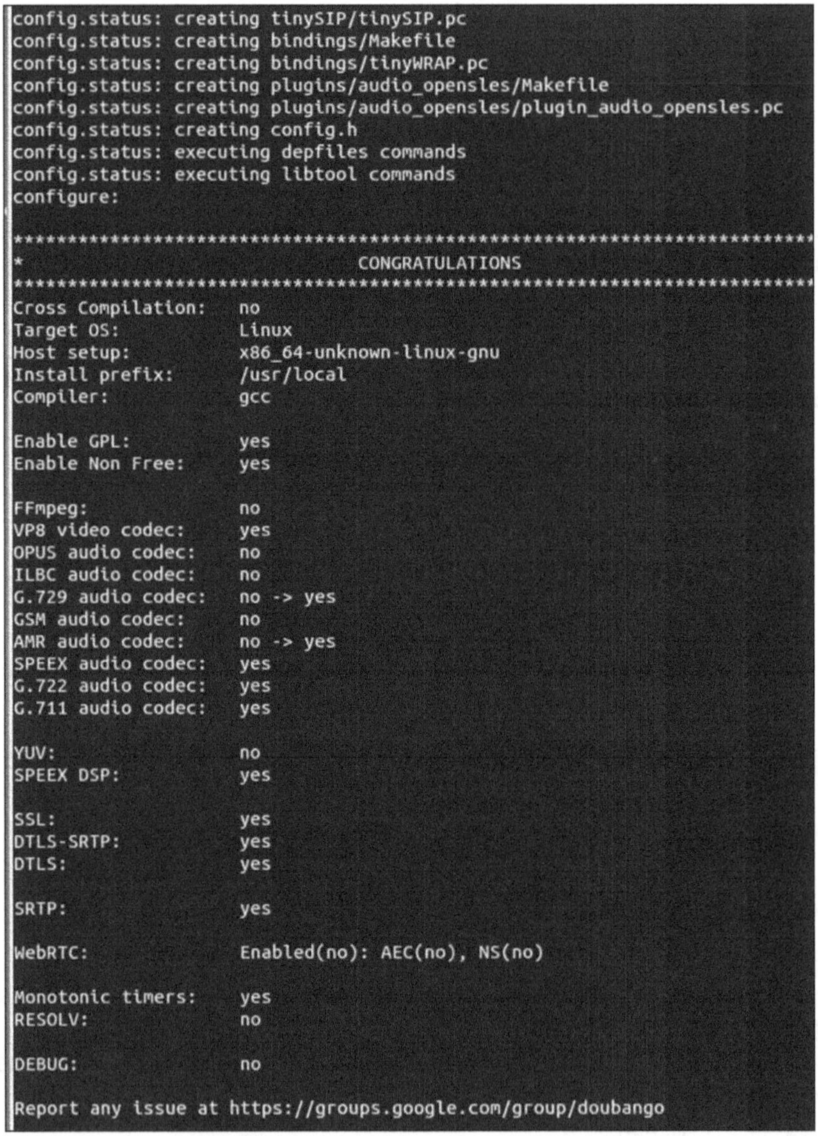

```
config.status: creating tinySIP/tinySIP.pc
config.status: creating bindings/Makefile
config.status: creating bindings/tinyWRAP.pc
config.status: creating plugins/audio_opensles/Makefile
config.status: creating plugins/audio_opensles/plugin_audio_opensles.pc
config.status: creating config.h
config.status: executing depfiles commands
config.status: executing libtool commands
configure:

********************************************************************
*                          CONGRATULATIONS
********************************************************************
Cross Compilation:    no
Target OS:            Linux
Host setup:           x86_64-unknown-linux-gnu
Install prefix:       /usr/local
Compiler:             gcc

Enable GPL:           yes
Enable Non Free:      yes

FFmpeg:               no
VP8 video codec:      yes
OPUS audio codec:     no
ILBC audio codec:     no
G.729 audio codec:    no -> yes
GSM audio codec:      no
AMR audio codec:      no -> yes
SPEEX audio codec:    yes
G.722 audio codec:    yes
G.711 audio codec:    yes

YUV:                  no
SPEEX DSP:            yes

SSL:                  yes
DTLS-SRTP:            yes
DTLS:                 yes

SRTP:                 yes

WebRTC:               Enabled(no): AEC(no), NS(no)

Monotonic timers:     yes
RESOLV:               no

DEBUG:                no

Report any issue at https://groups.google.com/group/doubango
```

5. Build and install the WebRTC2sip gateway using the following command lines:

```
export PREFIX=/opt/WebRTC2sip

cd WebRTC2sip && ./autogen.sh && ./configure --prefix=$PREFIX

make clean && make && make install
```

```
checking for TINYMSRP... yes
checking for TINYRTP... yes
checking for TINYIPSEC... yes
checking for libxml2... /usr
checking for libpthread... /usr
checking that generated files are newer than configure... done
configure: creating ./config.status
config.status: creating Makefile
config.status: creating config.h
config.status: config.h is unchanged
config.status: executing depfiles commands
configure:

********************************************************************
                         CONGRATULATIONS
********************************************************************
Host setup:
Install prefix:                 /opt/webrtc2sip
Compiler:                       gcc

DOUBANGO
     MIN_VER:                   2.0.898
     TINYSAK:                   yes
     TINYNET:                   yes
     TINYHTTP:                  yes
     TINYSIP:                   yes
     TINYDAV:                   yes
     TINYSDP:                   yes
     TINYSIGCOMP:               yes
     TINYMEDIA:                 yes
     TINYMEDIA:                 yes
     TINYSMS:                   yes
     TINYMSRP:                  yes
     TINYRTP:                   yes
     TINYIPSEC:                 yes

LIBXML2_INCLUDE:                /usr/include/libxml2
LIBXML2_LIB:                    /usr/lib

LIBPTHREAD_INCLUDE:             /usr/include
LIBPTHREAD_LIB:                 /usr/lib

Report issues at https://groups.google.com/group/doubango

--------------------------------------------------------------
Next steps
  1) run 'make' to build the source
  2) run 'make install' to install
--------------------------------------------------------------


altanai@tcs:~/Downloads/webrtc2sip-read-only$ sudo make
make  all-am
```

6. The gateway is configured using the following XML file named `config.xml`, and it is stored in the same folder where the gateway is running:

```xml
<?xml version="1.0" encoding="utf-8" ?>
<config>
 <debug-level>ERROR</debug-level>
 <transport>udp;*;10060</transport>
 <transport>WS;*;10060</transport>
 <transport>wss;*;10062</transport>
 <!--transport>tcp;*;10063</transport-->
 <!--transport>tls;*;10064</transport-->

 <video-size-pref>vga</video-size-pref>
 <rtp-buffsize>65535</rtp-buffsize>

 <srtp-type>sdes;dtls</srtp-type>

<codecs>opus;pcma;pcmu;gsm;vp8;h264-bp;h264-mp;h263;h263+</codecs>

<!--Few more fields omitted for clarity -->
</config>
```

The file specifies the ports for transport protocols. It also specifies the preference for video size and codecs supported, among others.

7. Register the WebRTC client with the `ws://` address that contains the WebRTC2sip gateway. To make the interaction of our WebRTC client with the SIP server without WebSocket support (in our case, Brekeke), we will use a WebRTC to SIP gateway.

The WebRTC client with Brekeke SIP server

Brekeke is also a popular SIP server that does not support WebSocket as yet. The following steps describe the process of configuring WebRTC to run through this SIP server with the help of the WebSocket gateway:

1. Download and run Brekeke on a Windows machine (refer to `http://www.brekeke.com/downloads/sip-server.php`).

2. Configure the Brekeke SIP server through the admin console in the local network/machine. Register the X-Lite phone through the Brekeke SIP registrar, as shown in the following screenshot:

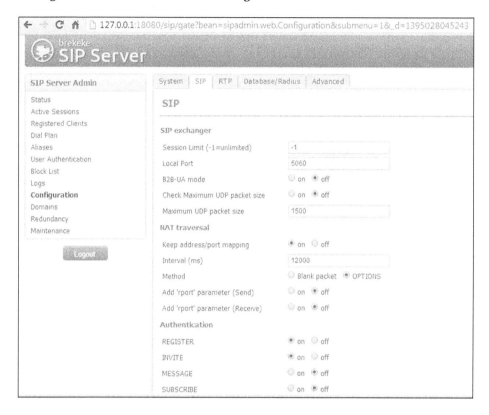

3. Register the WebRTC client through the WebRTC2sip server to the Brekeke SIP server as well.

   Enter the address of the WebRTC2sip gateway machine in the WS server input box of the **Expert settings** page, for example, ws://115:90:56:4:443.

   Enter the address of the SIP server machine that runs Brekeke in the outbound proxy input box of the **Expert settings** page, for example, udp:// 117:67:45:2:5060.

4. Run and test the X-Lite call to the WebRTC client using the WebRTC2sip gateway and SIP server.

The WebRTC client with the Kamailio SIP server

Kamailio is an open source SIP server that also supports SIP over WebSocket, among other features. It can be hosted only on Linux-based machines. Due to machine dependency of the gateway and scalability issues, I recommend that you use the Kamailio SIP server as an open source option to set up WebRTC to any SIPUA infrastructure. Let's try to get a basic configuration of Kamailio started.

Some prerequisites for the installation of the Kamailio SIP server should be installed on the machine before starting to build Kamailio from source. The following are the packages you need to install before installing Kamailio 4.1.1:

- Git client
- Gcc compile
- Flex
- Bison
- Make
- Libxlm2

Now, perform the following steps to install the Kamailio SIP server:

1. The first step to configure the Kamailio SIP server is to get the source, its compilation, and its installation. We should create a directory on the file system, where the sources will be stored, using the following command line:

   ```
   mkdir -p /usr/local/src/kamailio-4.0
   ```

2. We can download the sources from GIT using the following command lines:

   ```
   git clone git://git.SIP-router.org/SIP-router kamailio
   cd kamailio
   git checkout -b 4.0 origin/4.0
   ```

3. Generate the config files for the build system using the following command:

   ```
   make cfg
   ```

4. The next step is to enable the MySQL module. For this, edit the `modules.lst` file and add `db_mysql` to the variable `include_modules` as follows:

   ```
   include_modules= db_mysql
   ```

5. Once you add the `mysql` module to the list of enabled modules, you can now compile and install it using the following commands:

   make all

   make install

   You might get error messages in between the installation if some prerequisites were not installed. If so, just install these using `yum install`. The following screenshot shows the execution of the Kamailio `make all` and `make install` commands after the GIT checkout:

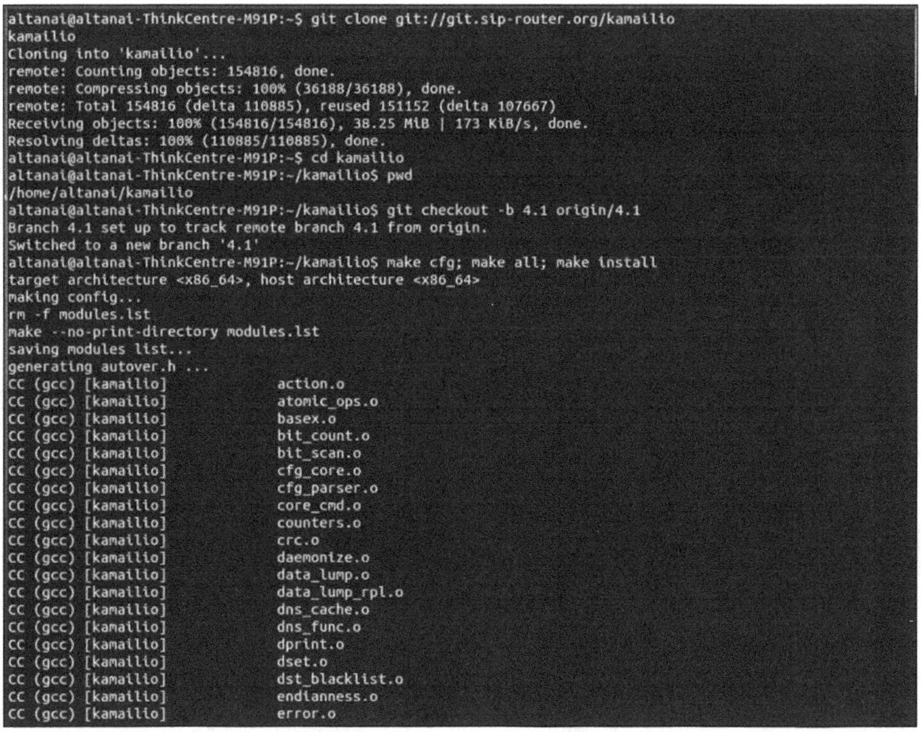

```
altanai@altanai-ThinkCentre-M91P:~$ git clone git://git.sip-router.org/kamailio
kamailio
Cloning into 'kamailio'...
remote: Counting objects: 154816, done.
remote: Compressing objects: 100% (36188/36188), done.
remote: Total 154816 (delta 110885), reused 151152 (delta 107667)
Receiving objects: 100% (154816/154816), 38.25 MiB | 173 KiB/s, done.
Resolving deltas: 100% (110885/110885), done.
altanai@altanai-ThinkCentre-M91P:~$ cd kamailio
altanai@altanai-ThinkCentre-M91P:~/kamailio$ pwd
/home/altanai/kamailio
altanai@altanai-ThinkCentre-M91P:~/kamailio$ git checkout -b 4.1 origin/4.1
Branch 4.1 set up to track remote branch 4.1 from origin.
Switched to a new branch '4.1'
altanai@altanai-ThinkCentre-M91P:~/kamailio$ make cfg; make all; make install
target architecture <x86_64>, host architecture <x86_64>
making config...
rm -f modules.lst
make --no-print-directory modules.lst
saving modules list...
generating autover.h ...
CC (gcc) [kamailio]          action.o
CC (gcc) [kamailio]          atomic_ops.o
CC (gcc) [kamailio]          basex.o
CC (gcc) [kamailio]          bit_count.o
CC (gcc) [kamailio]          bit_scan.o
CC (gcc) [kamailio]          cfg_core.o
CC (gcc) [kamailio]          cfg_parser.o
CC (gcc) [kamailio]          core_cmd.o
CC (gcc) [kamailio]          counters.o
CC (gcc) [kamailio]          crc.o
CC (gcc) [kamailio]          daemonize.o
CC (gcc) [kamailio]          data_lump.o
CC (gcc) [kamailio]          data_lump_rpl.o
CC (gcc) [kamailio]          dns_cache.o
CC (gcc) [kamailio]          dns_func.o
CC (gcc) [kamailio]          dprint.o
CC (gcc) [kamailio]          dset.o
CC (gcc) [kamailio]          dst_blacklist.o
CC (gcc) [kamailio]          endianness.o
CC (gcc) [kamailio]          error.o
```

6. The next step is to set the path to the installation directories. So, before we proceed further, let's have a look at the root directories and other installed paths. The binaries to execute Kamailio and add or delete users are installed inside the `sbin` folder of the Kamailio installation directory. These binaries are as follows:

   ° `kamailio`: This is the Kamailio SIP server

   ° `kamdbctl`: This is the script to create and manage the databases

- ° `kamctl`: This is the shell script to manage and control the Kamailio SIP server

- ° `sercmd`: This is the command line tool to interface with the Kamailio SIP server

The configuration files can be found inside the `etc` folder of the installation directory. Kamailio modules are installed inside the `module`, `modules_k`, and `modules_s` folders. One must ascertain that the installation path for modules match those inside the config files so that Kamailio doesn't yield an error when it starts or, at the worst, at runtime. The following screenshot shows the content of the `sbin` folder:

```
altanai@tcs:/usr/sbin$ ls
aa-status              e2freefrag             named-compilezone      select-default-ispell
accept                 e4defrag               named-journalprint     select-default-wordlist
accessdb               fdformat               netscsid               sendmail
acpid                  filefrag               NetworkManager         service
addgroup               gconf-schemas          newusers               setvesablank
add-shell              genrandom              node                   smtp-sink
adduser                gnome-menus-blacklist  nodeusers              smtp-source
alsactl                groupadd               nologin                split-logfile
anacron                groupdel               nsec3hash              tarcat
apparmor_status        groupmod               ntpdate                tcpd
aptd                   grpck                  ntpdate-debian         tcpdchk
arp                    grpconv                ownership              tcpdmatch
arpaname               grpunconv              pam-auth-update        tcpdump
arpd                   grub-bios-setup        pam_getenv             toshsat1800-irdasetup
aspell-autobuildhash   grub-install           pam_timestamp_check    try-from
avahi-autoipd          grub-mkconfig          paperconfig            tunelp
avahi-daemon           grub-mkdevicemap       pm-hibernate           tzconfig
avivotool              grub-mknetdir          pm-powersave           ufw
ax25-node              grub-probe             pm-suspend             unity-greeter
bccmd                  grub-reboot            pm-suspend-hybrid      update-alternatives
biosdecode             grub-set-default       popcon-largest-unused  update-apt-xapian-index
bluetoothd             guest-account          popularity-contest     update-binfmts
chat                   hciattach              postalias              update-ca-certificates
check_forensic         hciconfig              postcat                update-catalog
checkgid               hciemu                 postconf               update-cracklib
chgpasswd              hplj1000               postdrop               update-default-aspell
chpasswd               hplj1005               postfix                update-default-ispell
chroot                 hplj1018               postfix-add-filter     update-default-wordlist
ck-log-system-restart  hplj1020               postfix-add-policy     update-dictcommon-aspell
ck-log-system-start    hpljP1005              postkick               update-dictcommon-hunspell
ck-log-system-stop     hpljP1006              postlock               update-fonts-alias
console-kit-daemon     hpljP1007              postlog                update-fonts-dir
cpgr                   hpljP1008              postmap                update-fonts-scale
cppw                   hpljP1505              postmulti              update-grub
cracklib-check         htcacheclean           postqueue              update-grub2
cracklib-format        httxt2dbm              postsuper              update-grub-gfxpayload
cracklib-packer        iconvconfig            pppconfig              update-gsfontmap
cracklib-unpacker      inetd                  pppd                   update-icon-caches
```

7. To configure the Kamailio SIP server as per out environment needs, we must edit the config files. We have to add the IP address of the server in the `kamailio.cfg` file. Add the following lines to `kamailio.cfg`, if not already present:

```
#!define WITH_DEBUG
#!define WITH_MYSQL
#!define WITH_AUTH
#!define WITH_ALIASDB
#!define WITH_USRLOCDB
#!define WITH_PRESENCE
#!define WITH_XCAPSRV
#!define WITH_RLS
#!define WITH_XMLRPC
#!define WITH_TLS
#!define WITH_MULTIDOMAIN
#!define WITH_WEBSOCKETS
#!define WITH_REGINFO
```

Make sure that the following line regarding the SIP domain is uncommented in the `kamctlrc` file:

```
SIP_DOMAIN=<your domain name, for example, Somedomain.com>
```

The database type can be MYSQL, PGSQL, ORACLE, DB_BERKELEY, DBTEXT, or SQLITE, by default, none is loaded. Also, one has to specify the database host, database name, user, and password.

```
DBENGINE=MYSQLs
DBHOST=localhost
DBNAME=kamailio
DBRWUSER="kamailio"
DBRWPW="kamailiorw"
DBROUSER="kamailioro"
DBROPW="kamailioro"
ALIASES_TYPE="DB"
```

8. In the next step, we will cover the process of adding more modules to the existing setup. We must use the `make` and `configure` commands for this purpose. Once the `.so` file is created, copy it to the folder where modules are installed.

9. In the next and most crucial step, we must create the MySQL Kamailio database. To create the MySQL database, we have to use the database setup script. First, edit the kamctlrc file to set the database server type. Locate the DBENGINE variable and set it to MYSQL as follows:

```
DBENGINE=MYSQL
```

10. Once we are done updating the kamctlrc file, run the following script to create the database used by Kamailio. We can find kamdbctl inside the sbin folder of the installation directory.

```
# ./kamdbctl create
```

The preceding script will add two users in MySQL:

 ○ kamailio (with the default password as kamailiorw): This user has full access rights to the kamailio database

 ○ kamailioro (with the default password as kamailioro): This user has read-only access rights to the kamailio database

We can check the database created inside MySQL using the show database and show tables commands of MySQL.

11. To start Kamailio, go to sbin inside the Kamailio installation directory and run the following command:

```
./kamailio start
```

```
altanai@tcs:/usr/local/sbin$ sudo kamailio start
[sudo] password for altanai:
loading modules under /usr/local/lib64/kamailio/modules_k/:/usr/local/lib64/kamailio/modules/
 0(15261) INFO: tls [tls_init.c:385]: init_tls_compression(): tls: init_tls: disabling compression...
Listening on
                udp: 14.96.130.114:5060
                udp: 14.96.130.114:6060
                tcp: 14.96.130.114:5060
                tcp: 14.96.130.114:6060
                tcp: 14.96.130.114:443
Aliases:
                tcp: tcs.com:443
                tcp: tcs.com:6060
                tcp: tcs.com:5060
                udp: tcs.com:6060
                udp: tcs.com:5060
                *: 14.96.130.114:*

 0(15261) INFO: <core> [tcp_main.c:4836]: init_tcp(): init_tcp: using epoll_lt as the io watch method (auto
detected)
 0(15263) INFO: rr [../outbound/api.h:54]: ob_load_api(): Failed to import bind_ob
 0(15263) INFO: rr [rr_mod.c:159]: mod_init(): outbound module not available
 0(15263) INFO: usrloc [hslot.c:53]: ul_init_locks(): locks array size 512
 0(15263) INFO: cfgutils [cfgutils.c:784]: mod_init(): no hash_file given, disable hash functionality
 0(15263) INFO: auth [auth_mod.c:350]: mod_init(): auth: qop set, but nonce-count (nc_enabled) support disa
bled
 0(15263) WARNING: tls [tls_mod.c:273]: mod_init(): WARNING: tls: mod_init: tls support is disabled (set en
able_tls=1 in the config to enable it)
 0(15263) INFO: <core> [udp_server.c:176]: probe_max_receive_buffer(): INFO: udp_init: SO_RCVBUF is initial
ly 212992
 0(15263) INFO: <core> [udp_server.c:227]: probe_max_receive_buffer(): INFO: udp_init: SO_RCVBUF is finally
 425984
 0(15263) INFO: <core> [udp_server.c:176]: probe_max_receive_buffer(): INFO: udp_init: SO_RCVBUF is initial
ly 212992
 0(15263) INFO: <core> [udp_server.c:227]: probe_max_receive_buffer(): INFO: udp_init: SO_RCVBUF is finally
 425984
altanai@tcs:/usr/local/sbin$ 12(15285) INFO: ctl [io_listener.c:225]: io_listen_loop(): io_listen_loop: us
ing epoll_lt io watch method (config)
```

12. To add users to the database, use the `kamctl` command as follows:

```
./kamctl add <user><password>
```

```
altanai@homeMachine:/usr/local/sbin$ ls
kamailio kamcmd kamctl kamdbctl
altanai@homeMachine:/usr/local/sbin$ sudo ./kamctl add alice
alice
new user 'alice' added
```

13. Register the WebRTC clients with Kamailio by adding user details and domain information in the `call.htm` registration section. Add the address of the machine as `ws://ip:port`, for example, `ws://10.34.65.98.443`, under the WS server input box on the `register.htm` page. The status displayed on the `call.htm` page should read **Connected**.

14. Register another user, and one can make multiple calls between them.

Setting up the admin console for Kamailio is an optional task. However, it's recommended as it provides a graphical provisioning system to configure and alert the settings of the SIP server. The following screenshot shows the admin GUI SIREMIS, which gives a visual interface to server management rather than the command prompt to monitor user accounts and usage statistics:

We can also monitor the real-time traffic using the Wireshark protocol analyzer. The following screenshot depicts the flow graph generated from Wireshark, which captures on all interfaces using the SIP and the WebSocket filters. In the following screenshot, the flow graph traces the Kamailio SIP server:

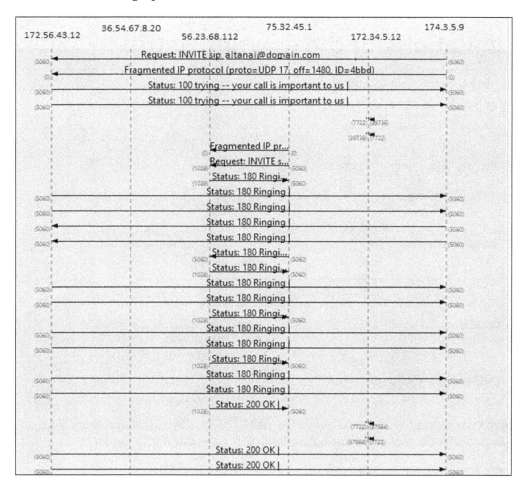

The flow depicts a call session that begins with an invite request traversing across various network nodes. It's not important to trace the path of the signal for now; however, the sequence of signal flows is a crucial task in determining that the WebRTC client server model is performing well.

Limitations of the existing setup

We saw how to develop a WebRTC client, install an SIP server, and configure a WebRTC to SIP environment. A sky view of our final, existing client-server solution setup for SIPWS signaling and WebRTC media so far is shown as follows:

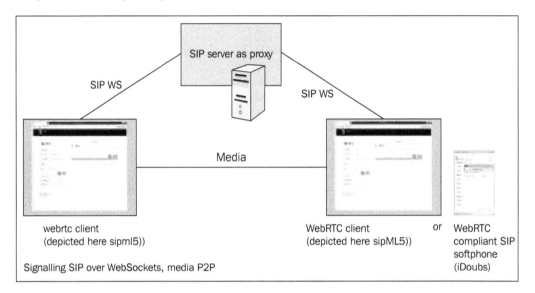

As per our current setup status, only the WebRTC-enabled client and servers can participate in the communication flow in an **offer/answer (O/A)** model.

There are, however, numerous limitations of the existing solution, some of which are mentioned in the following sections. In the upcoming chapters, we shall do away with most of the limitations.

Firewall and NAT issues

The existing architecture does not provide the **Network Address Translation** (**NAT**) technique to overcome the blockage due to firewalls and enterprise policies. As a solution, we must see the alternative for public IP discovery in the WebRTC client server setup. NAT is possible in the Kamailio server through RTP proxy modules and STUN.

Media transcoding

If the codecs on two endpoints do not match for audio and video communication, then it could lead to a session failure with an abrupt termination of calls when a user picks up a ringing call. There is where the media transcoder is required to support communication with non-WebRTC devices such as SIP phone and softphones. As a solution, we can either use the RTCWeb Breaker, which converts SDP and media streams for WebRTC and other UAs, or configure the media server such as FreeSWITCH, which provides the functionality. The following diagram shows the complete architecture with the STUN server and RTCWeb Breaker:

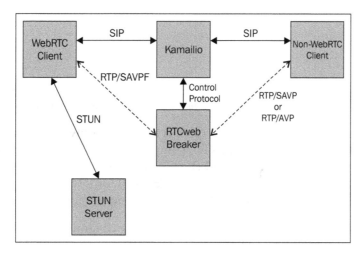

A call flow that depicts the flow of media from the WebRTC client to the non-WebRTC client (SIP phone) through the RTCWeb Breaker is shown as follows:

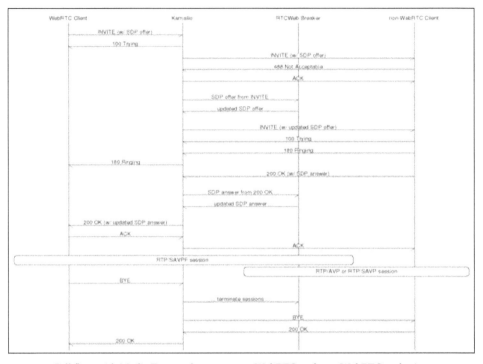

Call flow with Media Transcoder to connect WebRTC and non-WebRTC endpoints

Real time-Transport Protocol (RTP), which is the media flow mechanism in most SIP clients, including SIP-based WebRTC, comprises two parts: the RTP data transfer protocol and the **RTP Control Protocol (RTCP)**. In addition to this, WebRTC also mandates the use of **Secure RTP Profile (RTP/SAVP)** for RTCP-based feedback. An RTP profile defines media parameters such as compression and encoding.

The RTP/SAVPF profile, as depicted in the following diagram, is the combination of the basic RTP/AVP profile, the RTP profile for **RTCP-based feedback (RTP/AVPF)**, and the RTP/SAVP. The RTCP-based feedback extensions are needed for the improved RTCP timer that enables features such as more flexible transmission and report of congestion.

After fulfilling the limitations, there are some recommended enhancements in the existing architecture; they contribute to making a robust, secure communication platform. The limitations are described as follows:

- Media should not be free flowing between peer to peer but passing through a **media relay** mechanism. A media relay mechanism involves a media server to be in the path of the media flow. This way, the media server receives the audio/video from one end and relays it to the other end. This leads to a better control on the communication by centralized network nodes.

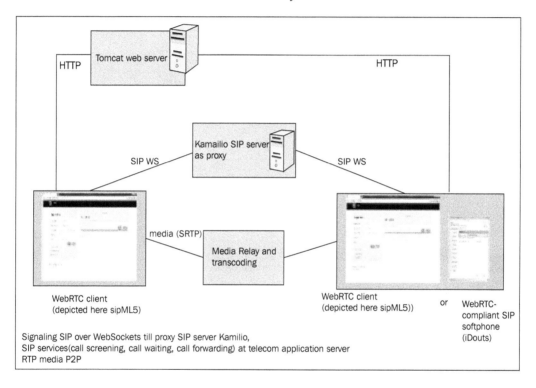

- Ipv4 and Ipv6 must be supported.

- The Telecom Application server is needed to embed the logic of SIP services such as call waiting, call forwarding, and call screening.

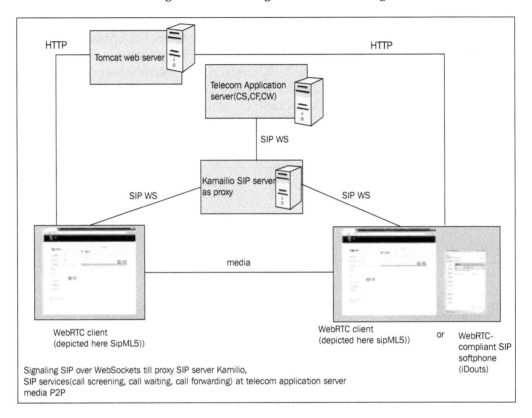

- Database implementation must happen to keep track of calls, user authentication, user profile, and so on.

- The monitoring tools allow for real-time statistics that, in turn, help the service provider to make predictive judgments and review the status at real time. This also aids in charging and billing if the service provider opts to bill the customer.

We will overcome these and a few more limitations when integrating with the **IP Multimedia Subsystem** (**IMS**) environment. They will be discussed in detail in the next chapter.

Summary

In this chapter, we learned how to make a dynamic web application for the WebRTC client using primitive building blocks such as CSS, JavaScript, SIP library, and HTML form elements. We also saw the setup of various kinds of SIP servers and their applicability in establishing an end-to-end call. In this process, we studied the implementation of WebSocket-supported SIP servers. We also studied the integration of the SIP WebRTC client with non-WebSocket supported SIP servers, through WebSocket gateways.

In essence, we learned about how client development and essential servers help to support the WebRTC SIP infrastructure. This includes the Tomcat web server, which caters to the loading of a web page and the HTTP handshake; the Kamailio SIP server, which acts as a registrar; and the SIP proxy node. The WebRTC client programs used open source libraries such as jsSIP and sipML5. The interaction and challenges inherent in communication between non-WebRTC sip endpoints, such as SIP phones and softphone, were also discussed.

3

WebRTC with SIP and IMS

IP Multimedia Subsystem (IMS) is an architectural framework for IP Multimedia communications and IP telephony based on Convergent applications. It specifies three layers in a telecom network:

- **Transport or Access layer**: This is the bottom-most segment responsible for interacting with end systems such as phones.
- **IMS layer**: This is the middleware responsible for authenticating and routing the traffic and facilitating call control through the Service layer.
- **Service or Application layer**: This is the top-most layer where all of the call control applications and **Value Added Services (VAS)** are hosted.

IMS standards are defined by **Third Generation Partnership Project (3GPP)** which adopt and promote **Internet Engineering Task Force (IETF) Request for Comments (RFCs)**. Refer to `http://www.3gpp.org/technologies/keywords-acronyms/109-ims` to learn more about 3GPP IMS specification releases.

This chapter will walk us through the interaction of WebRTC client with important IMS nodes and modules. The **WebRTC gateway** is the first point of contact for the SIP requests from the WebRTC client to enter into the IMS network. The WebRTC gateway converts SIP over WebSocket implementation to legacy/plain SIP, that is, a WebRTC to SIP gateway that connects to the IMS world and is able to communicate with a legacy SIP environment. It also can translate other REST- or JSON-based signaling protocols into SIP. The gateway also handles the media operation that involves DTLS, SRTP, RTP, transcoding, demuxing, and so on.

In the previous chapter, we saw how to create the WebRTC environment using the SIP server that has WebSocket capabilities. In this chapter, we will study a case where there exists a simple IMS core environment, and the WebRTC clients are meant to interact after the signals are traversed through core IMS nodes such as **Call Session Control Function (CSCF)**, **Home Subscriber Server (HSS)**, and **Telecom Application Server (TAS)**.

The Interaction with core IMS nodes

This section describes the sequence of steps that must be followed for the integration of the WebRTC client with IMS. Before you go ahead, set up a **Session Border Controller** (**SBC**) / WebRTC gateway / SIP proxy node for the WebRTC client to interact with the IMS control layer.

1. Direct the control towards the CSCF nodes of IMS, namely, Proxy-CSCF, Interrogating-CSCF, and Serving-CSCF.

2. The subscriber details and the location are updated in the HSS.

3. **Serving-CSCF** (**SCSCF**) routes the call through the **SIP Application Server** to invoke any services before the call is processed. The Application Server, which is part of the IMS service layer, is the point of adding logic to call processing in the form of VAS.

4. Additionally, we will uncover the process of integrating media server for an inter-codec conversion between legacy SIP phones and WebRTC clients.

The setup will allow us to support all SIP nodes and endpoints as part of the IMS landscape. We will follow the interaction of the WebRTC SIP client with IMS nodes, assuming that the SIPWS to SIP gateway is configured, as described in *Chapter 2, Making a Standalone WebRTC Communication Client.*

The following figure shows the placement of the SIPWS to SIP gateway in the IMS network:

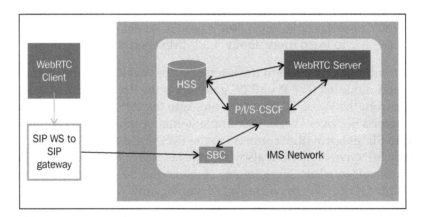

The WebRTC client is a web-based dynamic application that is run over a Web Application Server. For simplification, we can club the components of the WebRTC client and the Web Application Server together and address them jointly as the WebRTC client, as shown in the following diagram:

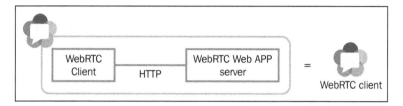

There are four major components of the OpenIMS core involved in this setup as described in the following sections. Along with these, two components of the WebRTC infrastructure (the client and the gateway) are also necessary to connect the WebRTC endpoints. Three optional entities are also described as part of this setup.

The components of Open IMS are CSCF nodes and HSS. More information on each component is given in the following sections.

The Call Session Control Function

The three parts of CSCF are described as follows:

- **Proxy-CSCF (P-CSCF)** is the first point of contact for a **user agent (UA)** to which all **user equipments (UEs)** are attached. It is responsible for routing an incoming SIP request to other IMS nodes, such as registrar and **Policy and Charging Rules Function (PCRF)**, among others.

- **Interrogating-CSCF (I-CSCF)** is the inbound SIP proxy server for querying the HSS as to which S-CSCF should be serving the incoming request.

- **Serving-CSCF (S-CFCS)** is the heart of the IMS core as it enables centralized IMS service control by defining routing paths that act like the registrar, interact with the Media Server, and much more.

Home Subscriber System

IMS core **Home Subscriber System (HSS)** is the database component responsible for maintaining user profiles, subscriptions, and location information. The data is used in functions such as authentication and authorization of users while using IM services.

The components of the WebRTC infrastructure primarily comprises of WebRTC Web Application Servers, WebRTC web-based clients, and the SIP gateway.

- **WebRTC Web Application Server and client**: The WebRTC client is intrinsically a web application that is composed of user interfaces, data access objects, and controllers to handle HTTP requests. A Web Application Server is where an application is hosted. As WebRTC is a browser-based technique, it is meant to be an HTML-based web application. The call functionalities are rendered through the SIP JavaScript files. The browser's native WebRTC capabilities are utilized to capture and transmit the data. A WebRTC service provider must embed the SIP call functions on a web page that has a call interface. It must provide values for the To and From SIP addresses, div to play audio/video content, and access to users' resources such as camera, mic, and speakers.

- **WebRTC to IMS gateway**: This is the point where the conversion of the signal from SIP over WebSockets to legacy/plain SIP takes place. It renders the signaling into a state that the IMS network nodes can understand. For media, it performs the transcoding from WebRTC standard codecs to others. It also performs decryption and demux of audio/video/RTCP/RTP.

There are other servers that act as IMS nodes as well, such as the STUN/TURN Server, Media Server, and Application Server. They are described as follows:

- **STUN/TURN Server**: These are employed for NAT traversals and overcoming firewall restrictions through ICE candidates. They might not be needed when the WebRTC client is on the Internet and the WebRTC gateway is also listening on a publicly accessible IP.

- **Media Server**: Media server plays a role when media relay is required between the UEs instead of a direct peer-to-peer communication. It also comes into picture for services such as voicemail, **Interactive Voice Response (IVR)**, playback, and recording.

- **Application Server (AS)**: Application Server is the point where developers can make customized logic for call control such as VAS in the form of call redirecting in cases when the receiver is absent and selective call screening.

The IP Multimedia Subsystem core

IMS is an architecture for real-time multimedia (voice, data, video, and messaging) services using a common IP network. It defines a layered architecture. According to the 3GPP specification, IMS entities are classified into six categories:

- Session management and route (CSCF, GGSN, and SGSN)
- Database (HSS and SLF)
- Interworking elements (BGCF, MGCF, IM-MGW, and SGW)
- Service (Application Server, MRFC, and MRFP)
- Strategy support entities (PDF)
- Billing

Interoperability with the SIP infrastructure requires a session border controller to decrypt the WebRTC control and media flows. A media node is also set up for transcoding between WebRTC codecs and other legacy phones. When a gateway is involved, the WebRTC voice and video peer connections are between the browser and the border controller. In our case, we have been using Kamailio in this role (refer to *Chapter 2, Making a Standalone WebRTC Communication Client*). Kamailio is an open source SIP server capable of processing both SIP and SIPWS signaling.

As WebRTC is made to function over SIP-based signaling, it is applicable to enjoy all of the services and solutions made for the IMS environment. The telecom operators can directly mount the services in the Service layer, and subscribers can avail the services right from their web browsers through the WebRTC client. This adds a new dimension to user accessibility and experience. A WebRTC client's true potential will come into effect only when it is integrated with the IMS framework.

We have some readymade, open IMS setups that have been tested for WebRTC-to-IMS integration. The setups are as follows:

- **3GPP IMS**: This is the IMS specification by 3GPP, which is an association of telecommunications group
- **OpenIMS**: This is the open source implementation of the IMS CSCFs and a lightweight HSS for the IMS core
- **DubangoIMS**: This is the cross-platform and open source 3GPP IMS/LTE framework
- **KamailioIMS**: Kamailio Version 4.0 and above incorporates IMS support by means of OpenIMS

We can also use any other IMS structure for the integration. In this chapter, we will demonstrate the use of OpenIMS. For this, it is required that a WebRTC client and a non-WebRTC client must be interoperable by means of signaling and media transcoding. Also, the essential components of IMS world, such as HSS, Media Server, and Application Server, should be integrated with the WebRTC setup.

The OpenIMS Core

The Open IMS Core is an open source implementation for core elements of the IMS network that includes IMS CSCFs nodes and HSS. The following diagram shows how a connection is made from WebRTC to CSCF:

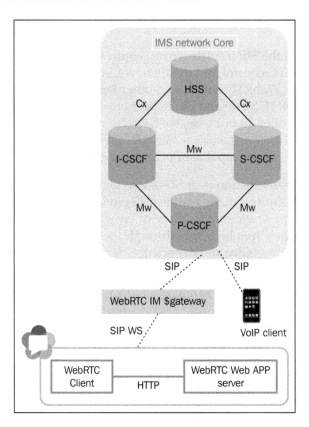

The following are the prerequisites to install the Open IMS core:

- Make sure that you have the following packages installed on your Linux machine, as their absence can hinder the IMS installation process:
    - ○ Git and Subversion
    - ○ GCC3/4, Make, JDK1.5, Ant
    - ○ MySQL as the database
    - ○ Bison and Flex, the Linux utilities
    - ○ libxml2 (Version 2.6 and above) and libmysql with development versions

    Install these packages from the Synaptic package manager or using the command prompt.

- For the LoST interface of E-CSCF, use the following command lines:

```
sudo apt-get install mysql-server libmysqlclient15-dev libxml2
libxml2-dev bind9 ant flex bison curl libcurl4-gnutls-dev
```

```
sudo apt-get install curl libcurl4-gnutls-dev
```

- The **Domain Name Server (DNS)**, bind9, should be installed and run. To do this, we can run the following command line:

```
sudo apt-get install bind9
```

- We need a web browser to review the status of the connection on the web console. To download a web browser, go to its download page. For example, Chrome can be downloaded from https://www.google.com/intl/en_in/chrome/browser/.

- We must verify that the Java version installed is above 1.5 so as to not break the compilation process in between, and set the path of JAVA_HOME as follows:

```
export JAVA_HOME=/usr/lib/jvm/java-7-openjdk-amd64/jre
```

The output of the command line that checks the Java version is as follows:

```
java version "1.7.0_40"
Java(TM) SE Runtime Environment (build 1.7.0_40-b43)
Java HotSpot(TM) 64-Bit Server VM (build 24.0-b56, mixed mode)
```

The following are the steps to install OpenIMS. As the source code is preconfigured to work from a standard file path of /opt, we will use the predefined directory for installation.

1. Go to the /opt folder and create a directory to store the OpenIMS core, using the following command lines:

    ```
    mkdir /opt/OpenIMSCore
    ```

    ```
    cd /opt/OpenIMSCore
    ```

2. Create a directory to store FHOSS, check out the HSS, and compile the source using the following command lines:

    ```
    mkdirFHoSS
    ```

    ```
    svn checkout http://svn.berlios.de/svnroot/repos/openimscore/
    FHoSS/trunk FHoSS
    ```

    ```
    cdFHoSS
    ```

    ```
    ant compile deploy
    ```

     Note that the code requires Java Version 7 or lower to work.

3. Also, create a directory to store ser_ims, check out the CFCs, and then install ser_ims using the following command lines:

    ```
    mkdirser_ims
    ```

    ```
    svn checkout http://svn.berlios.de/svnroot/repos/openimscore/ser_
    ims/trunk ser_ims
    ```

    ```
    cdser_ims
    ```

    ```
    make install-libs all
    ```

    After downloading and installing the OpenIMS installation directory, its contents are as follows:

By default, the nodes are configured to work only on the local loopback, and the default domain configured is open-ims.test. The MySQL access rights are also set only for local access. However, this can be modified using the following steps:

1. Run the following command line:

   ```
   ./opt/ser_ims/cfg/configurator.sh
   ```

2. Replace 127.0.0.1 (the default IP for the localhost) with the new IP address that is required to configure the IMS Core server.

3. Replace the home domain (open-ims.test) with the required domain name.

4. Change the database passwords.

   The following figure depicts the domain change process through configurator.sh:

```
altanai@tcs:/opt/OpenIMSCore/ser_ims/cfg$ sudo ./configurator.sh
Domain Name:tcs.com
IP Adress:10.1.5.20
File to change ["all" for everything, "exit" to quit]:all
changing: ecscf.cfg icscf.cfg icscf_pg.sql icscf.sql icscf.thig.cfg icscf.xml lrf.cfg mgcf.c
st_pg.sql scscf.cfg scscf.xml TGPPGq.xml TGPPRx.xml trcf.cfg
```

5. To resolve the domain name, we need to add a new IMS domain to bind the configuration directory. Change to the system's bind folder (cd /etc/bind) and copy the open-ims.dnszone file there after replacing the domain name.

   ```
   sudo cp /opt/OpenIMSCore/ser_ims/cfg/open-ims.dnszone /etc/bind/
   ```

6. Open the name.conf file and include open-ims.dnszone in the list that already exists:

   ```
   include "/etc/bind/named.conf.options";

   include "/etc/bind/named.conf.local";

   include "/etc/bind/named.conf.default-zones";

   include "/etc/bind/open-ims.dnszone";
   ```

 One can also add a reverse zone file, which, contrary to the DNS zone file, converts an address to a name.

7. Restart the naming server using the following command:

   ```
   sudo bind9 restart
   ```

8. On occasion of any failure or error note, the system logs/reports can be generated using the following command line:

```
tail -f /var/log/syslog
```

9. Open the MySQL client (`sudo mysql`) and add the SQL scripts for the creation of database and tables for HSS operations:

```
mysql -u root -p -h localhost<ser_ims/cfg/icscf.sql
mysql -u root -p -h localhost<FHoSS/scripts/hss_db.sql
mysql -u root -p -h localhost<FHoSS/scripts/userdata.sql
```

The following screenshot shows the tables for the HSS database:

```
mysql> show tables
    -> ;
+-------------------------+
| Tables_in_hss_db        |
+-------------------------+
| aliases_repository_data |
| application_server      |
| capabilities_set        |
| capability              |
| charging_info           |
| cx_events               |
| dsai                    |
| dsai_ifc                |
| dsai_impu               |
| ifc                     |
| impi                    |
| impi_impu               |
| impu                    |
| impu_visited_network    |
| imsu                    |
| preferred_scscf_set     |
| repository_data         |
| sh_notification         |
| sh_subscription         |
| shared_ifc_set          |
| sp                      |
| sp_ifc                  |
| sp_shared_ifc_set       |
| spt                     |
| tp                      |
| visited_network         |
| zh_uss                  |
+-------------------------+
27 rows in set (0.00 sec)
```

 Users should be registered with a domain (that is, one needs to make changes in the `userdata.sql` file by replacing the default domain name with the required domain name). Note that while it is not mandatory to change the domain, it is a good practice to add a new domain that describes the enterprise or service provider's name.

The following screenshot shows user domains changed from the default to the personal domain:

```
mysql> select * from impi;
+-----+---------+-----------+-------+-------------+-------------------+
| id | id_imsu | identity  | k     | auth_scheme | default_auth_scheme
er | zh_uicc_type | zh_key_life_time | zh_default_auth_scheme |
+-----+---------+-----------+-------+-------------+-------------------+
| 4 |       1 | alice@tcs.com | alice |         127 |                   1
   |       0 |    3600 |                 1 |
| 2 |       2 | bob@tcs.com  | bob   |         255 |                   1
   |       0 |    3600 |                 1 |
+-----+---------+-----------+-------+-------------+-------------------+
2 rows in set (0.00 sec)
```

10. Copy the `pcscf.cfg`, `pcscf.sh`, `icscf.cfg`, `icscf.xml`, `icscf.sh`, `scscf.cfg`, `scscf.xml`, and `scscf.sh` files to the `/opt/OpenIMSCore` location.

11. Start the **Policy Call Session Control Function (PCSCF)** by executing the `pcscf.sh` script. The default element port assigned for P-CSCF is `4060`.

    A screenshot of the running of PCSCF is as follows:

```
Listening on
         udp: 10.1.5.20 [10.1.5.20]:4060
         tcp: 10.1.5.20 [10.1.5.20]:4060
Aliases:
         tcp: tcs.com:4060
         udp: tcs.com:4060
         *: pcscf.tcs.com:4060

0(14564) init_tcp: using epoll_lt as the io watch method (auto detected)
0(14564) Maxfwd module- initializing
0(14564) INFO:P-CSCF:mod_init: Initialization of module
0(14564) INFOP-CSCF:mod_init: E-CSCF uri is sip:ecscf.tcs.com:7060
0(14564) DBG:P-CSCF:mod_init: Can not import load_client_rf. This module might
require client_rf module.
0(14564) DBG:P-CSCF:mod_init: Usage of the charging info in the pcscf module wi
ll be disabled, no charging correlation possible.
0(14564) INFOP-CSCFmod_init:E-CSCF uri is sip:ecscf.tcs.com:7060
0(14564) INFO: udp_init: SO_RCVBUF is initially 212992
0(14564) INFO: udp_init: SO_RCVBUF is finally 425984
2(14566)  1(14565)  3(14567) INFO:P-CSCF:mod_init: Initialization of module in
child [2]
INFO:P-CSCF:mod_init: Initialization of module in child [3]
0(14564) INFO:P-CSCF:mod_init: Initialization of module in child [0]
INFO:P-CSCF:mod_init: Initialization of module in child [1]
4(14568) INFO:P-CSCF:mod_init: Initialization of module in child [4]
6(14570) 10(14574)  7(14571) INFO:P-CSCF:mod_init: Initialization of module in
child [8]
8(14572) INFO:P-CSCF:mod_init: Initialization of module in child [6]
9(14573) 11(14575) INFO:P-CSCF:mod_init: Initialization of module in child [-4]

5(14569) INFO:P-CSCF:mod_init: Initialization of module in child [7]
INFO:P-CSCF:mod_init: Initialization of module in child [-1]
INFO:P-CSCF:mod_init: Initialization of module in child [5]
INFO:P-CSCF:mod_init: Initialization of module in child [-1]
5(14569) INF:P-CSCF:---------  Registrar Contents begin --------
5(14569) INF:P-CSCF:---------  Registrar Contents end ---------
5(14569) INF:P-CSCF:---------  Subscription list begin --------
5(14569) INF:P-CSCF:---------  Subscription list end ---------
5(14569) INF:P-CSCF:---------  Registrar Contents begin --------
5(14569) INF:P-CSCF:---------  Registrar Contents end ---------
5(14569) INF:P-CSCF:---------  Subscription list begin --------
5(14569) INF:P-CSCF:---------  Subscription list end ---------
5(14569) INF:P-CSCF:---------  Registrar Contents begin --------
5(14569) INF:P-CSCF:---------  Registrar Contents end ---------
5(14569) INF:P-CSCF:---------  Subscription list begin --------
5(14569) INF:P-CSCF:---------  Subscription list end ---------
^Y 5(14569) INF:P-CSCF:---------  Registrar Contents begin --------
5(14569) INF:P-CSCF:---------  Registrar Contents end ---------
5(14569) INF:P-CSCF:---------  Subscription list begin --------
5(14569) INF:P-CSCF:---------  Subscription list end ---------
```

12. Start the **Interrogating Call Session Control Function (I-CSCF)** by executing the `icscf.sh` script.

The default element port assigned to I-CSCF is `5060`. If the scripts display a warning about connection, it is just because the FHoSS client still needs to be started. A screenshot of the running I-CSCF is as follows:

```
altanai@tcs:/opt/OpenIMSCore$ sudo ./icscf.sh
[sudo] password for altanai:
listening on
            udp: 10.1.5.20 [10.1.5.20]:5060
            tcp: 10.1.5.20 [10.1.5.20]:5060
Aliases:
            *: tcs.com:*
            *: icscf.tcs.com:*

0(14729) init_tcp: using epoll_lt as the io watch method (auto detected)
0(14729) Maxfwd module- initializing
0(14729) INFO:I-CSCF:mod_init: Initialization of module
0(14729) INF:I-CSCF:icscf_db_get_nds: Loaded 1 trusted domains
0(14729) INF:I-CSCF:icscf_db_get_capabilities: Loaded 2 capabilities for 1 S-CSCFs (0 invalid entries in db)
0(14729) Twofish encryption ready
0(14729) INFO:cdp:cdp_init(): CDiameterPeer initializing
0(14729) Diameter Peer Config:
0(14729)        FQDN    : icscf.tcs.com
0(14729)        Realm   : tcs.com
0(14729)        VendorID: 10415
0(14729)        ProdName: CDiameterPeer
0(14729)        AcceptUn: [X]
0(14729)        DropUnkn: [X]
0(14729)        Tc      : 30
0(14729)        Workers : 4
0(14729)        QueueLen: 8
0(14729)        ConnTime: 5
0(14729)        TranTime: 5
0(14729)        SessHash: 128
0(14729)        DefAuthT: 60
0(14729)        MaxAuthT: 300
0(14729)        Peers   : 1
0(14729)            FQDN: hss.tcs.com      Realm: tcs.com        Port: 3868
0(14729)        Acceptors : 1
0(14729)            Port: 3869    Bind: 10.1.5.20
0(14729)        Applications : 4
0(14729)            Auth ID: 16777216      Vendor: 10415
0(14729)            Auth ID: 16777216      Vendor: 4491
0(14729)            Auth ID: 16777216      Vendor: 13019
0(14729)            Auth ID: 16777216      Vendor: 0
0(14729)        Supported Vendors : 0
0(14729)        Routing Table :
0(14729)            DefaultRoute: [  10] hss.tcs.com
0(14729) INFO: udp_init: SO_RCVBUF is initially 212992
0(14729) INFO: udp_init: SO_RCVBUF is finally 425984
1(14731)  2(14732) INFO:I-CSCF:mod_init: Initialization of module in child [2] receiver child=1 sock=10.1.5.20:5060
INFO:I-CSCF:mod_init: Initialization of module in child [1] receiver child=0 sock=10.1.5.20:5060
3(14733) INFO:I-CSCF:mod_init: Initialization of module in child [3] receiver child=2 sock=10.1.5.20:5060
4(14734) INFO:I-CSCF:mod_init: Initialization of module in child [4] receiver child=3 sock=10.1.5.20:5060
0(14729) INFO:I-CSCF:mod_init: Initialization of module in child [0] main
0(14729) INFO:cdp:cdp_child_init(): CDiameterPeer starting ...
6(14736) INFO:I-CSCF:mod_init: Initialization of module in child [-1] timer
```

13. Start SCSCF by executing the `scscf.sh` script. The default element port assignment for S-CSCF is `6060`.

A screenshot of the running SCSCF is as follows:

```
altanai@tcs:/opt/OpenIMSCore$ sudo ./scscf.sh
[sudo] password for altanai:
Listening on
              udp: 10.1.5.20 [10.1.5.20]:6060
              tcp: 10.1.5.20 [10.1.5.20]:6060
Aliases:
              tcp: tcs.com:6060
              udp: tcs.com:6060
               *: scscf.tcs.com:6060

0(14868) init_tcp: using epoll_lt as the io watch method (auto detected)
0(14868) Maxfwd module- initializing
0(14868) INFO:S-CSCF:mod_init: Initialization of module
0(14868) INFO:ISC: - init
0(14868) INFO:cdp:cdp_init(): CDiameterPeer initializing
0(14868) Diameter Peer Config:
0(14868)       FQDN    : scscf.tcs.com
0(14868)       Realm   : tcs.com
0(14868)       VendorID: 10415
0(14868)       ProdName: CDiameterPeer
0(14868)       AcceptUn: [X]
0(14868)       DropUnkn: [X]
0(14868)       Tc      : 30
0(14868)       Workers : 4
0(14868)       QueueLen: 8
0(14868)       ConnTime: 5
0(14868)       TranTime: 5
0(14868)       SessHash: 128
0(14868)       DefAuthT: 60
0(14868)       MaxAuthT: 300
0(14868)       Peers   : 1
0(14868)             FQDN: hss.tcs.com        Realm: tcs.com        Port: 3868
0(14868)       Acceptors : 1
0(14868)             Port: 3870     Bind: 10.1.5.20
0(14868)       Applications : 4
0(14868)             Auth ID:  16777216     Vendor: 10415
0(14868)             Auth ID:  16777216     Vendor: 4491
0(14868)             Auth ID:  16777216     Vendor: 13019
0(14868)             Auth ID:  16777216     Vendor: 0
0(14868)       Supported Vendors : 0
0(14868)       Routing Table :
0(14868)             DefaultRoute: [  10] hss.tcs.com
0(14868) INFO: udp_init: SO_RCVBUF is initially 212992
0(14868) INFO: udp_init: SO_RCVBUF is finally 425984
1(14869)  2(14870) INFO:S-CSCF:mod_child_init: Initialization of module in child [1]
INFO:S-CSCF:mod_child_init: Initialization of module in child [2]
3(14871)  4(14872) INFO:S-CSCF:mod_child_init: Initialization of module in child [4]
0(14868) INFO:S-CSCF:mod_child_init: Initialization of module in child [0]
0(14868) INFO:ISC: - child init [0]
0(14868) INFO:cdp:cdp_child_init(): CDiameterPeer starting ...
7(14875) INFO:S-CSCF:mod_child_init: Initialization of module in child [1001]
8(14876) INFO:S-CSCF:mod_child_init: Initialization of module in child [1002]
```

14. Start the **FOKUS Home Subscriber Server (FHoSS)** by executing `FHoss/deploy/startup.sh`.

    The HSS interacts using the diameter protocol. The ports used for this protocol are `3868`, `3869`, and `3870`.

    A screenshot of the running HSS is shown as follows:

```
altanai@tcs:/opt/OpenIMSCore/FHoSS/deploy$ sudo ./startup.sh
Building Classpath
Classpath is lib/xml-apis.jar:lib/xercesImpl.jar:lib/xerces-2.4.0.jar:lib/xalan-2.4.0.jar:lib/tomcat-util.jar:lib/tomcat-http.jar:lib/t
omcat-coyote.jar:lib/struts.jar:lib/servlets-default.jar:lib/servlet-api.jar:lib/naming-resources.jar:lib/naming-factory.jar:lib/mysql-
connector-java-3.1.12-bin.jar:lib/mx4j-3.0.1.jar:lib/log4j.jar:lib/junit.jar:lib/junitee.jar:lib/jta.jar:lib/jsp-api.jar:lib/jmx.jar:li
b/jdp.jar:lib/jasper-runtime.jar:lib/jasper-compiler-jdt.jar:lib/jasper-compiler.jar:lib/hibernate3.jar:lib/FHoSS.jar:lib/ehcache-1.1.j
ar:lib/dom4j-1.6.1.jar:lib/commons-validator.jar:lib/commons-modeler.jar:lib/commons-logging.jar:lib/commons-logging-1.0.4.jar:lib/comm
ons-lang.jar:lib/commons-fileupload.jar:lib/commons-el.jar:lib/commons-digester.jar:lib/commons-collections-3.1.jar:lib/commons-beanuti
ls.jar:lib/cglib-2.1.3.jar:lib/catalina-optional.jar:lib/catalina.jar:lib/c3p0-0.9.1.jar:lib/base64.jar:lib/asm.jar:lib/asm-attrs.jar:l
ib/antlr-2.7.6.jar::log4j.properties:..
2014-04-13 14:50:28,389 INFO  de.fhg.fokus.hss.main.TomcatServer - startTomcat Tomcat-Server is started.
2014-04-13 14:50:29,375 WARN  org.apache.catalina.connector.MapperListener - registerEngine Unknown default host: 127.0.0.1
2014-04-13 14:50:30,547 INFO  de.fhg.fokus.hss.web.servlet.ResponseFilter - init Response Filter Initialisation!
2014-04-13 14:50:30,988 INFO  de.fhg.fokus.hss.main.TomcatServer - startTomcat WebConsole of FHoSS was started !
2014-04-13 14:50:32,753 WARN  org.hibernate.impl.SessionFactoryObjectFactory - addInstance InitialContext did not implement EventContex
t
2014-04-13 14:50:32,791 INFO  de.fhg.fokus.diameter.DiameterPeer.DiameterPeer - <init> Bean style constructor called, don't forget to c
onfigure!
2014-04-13 14:50:32,795 INFO  de.fhg.fokus.diameter.DiameterPeer.DiameterPeer - configure FQDN: hss.open-ims.test
2014-04-13 14:50:32,795 INFO  de.fhg.fokus.diameter.DiameterPeer.DiameterPeer - configure Realm: open-ims.test
2014-04-13 14:50:32,795 INFO  de.fhg.fokus.diameter.DiameterPeer.DiameterPeer - configure Vendor_ID : 10415
2014-04-13 14:50:32,795 INFO  de.fhg.fokus.diameter.DiameterPeer.DiameterPeer - configure Product Name: JavaDiameterPeer
2014-04-13 14:50:32,796 INFO  de.fhg.fokus.diameter.DiameterPeer.DiameterPeer - configure AcceptUnknwonPeers: true
2014-04-13 14:50:32,796 INFO  de.fhg.fokus.diameter.DiameterPeer.DiameterPeer - configure DropUnknownOnDisconnect: true
2014-04-13 14:50:32,802 INFO  de.fhg.fokus.hss.main.HSSContainer - waitForExit
Type "exit" to stop FHoSS!
```

15. Go to `http://<yourip>:8080` and log in to the web console with `hssAdmin` as the username and `hss` as the password as shown in the following screenshot.

16. To register the WebRTC client with OpenIMS, we must use an IMS gateway that performs the function of converting the SIP over WebSocket format to SIP. In order to achieve this, use the IP port or domain of the PCSCF node while registering the client.

    The flow will be from the WebRTC client to the IMS gateway to the PCSCF of the IMS Core. The flow can also be from the SIPML5 WebRTC client to the webrtc2sip gateway to the PCSCF of the OpenIMS Core.

The subscribers are visible in the IMS subscription section of the portal of OpenIMS. The following screenshot shows the user identities and their statuses on a web-based admin console:

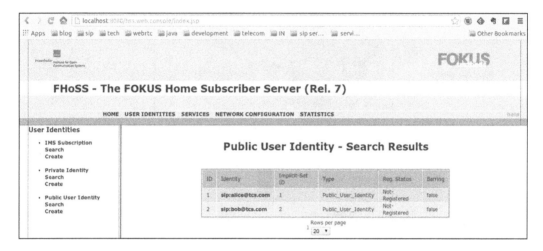

As far as other components are concerned, they can be subsequently added to the core network over their respective interfaces. We can study the integration of Policy Control Resource Function, Application Server, Media Server, and other vital components in *Chapter 7, WebRTC with Industry Standard Frameworks*.

The Telecom server

The TAS is where the logic for processing a call resides. It can be used to add applications such as call blocking, call forwarding, and call redirection according to the predefined values. The inputs can be assigned at runtime or stored in a database using a suitable provisioning system. The following diagram shows the connection between WebRTC and the IMS Core Server:

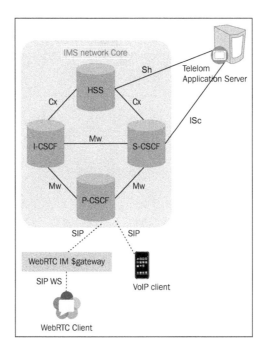

For demonstration purposes, we can use an Application Server that can host SIP servlets and integrate them with IMS core.

The Mobicents Telecom Application Server

Mobicents SIP Servlet and **Java APIs for Integrated Networks-Service Logic Execution Environment (JAIN-SLEE)** are open platforms to deploy new call controller logic and other converged applications. The steps to install Mobicents TAS are as follows:

1. Download the SIP Application Server logic package from https://code.google.com/p/sipservlets/wiki/Downloads.

2. Unzip the contents. Make sure that the Java environment variables are in place.

3. Start the JBoss container from mobicents\jboss-5.1.0.GA\bin

In case of MS Windows, click on `run.bat`, and for Linux, click on `run.sh`. The following figure displays the traces on the console when the server is started on JBoss:

```
altanai@tcs:~/mobicents-jainslee-2.7.0.FINAL-jboss-5.1.0.GA/jboss-5.1.0.GA/bin$ sudo ./run.sh
============================================================================

  JBoss Bootstrap Environment

  JBOSS_HOME: /home/altanai/mobicents-jainslee-2.7.0.FINAL-jboss-5.1.0.GA/jboss-5.1.0.GA

  JAVA: /usr/lib/jvm/java-7-openjdk-amd64/jre/bin/java

  JAVA_OPTS: -Dprogram.name=run.sh -Xms128m -Xmx512m -XX:MaxPermSize=256m -Dorg.jboss.resolver.warning=true -Dsun.rmi.dgc
rval=3600000 -Dsun.rmi.dgc.server.gcInterval=3600000 -Djava.net.preferIPv4Stack=true

  CLASSPATH: /home/altanai/mobicents-jainslee-2.7.0.FINAL-jboss-5.1.0.GA/jboss-5.1.0.GA/bin/run.jar

============================================================================

11:46:12,399 INFO  [ServerImpl] Starting JBoss (Microcontainer)...
11:46:12,400 INFO  [ServerImpl] Release ID: JBoss [The Oracle] 5.1.0.GA (build: SVNTag=JBoss_5_1_0_GA date=200905221634)
11:46:12,400 INFO  [ServerImpl] Bootstrap URL: null
11:46:12,401 INFO  [ServerImpl] Home Dir: /home/altanai/mobicents-jainslee-2.7.0.FINAL-jboss-5.1.0.GA/jboss-5.1.0.GA
```

4. The Mobicents application can also be developed by installing the Tomcat/Mobicents plugin in Eclipse IDE. The server can also be added for Mobicents instance, enabling quick deployment of applications.

5. Open the web console to review the settings. The following screenshot displays the process:

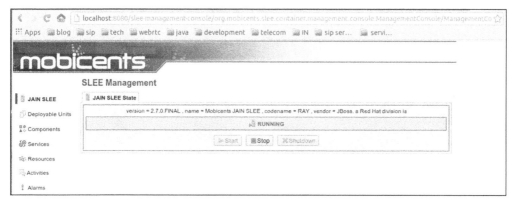

Mobicents SLEE Management console home screen in a web browser

6. In order to deploy Resource Adaptors, enter:

```
ant -f resources/<name of resource adapter>/build.xml deploy
```

7. To undeploy the resource adapters, execute `ant undeploy` with the name of the resource adapter:

```
ant -f resources/<name of resource adapter>/build.xml undeploy
```

Make sure that you have **Apache Ant 1.7**. The deployed instances should be visible in a web console as follows:

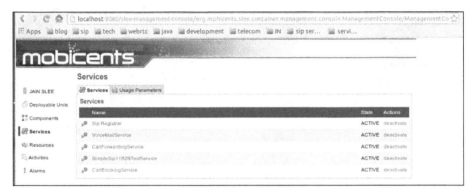

Services deployed on Mobicents Telecom Application Server

8. To deploy and run SIP Servlet applications, use the following command line:

```
ant -f examples/<name of application directory>/build.xml deploy-all
```

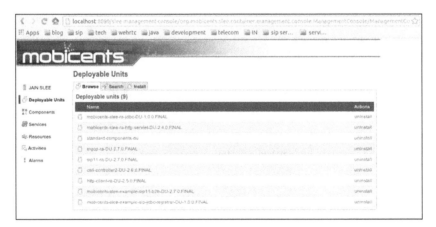

Resources hosted on Mobicents Telecom Application Server

9. Configure CSCF to include the Application Server in the path of every incoming SIP request and response.

With the introduction of TAS, it is now possible to provide customized call control logic to all subscribers or particular subscribers. The SIP solution and services can range from simple activities, such as call screening and call rerouting, to a complex call-handling application, such as selective call screening based on the user's calendar. Some more examples of SIP applications are given as follows:

- **Speed Dial**: This application lets the user make a call using pre-programmed numbers that map to actual SIPURIs of users.

- **Click to Dial**: This application makes a call using a web-based GUI. However, it is very different from WebRTC, as it makes/receives the call through an external SIP phone.

- **Find me Follow Me**: This application is beneficial if the user is registered on multiple devices simultaneously, for example, SIP phone, X-Lite, and WebRTC. In such a case, when there is an incoming call, each of the user's devices rings for few seconds in order of their recent use so that the user can pick the call from the device that is nearest to him.

These services are often referred to as VAS, which can be innovative and can take the user experience to new heights.

The Media Server

To enable various features such as **Interactive Voice Response** (**IVR**), record voice mails, and play announcements, the Media Server plays a critical role. The Media Server can be used as a standalone entity in the WebRTC infrastructure or it can be referenced from the SIP server in the IMS environment.

The FreeSWITCH Media Server

FreeSWITCH has powerful Media Server capabilities, including those for functions such as IVR, conferencing, and voice mails. We will first see how to use FreeSWITCH as a standalone entity that provides SIP and RTP proxy features.

Let's try to configure and install a basic setup of FreeSWITCH Media Server using the following steps:

1. Download and store the source code for compilation in the /usr/src folder, and run the following command lines:

```
cd usr/src

git clone -b v1.4 https://stash.freeswitch.org/scm/fs/freeswitch.git
```

2. A directory named `freeswitch` is made using the following command line and binaries will be stored in this folder. Assign all permissions to it.

```
sudo chown -R <username> /usr/local/freeswitch
```

Replace `<username>` with the name of the user who has the ownership of the folder.

3. Go to the directory where the source will be stored, that is, the following directory:

```
cd /usr/src/freeswitch
```

4. Then, run bootstrap using the following command line:

```
./bootstrap.sh
```

5. One can add additional modules by editing the configuration file using the vi editor. We can open our file using the following command line:

```
vi modules.conf
```

The names of the module are already listed. Remove the # symbol before the name to include the module at runtime, and add # to skip the module. Then, run the configure command:

```
./configure --enable-core-pgsql-support
```

6. Use the `make` command and install the components:

```
make && make install
```

7. Go to the Sofia profile and uncomment the parameters defined for WebSocket binding. By doing so, the WebRTC clients can register with FreeSWITCH on port `443`.

Sofia is an SIP stack used by FreeSWITCH. By default, it supports only pure SIP requests. To get WebRTC clients, register with FreeSWITCH's SIP Server.

```
<!-- uncomment for SIP over WebSocket support -->
<!-- <param name="ws-binding" value=":443"/>
```

8. Install the sound files using the following command line:

```
make all cd-sounds-install cd-moh-install
```

9. Go to the installation directory, and in the `vars.xml` file under `freeswitch/conf/` make sure that the codec preferences are set as follows:

```
<X-PRE-PROCESS cmd="set" data="global_codec_
prefs=G722,PCMA,PCMU,GSM"/>

<X-PRE-PROCESS cmd="set" data="outbound_codec_
prefs=G722,PCMA,PCMU,GSM"/>
```

10. Make sure that the SIP profile is directly using the codec values as follows:

```
<param name="inbound-codec-prefs" value="$${global_codec_prefs}"/>
<param name="outbound-codec-prefs" value="$${global_codec_prefs}"/>
```

We can later add more codecs such as vp8 for video calling/conferencing.

11. To start FreeSWITCH, go to the `/freeswitch/bin` installation directory and run FreeSWITCH.

12. Run the command-line console that will be used to control and monitor the passing SIP packets by going to the `/freeswitch/bin` installation directory and executing `fs_cli`.

The following is the screenshot of the FreeSWITCH client console:

13. Go to the `/freeswitch/conf/SIP_profile` installation-directory and look for the existing configuration files.

14. Load and start the SIP profile using the following command line:

```
sofia profile <name of profile> start load
```

15. Restart and reload the profile in case of changes using the following command line:

```
sofia profile <name of profile>restart reload
```

16. Check its working by executing the following command line:

```
Sofia status
```

17. We can check the status of the individual SIP profile by executing the following command line:

```
sofia status profile <name of profile> reg
```

```
freeswitch@internal> sofia status profile sipinterface_1 reg

Registrations:
=================================================================================
Call-ID:      b9f521ab-f06c-39a0-25a7-7d5e924d837b
User:         1018@10.1.5.2
Contact:      "1018" <sip:1018@df7jal23ls0d.invalid;rtcweb-breaker=yes;transport=ws;fs_nat=yes;fs_path=sip%3A1018%4010.1.5.11%3A495(
%3Brtcweb-breaker%3Dyes%3Btransport%3Dws>
Agent:        IM-client/OMA1.0 sipML5-v1.2014.04.18
Status:       Registered(WS-NAT)(unknown) EXP(2014-04-29 18:16:45) EXPSECS(173)
Host:         tcs.com
IP:           10.1.5.11
Port:         49502
Auth-User:    1018
Auth-Realm:   10.1.5.2
MWI-Account:  1018@10.1.5.2

Call-ID:      b91b5167-3b61-a1d6-a2cf-d74c5095ea63
User:         1004@10.1.5.2
Contact:      "1004" <sip:1004@df7jal23ls0d.invalid;rtcweb-breaker=yes;transport=ws;fs_nat=yes;fs_path=sip%3A1004%4010.1.5.10%3A357:
%3Brtcweb-breaker%3Dyes%3Btransport%3Dws>
Agent:        IM-client/OMA1.0 sipML5-v1.2014.04.18
Status:       Registered(WS-NAT)(unknown) EXP(2014-04-29 18:18:09) EXPSECS(257)
Host:         tcs.com
IP:           10.1.5.10
Port:         35715
Auth-User:    1004
Auth-Realm:   10.1.5.2
MWI-Account:  1004@10.1.5.2

Total items returned: 2
=================================================================================
```

The preceding figure depicts the status of the users registered with the server at one point of time.

Media Services

The following steps outline the process of using the FreeSWITCH media services:

1. Register the SIP softphone and WebRTC client using FreeSWITCH.

2. Use sample values between 1000 and 1020 initially. Later, we can configure for more users as specified by the `/freeswitch/conf/directory` installation directory.

3. The following are the sample values to register Kapanga:

   ○ **Username**: `1002`

   ○ **Display name**: `any`

   ○ **Domain/ Realm**: `14.67.87.45`

   ○ **Outbound proxy**: `14.67.87.45:5080`

   ○ **Authorization user**: `1002`

   ○ **Password**: `1234`

4. The sample value for WebRTC client registration, if, for example, we decide to use the Sipml5webrtc client, for example, will be as follows:

   ○ **Display name**: `any`

   ○ **Private identity**: `1001`

   ○ **Public identity**: `SIP:1001@14.67.87.45`

   ○ **Password**: `1234`

   ○ **Realm**: `14.67.87.45`

   ○ **WebSocket Server URL**: `ws://14.67.87.45:443`

 Note that the values used here are arbitrary for the purpose of understanding.

IP denotes the public IP of the FreeSWITCH machine and the port is the WebSocket configured port in the Sofia profile. As seen in the following screenshot, it is required that we tick the **Enable RTCWeb Breaker** option in **Expert settings** to compensate for the incompatibility between the WebSocket and SIP standards that might arise:

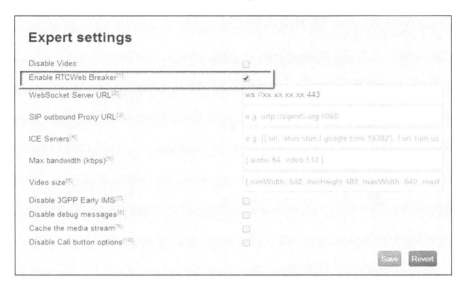

5. Make a call between the SIP softphone and WebRTC client. In this case, the signal and media are passing through FreeSWITCH as proxy.

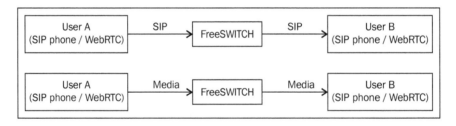

Call from a WebRTC client is depicted in the following screenshot, which consists of SIP messages passing through the FreeSWITCH server and are therefore visible in the FreeSWITCH client console. In this case, the server is operating in the default mode; other modes are bypass and proxy modes.

6. Make a call between two WebRTC clients, where SIP and RTP are passing through FreeSWITCH as proxy.

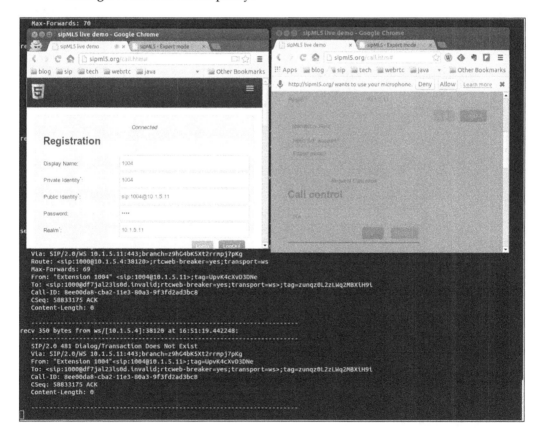

We can use other services of FreeSWITCH as well, such as voicemail, IVR, and conferencing. We will cover them in later chapters of the book.

We can also configure this setup in such a way that media passes through the FreeSWITCH Media Server, and the SIP signaling is via the Telecom Kamailio SIP server.

Use the RTP proxy in the SIP proxy server, in our case, Kamailio, to pass the RTP media through the Media Server. The RTP proxy module of Kamailio should be built in a format and configured in the `kamailio.cfg` file. The RTP proxy forces the RTP to pass through a node as specified in the settings parameters. It makes the communication between SIP user agents behind NAT and will also be used to set up a relaying host for RTP streams. Configure the RTP Engine as the media proxy agent for RTP. It will be used to force the WebRTC media through it and not in the old peer-to-peer fashion in which WebRTC is designed to operate. Perform the following steps to configure the RTP Engine:

1. Go to the Kamailio installation directory and then to the RTPProxy module. Run the `make` command and install the proxy engine:

    ```
    cd rtpproxy
    ./configure && make
    ```

2. Load the module and parameters in the `kamailio.cfg` file:

    ```
    listen=udp:<ip>:<port>
    . .
    loadmodule "rtpproxy.so"
    . .
    modparam("rtpproxy", "rtpproxy_sock",
      "unix:/var/run/rtpproxy/rtpproxy.sock")
    ```

3. Add `rtpproxy_manage()` for all of the requests and responses in the `kamailio.cfg` file. The example of `rtpproxy_manage` for INVITE is:

    ```
    if (is_method("INVITE")) {
    ...
    rtpproxy_manage();
    ...
    };
    ```

4. Get the source code for the RTP Engine using `git` as follows:

    ```
    https://github.com/sipwise/rtpengine.git
    ```

5. Go to the daemon folder in the installation directory and run the `make` command as follows:

    ```
    sudo make
    ```

6. Start `rtpengine` in the default user space mode on the local machine:

   ```
   sudo ./rtpengine --ip=10.1.5.14 --listen-ng=12334
   ```

7. Check the status of `rtpengine`, which is running, using the following command:

   ```
   ps -ef|greprtpengine
   ```

 Note that `rtpengine` must be installed on the same machine as the Kamailio SIP server.

8. In case of the sipml5 client, after configuring the modules described in the preceding section and before making a call through the Media Server, the flow for the media will become one of the following:

   ° In case of Voicemail/IVR, the flow is as follows:

     WebRTC client to RTP proxy node to Media Server

   ° In case of a call through media relay, the flow is as follows:

     WebRTC client A to RTP proxy node to Media Server to RTP Proxy to WebRTC client B

The following diagram shows the MediaProxy relay between WebRTC clients:

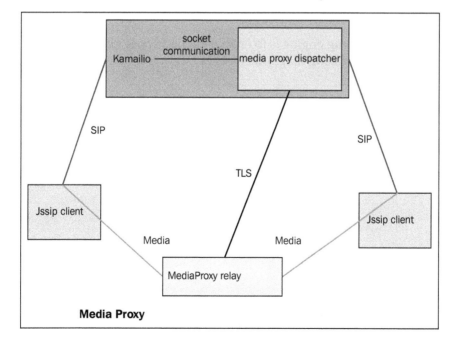

The potential of media server lies in its media transcoding of various codecs. Different phones / call clients / softwares that support SIP as the signaling protocol do not necessarily support the same media codecs. In the situation where Media Server is absent and the codecs do not match between a caller and receiver, the attempt to make a call is abruptly terminated when the media exchange needs to take place, that is, after `invite`, `success`, `response`, and `acknowledgement` are sent.

In the following figure, the setup to traverse media through the FreeSWITCH Media Server and signaling through the Kamailio SIP server is depicted:

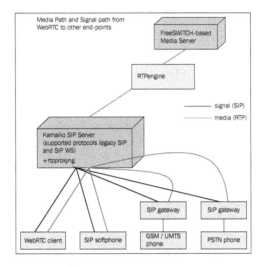

The role of the **rtpproxyng** engine is to enable media to pass via Media Server; this is shown in the following diagram:

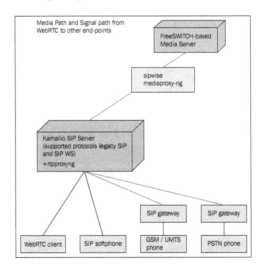

WebRTC over firewalls and proxies

There are many complicated issues involved with the correct working of WebRTC across domains, NATS, geographies, and so on. It is important for now that the firewall of a system, or any kind of port-blocking policy, should be turned off to be able to make a successful audio-video WebRTC call across any two parties that are not on the same **Local Area Network (LAN)**.

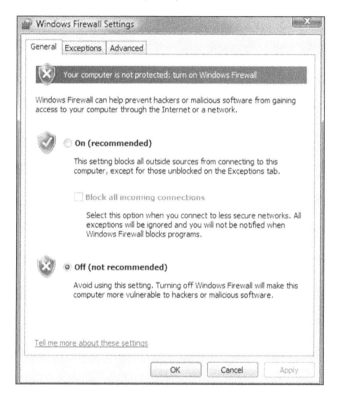

For the user to not have to switch the firewall off, we need to configure the **Simple Traversal of UDP through NAT (STUN)** server or modify the **Interactive Connectivity Establishment (ICE)** parameter in the SDP exchanged. STUN helps in packet routing of devices behind a NAT firewall. STUN only helps in device discoverability by assigning publicly accessible addresses to devices within a private local network.

Traversal Using Relay NAT (TURN) servers also serve to accomplish the task of interconnecting the endpoints behind NAT. As the name suggests, TURN forces media to be proxied through the server.

 To learn more about ICE as a NAT-traversal mechanism, refer to the official document named *RFC 5245*.

The ICE features are defined by sipML5 in the `sipml.js` file. It is added to SIP SDP during the initial phase of setting up the SIP stack. Snippets from the `sipml.js` file regarding ICE declaration are given as follows:

```
var configuration = {
...
  websocket_proxy_url: 'ws://192.168.0.10:5060',
  outbound_proxy_url: 'udp://192.168.0.12:5060',
  ice_servers: [{ url: 'stun:stun.l.google.com:19302'}, {
    url:'turn:user@numb.viagenie.ca', credential:'myPassword'}],
...
  };
```

Under the `postInit` function in the `call.htm` page add the following function:

```
oConfigCall = {
...
  events_listener: { events: '*', listener: onSipEventSession },
    SIP_caps: [
      { name: '+g.oma.SIP-im' },
      { name: '+SIP.ice' },
      { name: 'language', value: '\"en,fr\"' }
    ]
};
```

Therefore, the WebRTC client is able to reach the client behind the firewall itself; however, the media displays unpredicted behavior.

In the need to create our own STUN-TURN server, you can take the help of *RFC 5766*, or you can refer to open source implementations, such as the project at the following site:

```
https://code.google.com/p/rfc5766-turn-server/
```

When setting the parameters for WebRTC, we can add our own STUN/TURN server. The following screenshot shows the inputs suitable for **ICE Servers** if you are using your own TURN/STUN server:

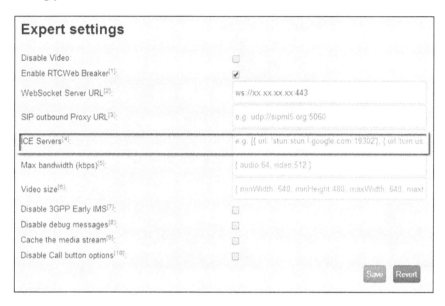

If there are no firewall restrictions, for example, if the users are on the same network without any corporate proxies and port blocks, we can omit the ICE by entering empty brackets, [], in the **ICE Servers** option on the **Expert settings** page in the WebRTC client.

The final architecture for the WebRTC-to-IMS integration

At the end of this chapter, we have arrived at an architecture similar to the following diagram. The diagram depicts a basic WebRTC-to-IMS architecture.

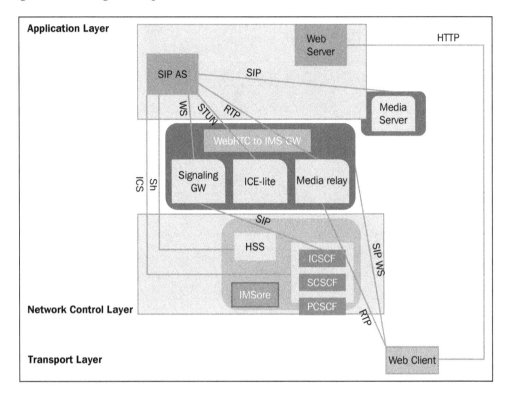

The diagram depicts the WebRTC client in the **Transport Layer** as it is the user endpoint. The IMS entities (**CSCF** and **HSS**), **WebRTC to IMS gateway**, and **Media Server** nodes are placed on the **Network Control Layer** as they help in signal and media routing. The applications for call control are placed in the top-most **Application Layer** that processes the call control logic. This architecture serves to provide a basic IMS-based setup for SIP-based WebRTC client interaction.

Summary

In this chapter, we saw how to interconnect the WebRTC setup with the IMS infrastructure. It included interaction with CSCF nodes, namely PCSCF, ICSCF, and SCSCF, after building and installing them from their sources. Also, FreeSWITCH Media Server was discussed, and the steps to build and integrate it were practiced. The Application Server to embed call control logic is Kamailio. NAT traversal via STUN / TURN server was also discussed and its importance was highlighted.

To deploy the WebRTC solution integrated with the IMS network, we must ensure that all of the required IMS nodes are consulted while making a call, the values are reflected in the HSS data store, and the incoming SIP request and responses are routed via call logic of the Application Server before connecting a call.

In the next chapter, we will see the interaction of the WebRTC client and server logic with **Intelligent Networks (IN)**. The process of establishing communication between the WebRTC client from the web browser and mobile handset will be discussed using the GSM and GPRS technologies.

4
WebRTC Integration with Intelligent Network

In the previous chapters, we saw the WebRTC client and server in a standalone environment. We also studied the WebRTC client integration with **IP Multimedia Subsystem (IMS)** Core and Media Server. In this chapter, we will discuss the WebRTC client's interaction with mobile handsets by utilizing the telecom service provider's GSM-based network, which is also known as **Intelligent Network (IN)**.

The chapter has been contracted from two main viewpoints: making a call to the WebRTC client through a mobile phone via the IMS network and applications and making calls between the WebRTC client and a mobile phone via the service logic of IN.

There are three ways one can make a call to a WebRTC client through a mobile phone:

- Using the mobile data packet, GPRS, to access the WebRTC client's web page in WebRTC-enabled mobile browsers (web view)

- Using the circuit-switched voice network, GSM, to call an SIP-based WebRTC client

- Using an Android-native SIP app to call a WebRTC client (this will be covered in *Chapter 9, Native SIP Application and Interaction with WebRTC Clients*)

We will be covering all of the preceding approaches in this chapter. We will look into every possible way to enable mobile phones to communicate with WebRTC endpoints. We will also touch on the process of sending SIP messages to GSM phones in the form of **Short Message Service (SMS)**.

The process of integrating the IN service logic to IMS/SIP and further to WebRTC endpoints is also discussed in detail in this chapter. There are two ways in which an IN application can be used by a WebRTC SIP client; they are as follows:

- Use of Reverse IMSSF to use IN service logic in IMS
- Use service broker for the orchestration of applications from the WebRTC SIP IMS and GSM IN worlds

We will begin the discussion on **General Packet Radio Services (GPRS)** usage to run WebRTC web pages in a mobile browser.

From mobiles to WebRTC client through GPRS

In this section, we will discuss the use of mobile data packets, GPRS, to access the WebRTC client in WebRTC-enabled mobile browsers. Through generations of telecom evolution, the connectivity to IP network has undergone a significant change. The first generation services, which comprised fixed line phones such as **Public Switched Telephone Network (PSTN)** / **Integrated Switched Digital Network (ISDN)**, had no connectivity to the packet-switched world. However, as the second generation of telecom arrived, there emerged GSM (2G) and GPRS (2.5G), which enabled a web phone to access the Internet through data packets. The speed and performance of IP connectivity accelerated with the introduction of 3G and 4G, which enable high-speed multimedia sharing and real-time streaming.

The GPRS support nodes are responsible for transmitting IP packets to GSM or **Universal Mobile Telecommunications System (UMTS)** devices. GPRS services are mainly provided through **GPRS Support Node (GSN)**. GSN also has two parts, Gateway GSN and Serving GSN, described as follows:

- **Gateway GPRS Support Node (GGSN)** manages the interworking between packets from the **Radio Access Network (RAN)** to the external IP world such as the Internet
- **Serving GPRS Support Node (SGSN)** is responsible for mobility, routing, authentication, and so on for the GPRS core

The following diagram shows the structure of the core **GPRS Support Nodes (GSNs)**:

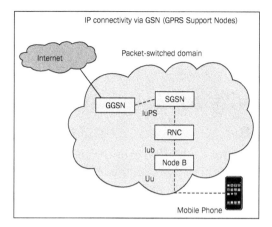

Use the GPRS functionality in GSM phones to access the WebRTC client through the mobile web browser. The process of making calls through the browser to another browser or SIP endpoint is already defined in *Chapter 2, Making a Standalone WebRTC Communication Client.*

 Only the phones that support WebRTC-enabled browsers will be able to support it, for example, the mobile browsers of Chrome and Mozilla.

The following is a diagrammatic representation of a WebRTC call that runs in the mobile browser of GSM phones through the GPRS connectivity:

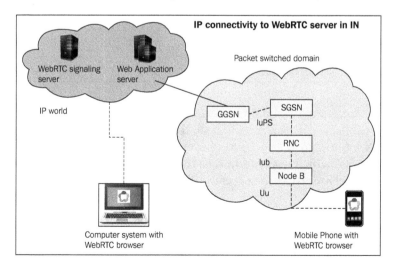

In this case, there are no alterations required in the telecom operator's landscape, except for the introduction of the web application server to host the WebRTC application. However, the operator can only charge for the data packets consumed by the end user in terms of data upload and download. This will be far less than the conventional voice call or video call rate.

IMS connectivity to Gateway GPRS Support Node

The WebRTC platform resides in the IP world of SIP and IMS. A mobile phone can connect to the IP world via data packets, that is, GPRS. The following figure gives an architectural representation of interconnecting a WebRTC IMS platform with a mobile phone through GGSN:

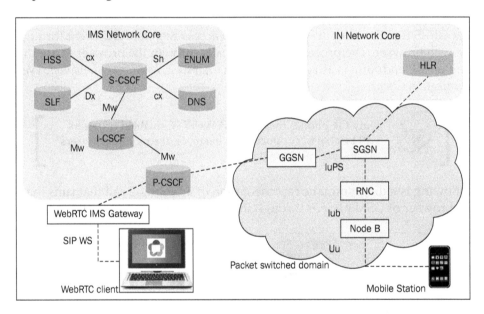

HSS in the IMS core network holds the profile of subscribers. CSCFs are the IMS entities responsible for call control. Overall, the preceding diagram gives a clear picture of GSN integrated with IMS to render GPRS packets to GSM mobile phones. It also mentions 3G, which uses **Node B** as the access node, and 4G, which uses **Evolved Node B (eNodeB)** as the access node.

Node B is the node responsible for connecting the mobile phones with the network in UMTS, which is the third generation of telecom (3G). It is controlled by a **Radio Network Controller (RNC)** in RAN.

eNodeB is the node responsible for connecting the mobile phones with the network in **Long Term Evolution (LTE)**, which is the fourth generation of telecom (4G).

Similar to BTS, in second-generation telecom networks, Node B and eNodeB have frequency transceivers, that is, transmitter and receivers, to connect the nearby mobile devices with a network.

The packet-switched domain provides the IP bearer with access to the IMS through the **Packet Data Protocol (PDP)** context. The phases of mobile access to the packet-switched network of IMS are as follows:

- In the first phase, the mobile registers with the packet-switched domain via **GPRS Attach**

- In the second phase, the mobile activates the PDP context and establishes **Radio Access Bearer (RAB)**

- The third phase consists of registering successfully with IMS and using the services

The following diagram shows the flow of the phases of mobile access to the packet-switched network of IMS:

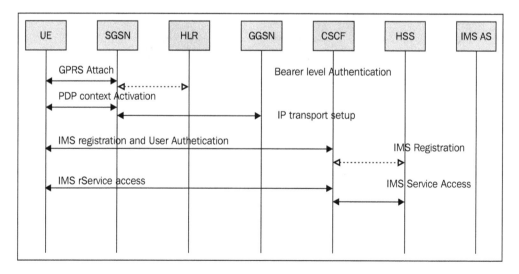

The preceding figure depicts the sequence flow between a **User Equipment** (**UE**), which is a mobile phone in this case, and a WebRTC client via **Serving GPRS Support Node** (**SGSN**) and **Gateway GPRS Support Node** (**GGSN**). As outlined, the first step is GPRS Attach and PDP context activation. At this stage, the authentication at the bearer level is achieved. In the next stage, the mobile phone will connect itself to CSCF, which is the core of the IMS network. Once this is achieved, the mobile phone can make calls, which will traverse through the IMS network. The IMS entities such as Application Server and Media Server will also apply to such signals. The following screenshot shows the sipML5 WebRTC client web page opened in a mobile browser:

From mobiles to WebRTC client through GSM

As we know that SIP IMS is a good way to implement a unifying technology (refer to the following diagram) between the legacy circuit-switched and the IP-based packet-switched networks, it is clear that the best approach to integrate WebRTC to the IN telecom network is via SIP IMS; this is illustrated in the following diagram:

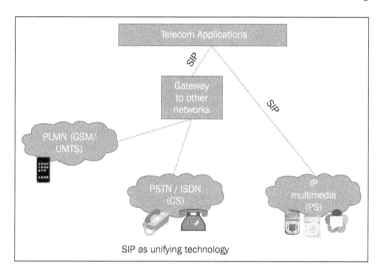

SIP as unifying technology

In the previous section, we saw the process of using the mobile packet-switched network to interact with the WebRTC client. This section describes the process of using the circuit-switched voice network to call a WebRTC client. To achieve this, there must be a point of translation between the voice network of the mobile and the IP network of IMS. This is often referred to as the GSM Gateway.

The difference between Circuit-Switching and Packet-Switching technologies is described in the following table:

Circuit-Switched (CS) network	Packet-Switched (PS) network
Circuit-Switching is a connection-oriented communication technology. In this case, a fixed bandwidth is allocated for every communication line, and this remains open throughout the session. It cannot be used by other data and phone calls.	In packet-switched communication network, the message gets broken into small data packets and is sent out to travel to its destination, seeking the most efficient route. Every packet might go a different route. The packets are reassembled in the correct order on reception.

Circuit-Switched (CS) network	Packet-Switched (PS) network
The biggest advantage of Circuit-Switching is the quality of service, which is due to a guaranteed full bandwidth for the duration of call.	The advantages of Packet-Switching are good use of bandwidth and high availability as it doesn't wait for a direct connection to be available
	The disadvantage of Packet-Switching is that the quality of service might be poor as there might be a delay in transmission. Also, there is a high risk of data packets being lost or corrupted.
Circuit-Switching is widely employed in voice communication in the telecom landscape. From the old PSTN phone to the current 3G phone, all mobile devices use a circuit-switched network to make calls.	Packet-Switching is used for data access such as Internet browsing and e-mails. Due to low reliability, there are still a lot of reservations to adopt packet switching in voice communication. However, IP communications such as WebRTC make use of the Packet-Switching protocol to make and receive audio/video calls.

There are various ways in which a WebRTC client can interact with the GSM endpoints that only understand ISUP. If the requirement is that of just connecting the endpoints without a centralized-server-level logic, then it is merely required to provide the interconnecting gateways that do media and protocol conversion between the WebRTC format in the IMS and GSM formats. The following figure depicts the components of this interconnecting gateway:

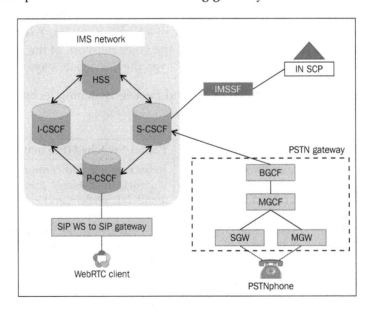

IMS provides interoperability with circuit-switched networks. This can be achieved in the following way:

1. **Signal Gateway (SGW)** transforms **ISDN User Part (ISUP)** to SIP, and **Media Gateway (MGW)** transforms data from CS to the IP–based data.

2. These are united and connected to the **Media Gateway Control Function (MGCF)**, which provides a protocol conversion between SIP and ISUP / **Bearer Independent Call Control (BICC)**. It also controls resources in the media gateway. **Bearer Independent Call Control (BICC)** is a signaling protocol based on ISUP that is used for supporting narrowband **Integrated Services Digital Network (ISDN)** service.

3. This in turn is connected to the **Border Gateway Control Function (BGCF)**, which is an SIP proxy responsible for processing requests which are telephone number and not DNS/ENUM types.

4. Finally, it's connected to **Serving Call Session Control Function (SCSCF)**, which is the very place responsible for central session control, activation/cancellation of bearer service, and so on.

Thus, it's said that IMS is a multi-access architecture and holds the door to seamless interconnectivity between current phones and futuristic SIP/WebRTC phones.

A call flow between a mobile phone and the WebRTC endpoint using the voice network of the mobile operator, as well as the IMS network of the service provider, is depicted in the following figure:

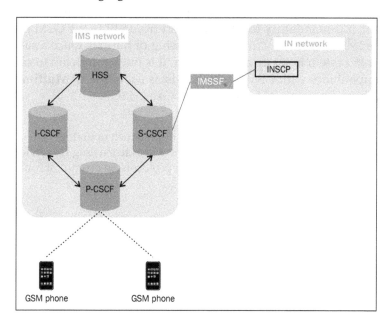

The SIP request is initiated from the WebRTC client that is in the SIP-over-WebSocket (SIP-WS) format. A WebRTC-to-SIP gateway is required to convert this request from the SIPWS format to the SIP format. Thereafter, the request is sent to the MCG/MG node, which is an ISUP to SIP interworking node that has also been described in detail in the previous section. Here, the SIP requests are converted to ISUP requests via SGW, and then proceed towards the ISUP switch, which interconnects to mobile phones. The request is generated from the mobile phone towards the WebRTC client flow in the exact opposite direction. The process is repeated for every other request and response. The media flow is also traversed via the MCG/MG node, which is responsible for codec conversion between WebRTC-supported formats and traditional media formats.

Call processed with the IN service logic

This part deals with WebRTC client communication through call control logic in **Service Control Point (INSCP)** of an IN. The use of this setup is that the operator does not need to introduce services such as call screening, forwarding, or VPN separately for WebRTC clients, as they can utilize the existing logic. If, however, there is a requirement for introducing logic in the form of an application program that resides on the telecom core, then there arise the following two cases:

- Logic resides in the IMS Network Application Server (seen in the previous chapter)
- Logic resides on the IN network in **Service Control Point (SCP)**

As we have embedded SIP as our signaling protocol in our instance of the WebRTC client, it is mandatory to either convert from SIP to the GSM protocol or provide the IMS core for any further processing of the call. Once a steadfast WebRTC-to-IMS system is set up and working, it is not a tough job to establish backward compatibility with GSM-based handsets using the **IP Multimedia Service Switching Function (IM SSF)** and reverse IM SSF.

What is IM SSF? It is a gateway through which operators can transparently provide IMS users the access to existing IN services using INAP and CAMEL signaling protocols. In essence, it connects the IMS network to IN services.

The following figure depicts the role of IM SSF in interconnecting the call flow from IMS network to IN network's SCP for logic processing. After executing the call control logic programmed within the SCP, the call is routed back to IMS network nodes.

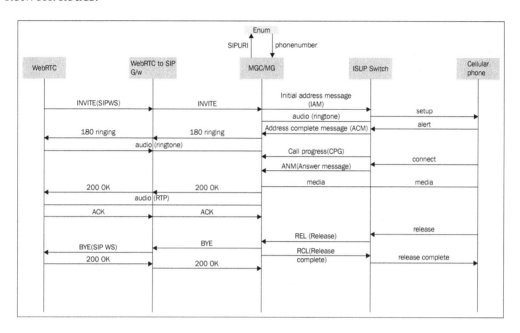

As shown in the preceding figure, the IM SSF node lies in the Application/Service layer and comes into picture when an SIP user from the IMS network wants to use an IN service, for example, old corporate **Virtual Private Networks (VPNs)**. Technically, IM SSF converts between ISC (the protocol used in the IMS network between the S-CSCF and SIP-AS) and CAP3 (the protocol used in the GSM network between the MSC and the Service layer).

Let's discuss the first case where logic resides within the IMS network's Application Server.

The WebRTC client's communication with the GSM phone through IMS

In this section, we will observe the call between a mobile phone and a WebRTC client; this call is processed by the application program hosted in IMS **Telecom Application Server (TAS)**. New age services such as Find-Me-Follow-Me, RingBack Tone Advertisement, and many innovative services can be mounted on the Application Server.

>
> In the Find-Me-Follow-Me Service, when the user receives an
> incoming call, their subscribed call agents such as phones, WebRTC
> clients, and desktop phones ring sequentially until any one of them
> is answered.
>
> In the RingBack Tone Advertisement services, while the call is in
> the ringing mode, that is, until the time the receiver doesn't pick
> the phone, the caller can enjoy the music played for them, instead
> of the ringing tone.

The following diagram shows the WebRTC-to-GSM phone using the IMS
Application server:

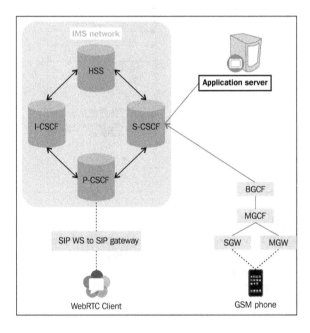

This instance depicts a setup where the call is routed from the CS domain to the PS
domain, but it is set up utilizing the call control logic and services installed in the
IMS application server.

The major four kinds of SIP programming for the Application Layer are as follows:

- **SIP Servlets**: These are Java extension APIs for SIP servers (SIP Servlet
  Request / Sip Servlet Response) and are similar to the HTTP Servlets (HTTP
  Servlet Request / HTTP Servlet Response)

- **JAIN SIP**: This is also a Java-based API for SIP signaling, however, it's more
  generic and low level

- **SIP CGI**: The **Common Gateway Interface** (**CGI**) for SIP is very similar to the HTTP CGI

- **CPL**: This is the **Common Programming Language**, which is an XML-based script for call control logic and needs to be validated and parsed by a CPL interpreter

Using high-end service orchestration tools, it is also possible to create various combinations and permutations of the services instead of putting fresh time and effort to create new ones from scratch.

This is the case where logic resides in the SCP of the IN, and the WebRTC client wishes to use this while placing a call to any endpoint, be it SIP WebRTC or GSM.

The WebRTC client's communication with a GSM phone with IN services

In the previous section, we observed the scenario where the service logic for call processing is derived from the application hosted on the IMS TAS. In this section, we will observe the case where the call control logic is embedded with the SCP in IN. The call originates from either a WebRTC client or a mobile phone and passes on to the IMS network for routing. The SCSCF node of IMS, which is responsible for negotiation with Application/Service Layer, sends across the signal to IN SCP via **IP Multimedia Service Switching Function** (**IMSSF**). The following diagram shows the WebRTC-to-GSM phone call control logic fetched from the SCP in IN via IM SSF:

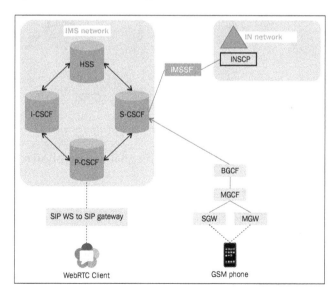

This instance of WebRTC to GSM phone connectivity signifies that while the call is traversed from the PS to CS network, the application logic is also used from the SCP of the IN by the means of IM SSF. This scenario is useful for making use of the existing IN service logic while routing calls, even if the call arrives from a GSM phone, SIP phone, or WebRTC client.

There could also be a third instance where both the networks, IN and IMS, intercommunicate with each other. To enable this, one needs a component called Service Broker.

A Service Broker is used to interoperate between multiple networks such as IN and IMS. The protocol understands the spans across the CS and PS calls. It is able to utilize the IMS services as well as the IN services in a transparent way. The end user doesn't come to know whether the service hit is an IN service of the IMS Application. This figure depicts call processing using the Service Broker as the Service Orchestrator of IN and IMS applications. The following diagram shows a typical Service Broker:

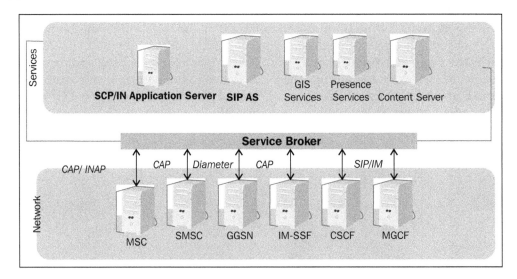

Now, the existing service brokers to achieve the goal are as follows:

- Oracle's Service Broker
- Open cloud's Service Broker

The services broker for endpoints and WebRTC in IMS to GSM phone in Intelligence Networks

The convergence of the Internet and Telecommunication Architectures is a key issue in today's telecommunication world. In present times, Intelligent Networks are used by telecom operators for creating and managing VAS in telecom networks for Circuit switched Access networks based on 2G/3G. Originally, IN was applied in telephone and voice services, but today its meaning is also growing in the service integration of mobile and fixed telephone networks and as a gateway to Internet-based networks.

This section particularly deals with WebRTC set up to Intelligent Networks communication that is between WebRTC clients and GSM phones through Service Broker. Service broker internetworking between GSM and SIP works seamlessly; this is illustrated in the following diagram:

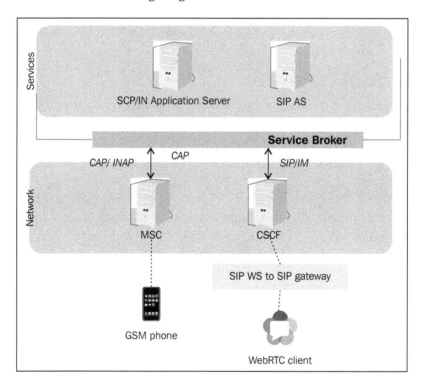

So far, we have discussed the interworking between SIP-based WebRTC client's call services and application logic with a mobile phone that is on the SS7 IN network. The next section describes the process of linking message services for SIP-based Instant Message to SMS in IN.

The WebRTC client's SIP messages to SMS in a GSM phone (SMSC)

Typical SMS service in Intelligent Networks can be achieved in the IMS environment via **Short Message Service Center** (**SMSC**). It sends an SMS message to a GSM phone and retires if the message is undelivered (usually stores it in a buffer and retires after a period of 2 days).

As we can extract content out of an SIP message and use the SMS gateway to deliver the message to a GSM phone, it is thus also practical to extract the WebRTC-based messages and send them over to a GSM phone as SMS. Another setup would be to store the message in a database and let Kannel send them out in succession.

The Kannel gateway

The Kannel gateway is a **Wireless Application Protocol** (**WAP**) and **SMS** (**Short Message Service**) gateway. It connects the HTTP Web Services to SMS centers. We will only make use of the SMS functionality.

To configure and install the Kannel gateway, follow the next steps:

1. Download the source code from `http://www.kannel.org/download.shtml`

2. Configure the downloaded content using the following command line:

    ```
    ./configure
    ```

The following screenshot shows the Kannel Configure running:

```
altanai@tcs:~/kannel/gateway-1.4.3$ configure

Configuring for Kannel gateway version 1.4.3 ...

Running system checks ...
checking build system type... x86_64-unknown-linux-gnu
checking host system type... x86_64-unknown-linux-gnu
checking for gcc... gcc
checking for C compiler default output file name... a.out
checking whether the C compiler works... yes
checking whether we are cross compiling... no
checking for suffix of executables...
checking for suffix of object files... o
checking whether we are using the GNU C compiler... yes
checking whether gcc accepts -g... yes
checking for gcc option to accept ISO C89... none needed
checking for gcc option to accept ISO C99... -std=gnu99
checking for a BSD-compatible install... /usr/bin/install -c
checking for ranlib... ranlib
checking for bison... bison -y
checking for flex... flex
checking lex output file root... lex.yy
checking lex library... -lfl
checking whether yytext is a pointer... yes
checking for ar... ar
checking for convert... /usr/bin/convert
checking for perl... /usr/bin/perl
checking for inline... inline
checking for special C compiler options needed for large files... no
checking for _FILE_OFFSET_BITS value needed for large files... no
checking how to run the C preprocessor... gcc -std=gnu99 -E
checking for grep that handles long lines and -e... /bin/grep
checking for egrep... /bin/grep -E
checking for ANSI C header files... yes
checking for sys/types.h... yes
checking for sys/stat.h... yes
checking for stdlib.h... yes
checking for string.h... yes
checking for memory.h... yes
checking for strings.h... yes
checking for inttypes.h... yes
checking for stdint.h... yes
checking for unistd.h... yes
checking size of short... █
```

3. Build the Kannel executables using the following command lines:

```
make
make bindir=/directory path for installation
```

```
altanai@tcs:~/kannel/gateway-1.4.3$ make
gcc -std=gnu99 -D_REENTRANT=1 -I. -Igw -g -O2 -D_XOPEN_SOURCE=600 -D_BSD_SOURCE -D_LARGE_FILES= -I/usr/incl
ude/libxml2 -o gw/bb_alog.o -c gw/bb_alog.c
gcc -std=gnu99 -D_REENTRANT=1 -I. -Igw -g -O2 -D_XOPEN_SOURCE=600 -D_BSD_SOURCE -D_LARGE_FILES= -I/usr/incl
ude/libxml2 -o gw/bb_boxc.o -c gw/bb_boxc.c
gcc -std=gnu99 -D_REENTRANT=1 -I. -Igw -g -O2 -D_XOPEN_SOURCE=600 -D_BSD_SOURCE -D_LARGE_FILES= -I/usr/incl
ude/libxml2 -o gw/bb_http.o -c gw/bb_http.c
gcc -std=gnu99 -D_REENTRANT=1 -I. -Igw -g -O2 -D_XOPEN_SOURCE=600 -D_BSD_SOURCE -D_LARGE_FILES= -I/usr/incl
ude/libxml2 -o gw/bb_smscconn.o -c gw/bb_smscconn.c
gcc -std=gnu99 -D_REENTRANT=1 -I. -Igw -g -O2 -D_XOPEN_SOURCE=600 -D_BSD_SOURCE -D_LARGE_FILES= -I/usr/incl
ude/libxml2 -o gw/bb_store.o -c gw/bb_store.c
gcc -std=gnu99 -D_REENTRANT=1 -I. -Igw -g -O2 -D_XOPEN_SOURCE=600 -D_BSD_SOURCE -D_LARGE_FILES= -I/usr/incl
ude/libxml2 -o gw/bb_store_file.o -c gw/bb_store_file.c
gcc -std=gnu99 -D_REENTRANT=1 -I. -Igw -g -O2 -D_XOPEN_SOURCE=600 -D_BSD_SOURCE -D_LARGE_FILES= -I/usr/incl
ude/libxml2 -o gw/bb_store_spool.o -c gw/bb_store_spool.c
gcc -std=gnu99 -D_REENTRANT=1 -I. -Igw -g -O2 -D_XOPEN_SOURCE=600 -D_BSD_SOURCE -D_LARGE_FILES= -I/usr/incl
ude/libxml2 -o gw/bb_udp.o -c gw/bb_udp.c
gcc -std=gnu99 -D_REENTRANT=1 -I. -Igw -g -O2 -D_XOPEN_SOURCE=600 -D_BSD_SOURCE -D_LARGE_FILES= -I/usr/incl
ude/libxml2 -o gw/dlr.o -c gw/dlr.c
gcc -std=gnu99 -D_REENTRANT=1 -I. -Igw -g -O2 -D_XOPEN_SOURCE=600 -D_BSD_SOURCE -D_LARGE_FILES= -I/usr/incl
ude/libxml2 -o gw/dlr_mem.o -c gw/dlr_mem.c
gcc -std=gnu99 -D_REENTRANT=1 -I. -Igw -g -O2 -D_XOPEN_SOURCE=600 -D_BSD_SOURCE -D_LARGE_FILES= -I/usr/incl
ude/libxml2 -o gw/dlr_mysql.o -c gw/dlr_mysql.c
gcc -std=gnu99 -D_REENTRANT=1 -I. -Igw -g -O2 -D_XOPEN_SOURCE=600 -D_BSD_SOURCE -D_LARGE_FILES= -I/usr/incl
ude/libxml2 -o gw/dlr_oracle.o -c gw/dlr_oracle.c
gcc -std=gnu99 -D_REENTRANT=1 -I. -Igw -g -O2 -D_XOPEN_SOURCE=600 -D_BSD_SOURCE -D_LARGE_FILES= -I/usr/incl
ude/libxml2 -o gw/dlr_pgsql.o -c gw/dlr_pgsql.c
gcc -std=gnu99 -D_REENTRANT=1 -I. -Igw -g -O2 -D_XOPEN_SOURCE=600 -D_BSD_SOURCE -D_LARGE_FILES= -I/usr/incl
ude/libxml2 -o gw/dlr_sdb.o -c gw/dlr_sdb.c
gcc -std=gnu99 -D_REENTRANT=1 -I. -Igw -g -O2 -D_XOPEN_SOURCE=600 -D_BSD_SOURCE -D_LARGE_FILES= -I/usr/incl
ude/libxml2 -o gw/heartbeat.o -c gw/heartbeat.c
gcc -std=gnu99 -D_REENTRANT=1 -I. -Igw -g -O2 -D_XOPEN_SOURCE=600 -D_BSD_SOURCE -D_LARGE_FILES= -I/usr/incl
ude/libxml2 -o gw/html.o -c gw/html.c
```

4. Define an SMS box group into the configuration file.

```
group = sms-service
keyword = complex
get-url = "http://host/service?sender=%p&text=%r"
accept-x-kannel-headers = true
max-messages = 3
concatenation = true
Start kannel
```

5. It requires a physical GSM handset to achieve this. We must connect the phone to the machine that runs the Kannel gateway and modify the config file for the phone specification. The phone must bear a valid SIM. Also, the amount per message is deducted from the balance of the SIM holders' account.

6. Send the content from the WebRTC application in the HTTP format and pass it on to the Kannel gateway. The content will be delivered to the phone in the form of an SMS. For example, consider the following content:

```
http://smsbox.host.name:13013/cgi-bin/sendsms?
username=foo&password=bar&to=0123456&text=Hello+world
```

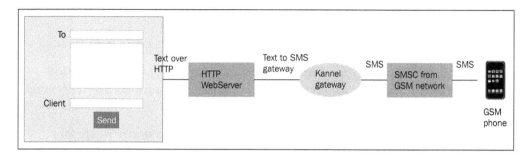

For the service to look seamless, we can encrypt the logic in a telecom application and install it in Application Servlet in the form of JAIN-SLEE with HTTP **Resource Adapter (RA)** or just use SIP Servlet to pass an HTTP request. This way, when an SIP message is sent from the WebRTC client/SIP phone, on the server end, we can extract the message content, append it to the SMS box URL, and send it across to the Kannel gateway to deliver it as an SMS to the destination phone.

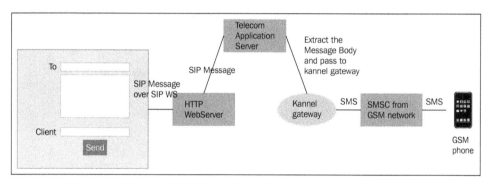

SIP message from the WebRTC application/Sip phone to SMS in a GSM phone

There are other options to build an SMS gateway; for instance, consider the following:

- The OpenSIPS SMS module also supports sending and receiving SMS directly from a GSM network.

- The Kamailio SMS module performs SIP message to GSMS and SMS delivery too. It requires a GSMS telephone to act as the modem. The format of the SIP address header should be as follows:

  ```
  sip:<number>@domain, for example sip:988768238@tcs.com.
  ```

- One can also opt for an enhanced SMSC gateway such as Mobicents SMSC built over Mobicents SS7 and Mobicents JSLEE. They support **Short Message Peer-to-Peer Protocol (SMPP)**, SIP IM, and legacy SS7 MAP interfaces as well.

At the end of this chapter, we have arrived at an architecture similar to the one shown in the following diagram:

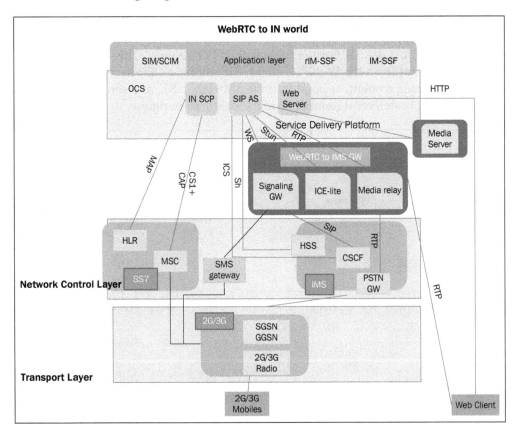

The figure depicts that the WebRTC client can make a call to a mobile phone in many ways. It can either be through IDP to invite conversion or via GPRS nodes. The application logic of IN SCP can also be integrated with SIP Application layer through RIMSSF.

Summary

So far, we have discovered various ways of integrating the IN application logic to the WebRTC call flow(IMSSF), making a call to the GSM client from the WebRTC client (SGW, MGW) and delivering an SIP message from the WebRTC client to a GSM phone (SMS gateway).

The implementations of these are meant to prove the feasibility of the proposal and not necessarily signify how the production environment must be. In order to construct a stable, scalable, and resilient communication system, one must ensure that the signal is well connected to all nodes via their interfaces and that the media is flowing smoothly. Interoperability issues usually arise on the border of these networks where issues such as protocol conversion and media codec conversion take place. The placement of appropriate gateways helps prevent these errors and smoothens out the differences.

The next chapter deals with WebRTC interconnectivity with old telephone systems such as PSTN. This shall be carried out through interoperable hooks provided in the IMS environment itself.

5
WebRTC Integration with PSTN

The **Voice over Internet Protocol (VoIP)** telephony is one of the coolest things ever invented. It gives us the ability to use the power of Internet in the context of communication such as user discovery; user presence; virtual conferences; file sharing; notifications based on web feeds such as news updates, parental control, and IPTV / Video On Demand; extensive option of call control; and, most importantly, the ability to take our call from any place where there is IP connectivity. However, what if there is no IP connectivity? What if there is just a fixed cable connection that supplies analog outputs?

There are still many such analog connections (called **Public Switched Telephone Network (PSTN)** endpoints) in the world even today that only have a dialer as the user interface and a handle with an embedded speaker and microphone.

As WebRTC is not intended to be just a web-only communication tool but to also connect to all other devices capable of communication, there will be occasions when a WebRTC user has to make a call to a PSTN endpoint. In such a scenario, the described approach in this chapter (from WebRTC to the PSTN via the IMS network) is the ideal way to achieve this goal.

So far, we have seen how WebRTC users can connect with other WebRTC users, SIP phone users, and mobile phone users. This chapter will take us through the detailed course of connecting the WebRTC signal and media to the PSTN signal and media via IMS. We know that IMS systems have hooks for PSTN terminals through the PSTN gateway. The first part of the chapter will discuss the direct approach to connect WebRTC clients to PSTN terminals through the IMS setup. The later part of this chapter is a continuation from the previous chapter, where we discussed the WebRTC connectivity to mobile stations in GSM/UMTS access technologies.

The IN setup, which is based on SS7 signaling, not only includes GSM/UMTS access networks, but also includes legacy networks such as the **Integrated Service Digital Network (ISDN)**, the PSTN, and the **Public Land Mobile Network (PLMN)**.

Here, the most primitive analog PSTN phones to slightly more sophisticated digital ISDN phones are considered in order to discuss the complete interconnectivity between the latest version of WebRTC and legacy telephones. The advanced tunneling and PBX system can be further derived from this setup.

In this chapter, we will cover the following topics:

- The PSTN system
- The WebRTC connectivity to the PSTN
- Challenges in connecting the WebRTC world to the PSTN landscape
- The service logic

What is PSTN?

PSTN is the connection of many wired communication endpoints. The communication is circuit-switched in nature. Originally, PSTN endpoints were fixed-line analog telephone systems, also referred to as **Plain Old Telephone Systems (POTS)**. However, most have completely converted to digital systems such as ISDN, and some of them are digital towards the core side but have wired analog function on the last mile, from the exchange center to the user location.

> A Circuit-Switched system has a dedicated path for communication. It offers a high quality of service and constant bit delay, as all the data traverses the same path. On the other hand, packet-switched systems move data in packets where each packet is independently transmitted through a different path that is dynamically decided. At the destination, the original message is reassembled from the received packet in the proper sequence.

The following diagram shows a typical PSTN setup for home subscribers and enterprise network:

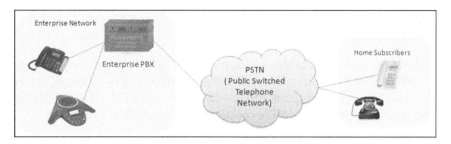

A **Private Brach Exchange (PBX)** is a telephone-switching system that comprises cables and micro controllers. The modern IP PBX is also capable of switching between VoIP and the traditional telephone system; however, we are only considering the traditional PBX and PSTN setup in this chapter.

 Just as GSM and UMTS are network access technologies, the PSTN system is also an access network technology. The core existing networks, such as IN, and the evolving networks, such as NGN IMS, have specified gateways and are switched to provide interconnectivity with the legacy communication endpoints.

WebRTC connectivity to the PSTN

For WebRTC connectivity to the PSTN phone, we can adopt one of two approaches: while the first approach is suited to an evolving next generation IMS landscape, the second approach depicts an IN setup. The IN approach is discussed not because all service providers have completely migrated to the IMS landscape, but because the IN service flow and call execution still holds good for many phones. The existing INs have hooks for interconnectivity between cellular phones and old analog phones. This was established using legacy PSTN gateways that took care of the digital-to-analog conversion. The ISUP switch provides the conversion to ISUP, which is responsible for setting up telephone calls in the IN network.

The next generation network that revolves around the IMS setup also provides interoperability with the PSTN system. This will be discussed in detail here. The methodology is adopted from RFC 3398 Integrated Services Digital Network (ISDN) User Part (ISUP) to Session Initiation Protocol (SIP) Mapping, and the call flows depicted here are derived from RFC 366 SIP PSTN Call Flows

Now that we have the basic translation from SIP-WS to SIP via the WebRTC-to-IMS gateway, such as WebRTC2SIP / OverSIP / the Kamailio proxy server, we can extend this setup further and connect to the PSTN phone via the PSTN gateway. The following diagram shows the WebRTC-to-PSTN connectivity via the PSTN gateway:

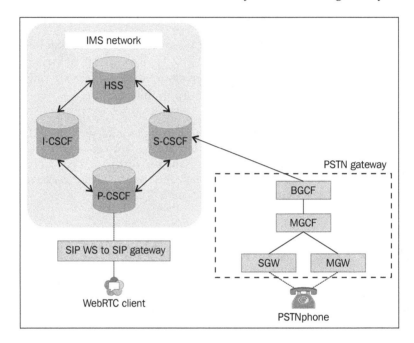

IMS is the standard platform for the IP/SIP protocol communication; SIP is integrated as the signaling protocol with the WebRTC client. For sound telecom infrastructure, we have to set up a WebRTC-to-IMS link first before extending the connection to the PSTN domain (refer to *Chapter 3, WebRTC with SIP and IMS*).

Once we are through with this, we will then use the PSTN gateway to provide the necessary signaling and media interoperability.

The PSTN gateway

PSTN gateways are the major game players in this setup. They are the entry point to the PSTN world, translating signal and media between the IP infrastructure and the Circuit-Switched network of the PSTN.

As described in the previous chapter, a gateway primarily consists of three components:

- **Signaling Gateway (SGW)**
- **Media Gateway (MGW)**
- **Media Gateway Controller (MGC)**

The following diagram shows the parts of the PSTN gateway interconnecting the IMS and PSTN worlds:

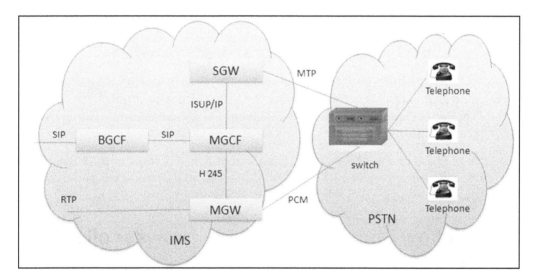

In the preceding diagram, **SGW** provides the protocol for interconversion between the new-age VoIP and the legacy network, **MGW** takes care of the media transcoding between the different codec standards supported on two ends, and **MGC** controls the call.

The PSTN connectivity to IMS via PSTN gateways

A PSTN/CS gateway interfaces with PSTN Circuit-Switched networks.

A **Media Gateway Control Function** (**MGCF**) is a SIP endpoint that does call control protocol conversion between SIP and ISUP/BICC and interfaces with the SGW over SCTP. It also controls the resources in a Media Gateway (MGW) across an H.248 interface. Let's take a look at the signal and media flow from IMS to PSTN separately.

- **IMS signaling to PSTN signaling**: For signaling, CS networks use ISDN User Part (ISUP) (or BICC) over Message Transfer Part (MTP), while IMS uses SIP over IP.

  A Signaling Gateway (SGW) interfaces with the signaling plane of the CS. It transforms lower layer protocols such as Stream Control Transmission Protocol which is a transport layer protocol over IP, into Message Transfer Part which is a Signaling System 7 protocol. This is done in order to pass ISDN User Part (ISUP) from the MGCF to the CS network.

- **IMS Media to PSTN Media**: For media, CS networks use Pulse-code modulation (PCM), while IMS uses Real-time Transport Protocol (RTP). The codecs required for this are G.711 and G.729, which can be configured with Media Server.

  A Media Gateway (MGW) interfaces with the media plane of the CS network, by converting between RTP and PCM. It can also transcode when the codecs don't match (e.g., IMS might use AMR, PSTN might use G.711).

The call flow from a WebRTC SIP browser client to a fixed landline phone

The SIP signals that originate from the WebRTC clients are proxied through the IMS nodes. After the service logic is executed by the Application Server, the signal arrives at the PSTN gateway, which is the entry point to the PSTN world. The interconversion form IP standard protocols and codecs to PSTN accepted values take place here. The modified version is sent across the PSTN network to the addressed telephone device. The flow among nodes is demonstrated in the following sequence:

WebRTC browser | WebRTC to SIP gateway | MGC / PSTN Gateway | ISUP Switch | Fixed Landline phone

The following diagram shows the call flow between the WebRTC and PSTN endpoints:

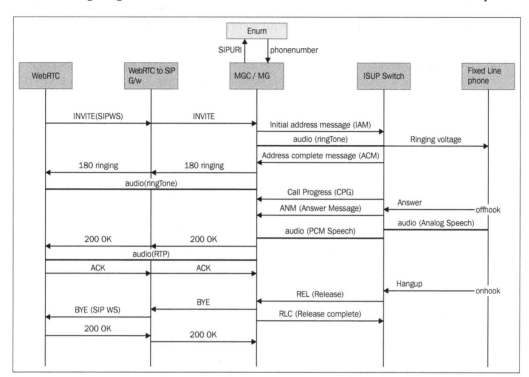

We have seen the role of the WebRTC-to-SIP gateway in *Chapter 2, Making a Standalone WebRTC Communication Client*. In brief, it converts the SIP-over-WebSocket signals to legacy plain SIP signals that IMS nodes can understand.

The MGC node handles all call signaling (SIP and ISUP), while MG handles media under the control of MGC. For ease of understanding, they are depicted together. They can be considered as the components of the PSTN gateway. The ISUP switch further converts the ISUP signals from MGC into the analog format expected by the PSTN endpoint. The ISUP switch is responsible for converting the incoming as well as the outgoing call format from the analog to the digital ISUP format as understood by the back network.

A step-by-step description of the call flow is given as follows:

1. The WebRTC client initiates a call through a click of a button on the call page. On doing so, a SIP-over-WebSocket `INVITE` request message is sent to the WebRTC gateway.

2. The WebRTC gateway converts it into a true SIP message and forwards it to the IMS core nodes.

3. The IMS network checks the address in the "To" header of the SIP message. The request URI in INVITE contains a telephone number. The IMS network understands that the signal is for a PSTN endpoint and forwards it to the PSTN gateway (refer to the *Address Mapping* section).

4. The PSTN Gateway maps INVITE to an SS7 ISUP **Initial Address Message (IAM)** along with other essential headers (refer to the *Translation from SIP to ISUP* section).

5. The ISUP switch is used to convert the signal from the digital to the analog format. At this point, a ringing voltage is sent to the fixed line phone for ringing.

6. Until the user answers the call, the PSTN gateway receives the call-in–progress message from the PSTN network and sends forth 180 ringing SIP responses to the IMS network, which passes through the WebRTC gateway, and the status is displayed on the WebRTC client's user interface.

7. In case of a successful call answer, that is, when the telephone is picked off the hook, an **answer message (ANM)** is generated and sent to the PSTN gateway from the PSTN network.

8. The PSTN gateway further sends out 200 OK SIP responses for the WebRTC client.

9. The two-way speech path is generated right after that. The Media Server is used to perform the codec conversion from legacy codecs such as G711/G729 to the WebRTC standard codecs such as PCMA/PCMU or Opus. We will speak of only the audio codecs here as PSTN terminals do not have a video call support unless they are customized to do so.

 Note that the media flow is not depicted in the preceding diagram for the sake of simplicity and ease of understanding.

10. To terminate the call, the user hooks up the PSTN telephone. As they do so, a **release (REL)** message is sent to the PSTN gateway. The PSTN gateway transforms the REL ISUP message to the BYE SIP message and forwards it to the IMS network.

11. The IMS network routes it to the WebRTC gateway where the SIP message is converted into the SIP over WebSockets message. BYE is forwarded to the WebRTC client.

12. The call hung up status is updated on the WebRTC client user interface. The WebRTC SIP session is prepared to be ready to make/receive another call.

This way, a call that originates from the PSTN endpoint can reach a WebRTC client, and both the parties can communicate.

The challenges in connecting the WebRTC world to the PSTN landscape

There are many big/small problems that arise or may arise when interconnecting the different networks of WebSocket, SIP, and PSTN. The most basic aspects of address mapping and protocol conversion from SIP to ISUP are mentioned here. Other challenges, such as policy control, billing, charging, and so on, are left to the reader to implement as they wish.

Address mapping

The PSTN scenario is much different from VoIP, as in the PSTN, the user ID is in the numeric form, while in VoIP networks, the username is followed by @domain name. To resolve the intermapping between both the worlds, DNS and Enum servers are used; this setup is depicted in the following diagram:

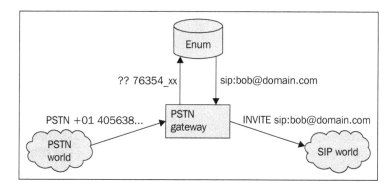

Translation from SIP to ISUP

This section describes the various ISUP call status responses and requests. It also describes the translated SIP messages. We need to have a basic understanding of ISUP messages before proceeding further. As the first call setup request is INVITE, we will begin describing the process of forming IAM from the INVITE message through the gateway.

The call setup

This section describes the mapping of the SIP headers in an `INVITE` message to the ISUP parameters in an IAM. An IAM ISUP message bears these five essential parameters:

- **Nature of Connection Indicators (NCI)**
- **Forward Call Indicators (FCI)**

    This can further be classified in the following types:

    - End-to-end method indicator
    - Interworking indicator
    - End-to-end information indicator
    - ISDN user part indicator
    - ISDN user part preference indicator
    - ISDN access indicator
    - SCCP method indicator

- **Calling Party's Category (CPC)**
- **Transmission Medium Requirement (TMR)**
- **Called Party's Number (CPN)**

A major task involved in the translation of the fields of an `INVITE` message to the parameters of an IAM is the inspection of the Request-URI and the construction of the telephony URL. When an SIP `INVITE` arrives at a PSTN gateway, the gateway *should* attempt to make use of the encapsulated ISUP, if any, within `INVITE` to assist in the formulation of outbound PSTN signaling.

If suitable ISUP headers encapsulated within the SIP request body are not found or the gateway ID is not able to decipher them anyway, then MGC formulates one on its own.

The MGC gateway sets the Interworking Indicator bit of the FCI to "No Interworking" and the ISDN User Part Indicator to "ISUP used all the way"; the gateway *might* also set the Originating Access Indicator to "Originating access non-ISDN".

The call termination

In case of no response, abrupt termination, or purposeful call termination, the SIP network is sent an appropriate response, and all the resources in MG are released.

For example, when no answer is received by the PSTN terminal or the ISUP timeout SIP Response is **504 gateway timeout**, the `Release` and `Release complete` messages are used by the ISDN to make the network ready for fresh reuse.

The `REL` message contains a cause value. The SIP response is sent based on this cause value. If a cause value other than what is listed in the following table is received, the default response of "500 Server internal error" will be used.

In the instances of **Normal event**, the following cause values might be generated; the column alongside depicts the SIP response message they would be translated into:

ISUP Cause value	SIP response
`1`: unallocated number	410 Gone
`2`: no route to network	404 Not found
`3`: no route to destination	404 Not found
`4`: send special information tone	---
`16`: normal call clearing	---
`17`: user busy	486 Busy here
`18`: no user responding	480 Temporarily unavailable
`19`: no answer from the user	480 Temporarily unavailable
`21`: call rejected	603 Decline
`22`: number changed	301 Moved permanently
`27`: destination out of order	404 Not found
`28`: address incomplete	484 Address incomplete
`29`: facility rejected	501 Not implemented
`31`: normal unspecified	480 Temporarily unavailable

The resource unavailable kind of cause value indicates a nonpermanent situation. A `Retry-After` header has to be added to the response.

ISUP Cause value	SIP response
34: no circuit available	503 Service unavailable
38: network out of order	503 Service unavailable
41: temporary failure	503 Service unavailable
42: switching equipment congestion	503 Service unavailable
44: requested channel not available	503 Service unavailable
47: resource unavailable	503 Service unavailable

The instances where the service or option not available status is generated, indicating a permanent solution, are discussed here. It is not appended by a `Retry-After` header, as in the previous case.

The service or option not available option indicates a permanent solution:

ISUP Cause value	SIP response
55: incoming calls bared within CUG	603 Decline
57: bearer capability not authorized	503 Service unavailable
58: bearer capability not presently available	503 Service unavailable
63: service/option not available	503 Service unavailable

The instances where service or option not implemented status is generated are discussed here. For enhanced SIP services such as SUBSCRIBE, NOTIFY, PUBLISH, and MESSAGE, there is no equivalent service on the PSTN front. Such requests are generally replied to with a "Not Implemented" cause value. The same is translated into the SIP response message and shared with the WebRTC client.

ISUP Cause value	SIP response
65: bearer capability not implemented	501 Not implemented
79: service or option not implemented	501 Not implemented

For the cases where ISU receives an invalid message, the response and cause values are given as follows. These are also translated into the SIP response, **503 Service unavailable**.

ISUP Cause value	SIP response
87: user not member of CUG	503 Service unavailable
88: incompatible destination	503 Service unavailable
95: invalid message	503 Service unavailable

In the event of protocol error and timer expiry, the ISUP response and equivalent SIP response generated are shown as follows.

ISUP Cause value	SIP response
102: recovery of timer expiry	408 Request timeout
111: protocol error	500 Server internal error

For instances where the interworking rules are not specified clearly, the cause of the generated ISUP error is "Interworking, unspecified". It is translated to "Server internal error" in the SIP message format.

ISUP Cause value	SIP response
127: interworking unspecified	500 Server internal error

The call in progress

This section describes the response generated for the occasions where the call is successfully routed across the network nodes from IMS to PSTN. Once the call signal reaches the PSTN phone, it might send a busy tone if it is engaged in another call or start ringing if it is free. In some cases, the telephones are configured just to record the voicemail; in such cases, the status sent back to the SIP world is "Call is being forwarded". Thus, in case of **Call in Progress** (**CPG**) message format, the following are the responses sent back to the SIP network:

ISUP event code	SIP response
1: Alerting	180 Ringing
2: Progress	183 Call progress
3: In-band information	183 Call progress

4: Call forward; line busy	181 Call is being forwarded
5: Call forward; no reply	181 Call is being forwarded
6: Call forward; unconditional	181 Call is being forwarded
-: (no event code present)	183 Call progress

When a **Conference (CON)** call is encountered, 200 OK success responses are sent back to the SIP network. After the receipt of acknowledgement, the media session is established between both the end points.

The service logic

Just as explained in the previous chapter, the service logic execution for various services such as conferencing, **Virtual Private Network (VPN)**, announcements, and other services applicable to PSTN systems, can be scripted in IN **Service Control Point (SCP)** or IMS SIP Application Server, or both. We will discuss these three approaches in brief here.

SIP service logic through application server

When the SIP call control logic is defined in the form of the SIP Servlet or the JAIN-SLEE program or, in a similar way, it is loaded and deployed onto the SIP application Server; the SCSCF consults the SIP application server for every call. The following diagram shows the IMS-to-PSTN connectivity using the Application Server call control:

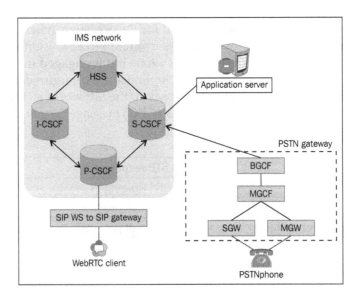

Many SIP applications such as call screening, Music on Hold, and the ring back tone advertisement are applicable for use with PSTN systems and can be integrated with the approach mentioned in the previous section.

IN services via IMSSF

As majority of service providers have not adopted the IMS platform or have adopted it partially and want to keep using the service logic defined in SCP for call control, it becomes feasible if we use a Reverse **IMSSF** (**IP Multimedia Service Switching Function**) node to convert SIP from INAP and deduce the logic from SCP. It happens in a transparent manner, and the end user on both the PSTN front and the WebRTC sides do not come to realize which node provides the call control services. The following diagram shows the IMS-to-PSTN connectivity using SCP call control:

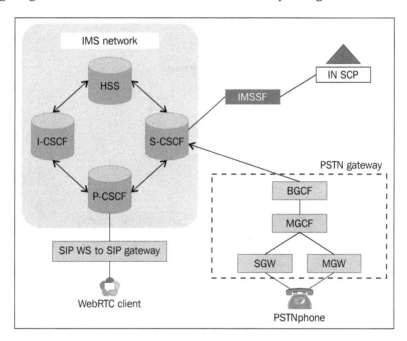

The Service Broker for the orchestration of services

A Service Broker, as discussed in the previous chapter, can interlink the services of IN's **Service Control Point** (**SCP**) and IMS Application Server. It can call the services in any permutation or combination. It can execute a service individually too. The following diagram depicts the role of a Service Broker in orchestrating the services of the SIP IMS and PSTN IN worlds:

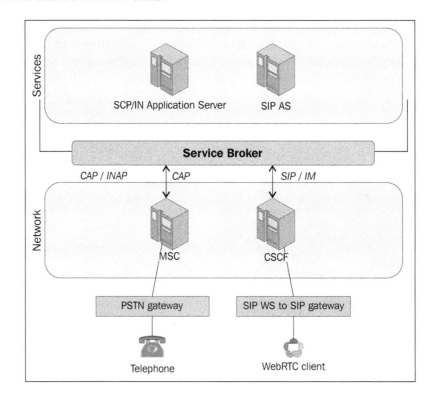

At the end of this chapter, we have arrived at an architecture similar to the one shown in the following diagram. The solution diagram for PSTN-to-WebRTC connectivity consists of SS7 and IMS network layer nodes. It might also be integrated with service logic embedded in the application layer components and **Service Delivery Platform** (**SDP**). The following diagram shows the IMS-to-PSTN connectivity using a Service Broker:

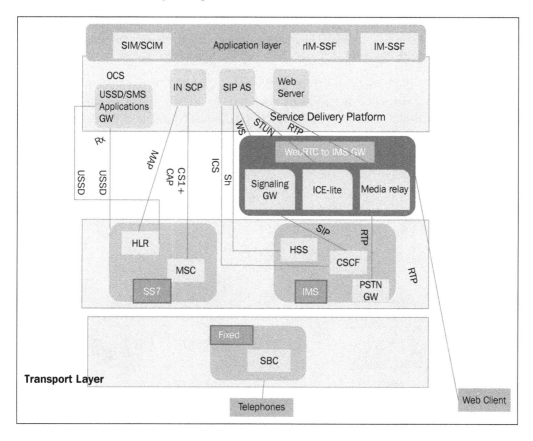

A **Session Border Controller** (**SBC**) is used for a variety of reasons that include security through network hiding, transcoding, offloading VoIP traffic, and so on. It is recommended that you use a standard grade SBC for PSTN network integration.

Summary

The process described in the book establishes an ideal way to interconnect a legacy telephone system with WebRTC. We discussed interworking based on the SS7 IN setup as well as the IMS-based environment. We saw how PSTN gateways function with the help of MGW and SGW, which take care of media and signaling conversions, respectively. We listed a few challenges that can occur when an SIP network is made to function with the PSTN system; these challenges included address mapping and SIP-to-ISUP headers. We saw the approach to integrating call control logic with the WebRTC PSTN setup build so far.

After establishing the interconnectivity of a typical WebRTC ecosystem with all the other useful networks, we can now shift our focus to deliver a robust, feature-rich WebRTC application architecture, which will be discussed in the upcoming chapters.

6
Basic Features of WebRTC over SIP

In the previous chapters, we had encountered the WebRTC integration architecture with and without the solution design. We will now draw our attention to the development of the full-fledged WebRTC client; this includes the basic features and rich communication services that must be implemented to put our WebRTC client in the ranks of a standard communication body.

This chapter only describes the basic features expected from a SIP-based WebRTC client. I have grouped the services into categories that best describe the implementation. The basic SIP services such as registration, call, instant message, call transfer, as well as enhanced SIP services, such as Presence and user capability, are also explained. The Media Server plays a crucial role in the development of some of the other SIP services, such as voicemail, IVR, Conferencing, Music on Hold, among others. This chapter explains the introduction of Media Services in the WebRTC client as well.

As the WebRTC is a web-based communication agent, it would be unfair if we do not integrate interactive web application features such as user-friendly GUIs and OAuth for token-based authentication, with other social networking platforms such as Facebook or Google+. The integration of such web-based services will also be covered as part of this chapter.

SIP services

SIP services are communication features that are intrinsic to SIP requests itself. These services include the following:

- Registration
- Audio/video call
- Instant message
- Presence

We will discuss all of them in detail, accompanied by a call-flow diagram.

Registering a SIP client

A SIP client, such as a SIP phone, SIP soft client, and SIP WebRTC web page, ought to register itself with the **Registrar**. The Registrar informs the VoIP systems about how you can be reached for an incoming event such as a call, instant message, and Presence update.

A Registrar notes down the physical address of each of the clients through the SIP REGISTER request and confirms their registration with a 200 OK response. The values obtained are copied to the **HSS/Location Server** as well.

The ideal scenario for the SIP Registration call flow without any authentication challenge is shown in the following diagram:

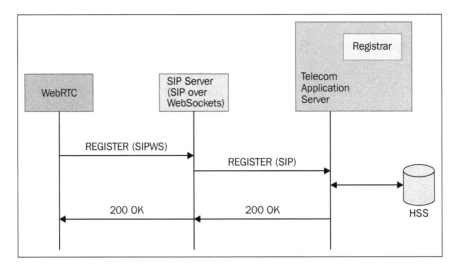

However, with the introduction of secure registration with authentication, the server throws an authentication challenge in the form of a **407 Proxy Authentication Required** response. It is for the request initiator to provide the assurance of its identity. For this purpose, a nonce (such as HTTP Digest) is computed and carried out in order to validate its identity. The following diagram shows the SIP Registration call flow with the authentication challenge:

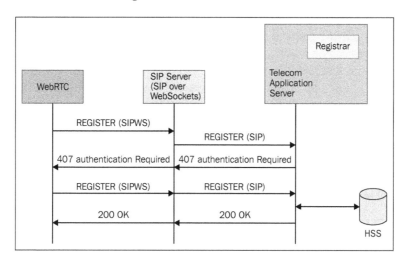

During the processing of a call, the Location Server is queried to find out which **Serving Call Session Control Function (SCSCF)** should be used in order to forward the request. We discussed the role of CSCF nodes in *Chapter 3, WebRTC with SIP and IMS*.

The SIP Traces for the Registration request by WebRTC is as follows:

```
SEND: REGISTER sip:domain.com SIP/2.0
Via: SIP/2.0/WS df7jal231s0d.invalid;branch=z9hG4bKkKS7wNb4eUtrGC4eqAcsLk
FtwdmmcUhr;report
From: "userA"<sip:userA@domain.com>;tag=QprEnFLGbLoZ1JzOAZro
To: "userA"<sip:userA@domain.com>
Contact: "userA"<sip:userA@df7jal231s0d.invalid;rtcweb-breaker=yes;transp
ort=ws>;expires=200;click2call=no;+g.oma.sip-im;+audio;language="en,fr"
Call-ID: 45771a0b-a074-a703-137e-95732a99422c
CSeq: 40303 REGISTER
Content-Length: 0
Max-Forwards: 70
Authorization: Digest username="userA",realm="domain.com",nonce="U3mcb1N5
m0PhCzqVWIgBxQPNuPAzfYMy",uri="sip:domain.com",response="cabd8882851165fb
d23f2de7410ee4c1",algorithm=MD5
```

```
User-Agent: IM-client/OMA1.0 sipML5-v1.2013.08.10B
Organization:
Supported: path
```

The first line tells us that this is a REGISTER message. It also specifies the Request-URI, which, in this case, is the domain for which the registration is meant .This line also identifies the version of the protocol, which is SIP/2.0. The To and From headers denote the address of the record; in case of REGISTER, these two are same unless it is a third-party registration. The Call-ID header field is mainly for dialog identification. For registration, a SIP or WebRTC client will use the same Call-ID value to register with a particular registrar. The Contact header holds the address bindings. The expires header indicates how long the registration should be valid, with the value given in seconds. Other headers are not mandatory.

The authentication challenge with the 407 Proxy Authentication Required response is thrown by the server. This is depicted in the following SIP RESPONSE trace:

```
recv=SIP/2.0 407 Proxy Authentication Required
Via: SIP/2.0/WS df7jal231s0d.invalid;report=52131;
received=122.160.87.159;branch=
z9hG4bKgpH8F0UP8eOnWOKKQ9TZIKEgKnSy7FnN
From: "userA"<sip:userA@domain.com>;tag=nBAgXU4kKmnC7Xx2JEpr
To: <sip:userB@domain.com>;tag=38aee63c0935fb6b672c4ad12db0cc71.0f98
Call-ID: ac8d4e18-3c8b-5a3f-45c9-f236112e8d69
CSeq: 60293 INVITE
Content-Length: 0
Proxy-Authenticate: Digest realm="domain.com",
nonce="U3ml01N5pKcIQXLqXHRThzGzj+erPWIK",stale=FALSE
Server: kamailio (4.1.1 (x86_64/linux))

SEND: ACK sip:userB@domain.com SIP/2.0
Via: SIP/2.0/WS df7jal231s0d.invalid;branch=
z9hG4bKgpH8F0UP8eOnWOKKQ9TZIKEgKnSy7FnN;rport
From: "userA"<sip:userA@domain.com>;tag=nBAgXU4kKmnC7Xx2JEpr
To: <sip:userB@domain.com>;tag=38aee63c0935fb6b672c4ad12db0cc71.0f98
Call-ID: ac8d4e18-3c8b-5a3f-45c9-f236112e8d69
CSeq: 60293 ACK
Content-Length: 0
Max-Forwards: 70
```

 Please note that **401 Unauthorized** or **407 Proxy Authentication Required** is present before almost all the SIP requests such as Register, Subscribe, and Invite. We have henceforth excluded them from traces to provide simplicity and clarity.

Making audio and video calls using SIP

This is primarily the most crucial and important part of any communication client. We have already made sure of this feature in *Chapter 2, Making a Standalone WebRTC Communication Client*. To refresh the concept of a call on SIP clients, we can recall the SIP requests that are sent out when a party wants to invite the other side for a communication session.

The overall working principle for a SIP call based on requests revolves around the following four requests:

- The Invite SIP request for session request
- The Ack SIP request confirms a request
- The Cancel SIP request is to end a pending request
- The Bye SIP request is to end a session

A 200 OK SIP response to the Invite SIP request is followed by the transmission of the Ack SIP request. The Ack SIP request is used to transport the **Session Description Protocol (SDP)** for media negotiation. This leads to successful call establishment between the caller and receiver parties. A call request that does not receive a success response of 200 OK is gracefully ended with a Cancel SIP request. An ongoing call is ended with a Bye SIP request.

SIP employs the Request-Response Model in a fashion similar to HTTP. The transactions are used to keep an account of the internal state and keep timers for every request/response. A dialog is a complete set of signaling protocols exchanged between both parties, and every subset of requests and final responses inside this is considered as a single transaction. This implies that a dialog can consists of many transactions.

To brush up our understanding of the SIP communication sessions, let's go through the difference between SIP Transaction and SIP Dialog.

SIP Transaction	SIP Dialog
This occurs between a client and a server and comprises all messages from the first request sent from the client to the server up to the final response sent from the server to the client.	This is a peer-to-peer SIP relationship between two UAs that persist for some time. A dialog is identified by a Call-ID header, a local tag, and a remote tag.

The following diagram gives a description of the SIP Dialog and SIP Transaction:

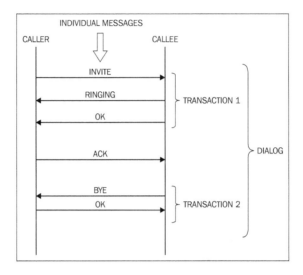

The call setup process, shown as follows, depicts a call between two WebRTC clients through a WebSocket-capable SIP Server. These kinds of calls can operate solely on SIP over WebSockets (SIP-WS) protocol and do not require a SIP-WS to SIP gateway. The following diagram shows a call between WebRTC clients using the SIP-over-WebSockets server:

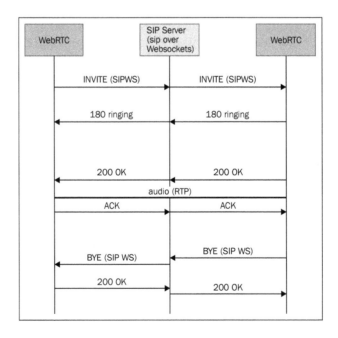

For interoperability of WebRTC clients with SIP agents such as hard phones, other desktop SIP phones, and mobile SIP phones, we require the WebRTC to SIP gateway (SIP-WS to SIP convertor). A call flow depicting such cases is shown as follows; here, the call is between the SIP agent and the WebRTC client using the SIP Server with a SIP-over-WebSockets support/gateway:

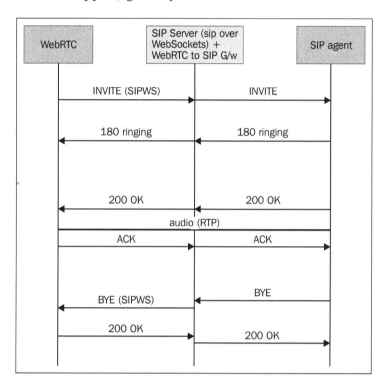

As visible from the preceding two diagrams, to call a WebRTC-only client, a SIP-over-WebSocket server is sufficient. However, to be able to call any true SIP agent such as hard SIP phone or a desktop-based soft SIP phone (Kapanga, X-Lite, Twinkle, and so on), we need to have the SIP flow passed through a SIP Server, which is capable of performing the inter-transformation from the WebSocket request to a true SIP.

Assuming that we have such a server deployed, as discussed in *Chapter 2, Making a Standalone WebRTC Communication Client*, we will focus on other services such as Presence, message, and information for WebRTC clients.

Before establishing a call, the browser's WebRTC stack requests permission to access the webcam and microphone to enable an audio/video call. The following screenshot shows a browser requesting permission to allow the usage of the camera and microphone for WebRTC calls:

The browser's WebRTC stack might also set the ICE parameters with the STUN and TURN servers for network discovery, as shown in the following trace:

```
State machine: c0000_Started_2_Outgoing_X_oINVITE SIPml-api.js:1

PeerConnectionClass = function RTCPeerConnection() { [native code] }
SessionDescriptionClass = function RDOMAINessionDescription() { [native
code] } IceCandidateClass = function RTCIceCandidate() { [native code] }
SIPml-api.js:1

Video Constraints:{"mandatory":{},"optional":[]} SIPml-api.js:1

ICE servers:[{"url":"stun:stun.l.google.com:19302"},{"url":"stun:stun.
counterpath.net:3478"},{"url":"stun:numb.viagenie.ca:3478"}] SIPml-api.
js:1

==stack event = m_permission_requested

ICE GATHERING COMPLETED! SIPml-api.js:1

onIceGatheringCompleted SIPml-api.js:1
```

Let's look at the SIP traces for a single side in a call between WebRTC clients in a sequential order:

1. The INVITE request sent from user A to user B WebRTC client is as follows:

```
SEND: INVITE sip:userB@domain.com SIP/2.0

Via: SIP/2.0/WS df7jal23ls0d.invalid;branch=z9hG4bKNK4lzTbVKKnbk7c
yp3zrSPiqsHatMFuL;rport

From: "userA"<sip:userA@domain.com>;tag=nBAgXU4kKmnC7Xx2JEpr

To: <sip:userB@domain.com>

Contact: "userA"<sip:userA@df7jal23ls0d.invalid;rtcweb-breaker=yes
;click2call=no;transport=ws>;impi=userA;ha1=ea46f66c4fd9c7e4493d59
a22810cd95;+g.oma.sip-im;+sip.ice;language="en,fr"

Call-ID: ac8d4e18-3c8b-5a3f-45c9-f236112e8d69

CSeq: 60294 INVITE

Content-Type: application/sdp

Content-Length: 3022

Max-Forwards: 70
```

```
Proxy-Authorization: Digest username="userA",realm="domain.com",no
nce="U3ml01N5pKcIQXLqXHRThzGzj+erPWIK",uri="sip:userB@domain.com",
response="765b3dcd317f55f05b60e3388a4740dd",algorithm=MD5
User-Agent: IM-client/OMA1.0 sipML5-v1.2013.08.10B
Organization: DOMAIN

/* SDP truncated */
```

Like the REGISTER SIP request message, INVITE also bears the same header fields. The topmost line tells us that this SIP message is an INVITE message that is used to establish call sessions. It contains the Request-URI, which is same as the To header in case of INVITE. The From and To header fields identify the caller and receiver, respectively. All the messages inside of a dialog, in our case, a call, will bear the same unique Call-ID.

The CSeq fields maintain the order of transactions. The Contact header is the address on which the sender is awaiting the next request/response. The Content-Type header field holds information about the message body. In case of INVITE, it's SDP.

2. The 100 trying response for the invitation sent from user A to user B is as follows:

```
recv=SIP/2.0 100 trying -- your call is important to us
Via: SIP/2.0/WS df7jal231s0d.invalid;rport=52131;
received=122.160.87.159;branch=
z9hG4bKNK41zTbVKKnbk7cyp3zrSPiqsHatMFuL
From: "userA"<sip:userA@domain.com>;tag=nBAgXU4kKmnC7Xx2JEpr
To: <sip:userB@domain.com>
Call-ID: ac8d4e18-3c8b-5a3f-45c9-f236112e8d69
CSeq: 60294 INVITE
Content-Length: 0
Server: kamailio (4.1.1 (x86_64/linux))
```

3. The 180 Ringing response for the invitation sent from user A to user B is as follows:

```
recv=SIP/2.0 180 Ringing
Via: SIP/2.0/WS df7jal231s0d.invalid;rport=52131;
received=122.160.87.159;branch=
z9hG4bKNK41zTbVKKnbk7cyp3zrSPiqsHatMFuL
From: "userA"<sip:userA@domain.com>;tag=nBAgXU4kKmnC7Xx2JEpr
To: <sip:userB@domain.com>;tag=RwaGGC5SWWopJkgqeBRU
Contact: <sip:userB@df7jal231s0d.invalid;alias=
122.160.87.159~49920~5;transport=ws>
Call-ID: ac8d4e18-3c8b-5a3f-45c9-f236112e8d69
```

```
CSeq: 60294 INVITE
Content-Length: 0
Record-Route: <sip:192.66.36.206:443;transport=ws;lr=on>
Allow: ACK,BYE,CANCEL,INVITE,MESSAGE,NOTIFY,OPTIONS,PRACK,REFER,UP
DATE
```

4. The 200 OK success response sent to user A by user B is as follows:

```
recv=SIP/2.0 200 OK
Via: SIP/2.0/WS df7jal231s0d.invalid;
rport=51627;received=122.160.87.159;
branch=z9hG4bKpSqUe9xfyp0eK8VBlOKAQCpL1WGTPavh
From: "userA"<sip:userA@domain.com>;tag=NXEl7RIgwL9Xq7RnOJVw
To: <sip:userB@domain.com>;tag=MHeTUftnAEUCVdzfd908
Contact: <sip:userB@df7jal231s0d.invalid;alias=
122.160.87.159~52719~5;transport=ws>
Call-ID: fe8e54e7-c04b-1064-4b4a-b3394fd06653
CSeq: 18645 INVITE
Content-Type: application/sdp
Content-Length: 2244
Record-Route: <sip:192.66.36.206:443;transport=ws;lr=on>
Allow: ACK,BYE,CANCEL,INVITE,MESSAGE,NOTIFY,OPTIONS,PRACK,REFER,UP
DATE

/* SDP truncated */
```

5. The ACK response sent by user A to user B is as follows:

```
SEND: ACK sip:userB@df7jal231s0d.invalid;alias=122.160.87.159~5271
9~5;transport=ws SIP/2.0
Via: SIP/2.0/WS df7jal231s0d.invalid;branch=z9hG4bKERC7ZDrc2OEGAB3
Q2ii0;rport
From: "userA"<sip:userA@domain.com>;tag=NXEl7RIgwL9Xq7RnOJVw
To: <sip:userB@domain.com>;tag=MHeTUftnAEUCVdzfd908
Contact: "userA"<sip:userA@df7jal231s0d.invalid;
rtcweb-breaker=yes;click2call=no;transport=ws>;
+g.oma.sip-im;+sip.ice;language="en,fr"
Call-ID: fe8e54e7-c04b-1064-4b4a-b3394fd06653
CSeq: 18645 ACK
Content-Length: 0
Max-Forwards: 70
Proxy-Authorization: Digest username="userA",realm="domain.co
m",nonce="U3nPOlN5zg7IV2Ka9IFh+5VqqWZRi5rU",uri="sip:userB@
df7jal231s0d.invalid;alias=122.160.87.159~52719~5;transport=ws",re
sponse="de1e4564c2938880095957dad6649d58",algorithm=MD5
```

```
Route: <sip:192.66.36.206:443;transport=ws;lr=on>
User-Agent: IM-client/OMA1.0 sipML5-v1.2013.08.10B
Organization: DOMAIN
```

Similarly, a call between a WebRTC client and SIP phone is established via the WebRTC-to-SIP gateway. Interoperability with various native mobile and desktop-based SIP phones is described in *Chapter 9, Native SIP Application and Interaction with WebRTC Clients*.

> Note that the Media Gateway is required for demultiplexing, and the Media Server is required for inter-codec conversion (transcoding) between legacy audio/video codecs supported by SIP phones and WebRTC-standard codecs. The process of integrating a Media Server with a WebRTC is detailed in *Chapter 3, WebRTC with SIP and IMS*.

Text Chat using SIP

The MESSAGE SIP request is the way through which messages are delivered to the SIP Server. The frontend of the WebRTC client issues a MESSAGE SIP request from the sender to the receiver who carries the message body, which is sent through the SIP signaling server infrastructure. The text of the instant message is transported in the body of the SIP request. A call-flow diagram depicting the traversal of SIP MESSAGE requests and subsequent responses is shown as follows:

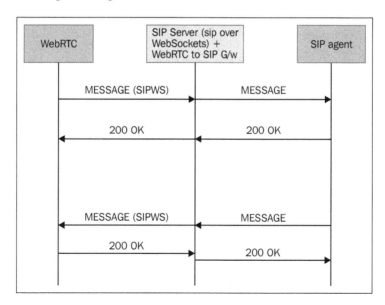

The SIP traces for instant messages in the form of text chats are shown through the SIP request and response messages. The sent and received messages between two parties using WebRTC clients are shown in a sequential order as follows:

1. The SIP message from user A to user B is as follows:

```
SEND: MESSAGE sip:userB@domain.com SIP/2.0
Via: SIP/2.0/WS df7jal231s0d.invalid;branch=z9hG4bKBd24tswZZnBxamA
STFhaaUOCwGhkeBlo;rport
From: "userA"<sip:userA@domain.com>;tag=kkDy7bqurNd3XV10dlAO
To: <sip:userB@domain.com>
Call-ID: a0db8770-9489-4fca-78c1-0ce6d839f4e8
CSeq: 17363 MESSAGE
Content-Type: text/plain;charset=utf8
Content-Length: 16
Max-Forwards: 70
Accept-Contact: *;+g.oma.sip-im
Accept-Contact: *;+sip.ice
Accept-Contact: *;language="en,fr"
Proxy-Authorization: Digest username="userA",realm="domain.com",
nonce="U3nSa1N50T91hzNQVe2ejTEtDFA4mTSh",uri="sip:userB@domain.
com",
response="5ae615b39ce4b6ba3e91617f3b5dab05",algorithm=MD5
User-Agent: IM-client/OMA1.0 sipML5-v1.2013.08.10B
Organization: DOMAIN

hello[{trxnid}]0
```

2. The RESPONSE SIP message for the message sent from user A to user B is as follows:

```
recv=SIP/2.0 200 OK
Via: SIP/2.0/WS df7jal231s0d.invalid;rport=51627;
received=122.160.87.159;
branch=z9hG4bKBd24tswZZnBxamASTFhaaUOCwGhkeBlo
From: "userA"<sip:userA@domain.com>;tag=kkDy7bqurNd3XV10dlAO
To: <sip:userB@domain.com>
Call-ID: a0db8770-9489-4fca-78c1-0ce6d839f4e8
CSeq: 17363 MESSAGE
Content-Length: 0
```

The MESSAGE requests do not establish a dialog and will always traverse the same set of proxies. There are not one but many ways to implement text. We discussed the SIP message in this section. It can also be implemented via the **Message Session Relay Protocol (MSRP)**. We will discuss this in greater detail in *Chapter 8, WebRTC and Rich Communication Services*.

Obtaining the online/offline status of users using SIP

The availability of users is determined by a SIP process called **Presence**. Depending on their registration validation and reachability, a SIP or WebRTC client might send online or offline status notifications. This is used to notify others that the particular user is unavailable to take messages or calls right now.

The PUBLISH SIP request publishes the status of a user to the **SIP Server**, which might either be online or offline. Let's assume that user X has published their status to the Server. The SIP Server also receives the SUBSCRIBE SIP request, which indicates that the other users would like to know about the status update of this particular user (user X). The Server then sends out the NOTIFY SIP request to update the subscribed users about the current status of user X. This process is replicated and repeated for all users. A person might like to subscribe for status updates of all their contacts in the phonebook so that they can view their online or offline status with a green or red indicator alongside their address entries in their phonebook.

The call flow depicted in the following diagram is derived from *SIP Extension for Event State Publication* of *RFC 3903*. The following diagram shows the call flow for the Presence service, using the PUBLISH, SUBSCRIBE, and NOTIFY requests:

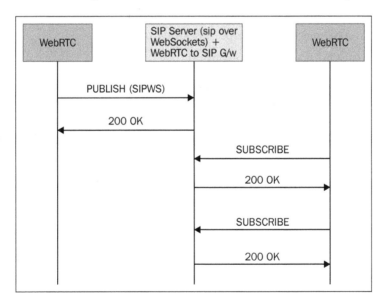

The working principle for the Presence service is described in this section. The participating entities in this scenario are described as in the following figure:

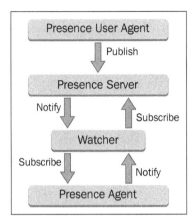

The **Presence Agent** publishes its current state to the **Presence Server** via the **Watcher**, which continuously monitors the state change for users. The other user agent listens for notifications from the Presence Server .The three major SIP requests for the Presence service are given as follows:

- Publish for event state update
- Subscribe to enable the receipt of notifications
- Notify to send updated information

The SUBSCRIBE message establishes a dialog and is immediately replied by the server using the 200 OK response. At this point, the dialog is established. The server sends a NOTIFY request to the user every time the event to which the user is subscribed to changes. The NOTIFY messages are sent within the dialog established by the SUBSCRIBE message.

Presence is a user's reachability and willingness to communicate its current status information. Once subscribed, the user receives notifications for every state change of the agent. This is a way to have sustained stateful communication.

The trace for WebRTC SIP Presence requests and responses are given as follows in a sequential order:

1. The PUBLISH request is sent by user A to publish its current state, and it is given as follows. It varies from offline (user is not available) to online (user is available) users:

```
SEND: PUBLISH sip:userA@domain.com SIP/2.0

Via: SIP/2.0/WS df7jal231s0d.invalid;
branch=z9hG4bKhGVaEAS182b5fsIlWufL8n6NiTbbDk6z;rport

From: "userA"<sip:userA@domain.com>;tag=gr4hcygvktExiuzDinch

To: "userA"<sip:userA@domain.com>

Call-ID: ce1e656e-fbb4-12a5-95dc-392ed1fe9519

CSeq: 23378 PUBLISH

Expires: 100

Content-Type: application/pidf+xml

Content-Length: 216

Max-Forwards: 70

Accept-Contact: *;+g.oma.sip-im

Accept-Contact: *;+sip.ice

Accept-Contact: *;language="en,fr"

Proxy-Authorization: Digest username="userA",
realm="domain.com",nonce="U3mcb1N5m0PhCzqVWIgBxQPNuPAzfYMy",
uri="sip:userA@domain.com",
response="487d9b6bb51693d7152d85bc52b23f2d",algorithm=MD5

Event: presence

User-Agent: IM-client/OMA1.0 sipML5-v1.2013.08.10B

Organization:


<?xml version="1.0" encoding="UTF-8"?>

<presence xmlns="urn:ietf:params:xml:ns:pidf">

<tuple id="a">

<status>

<basic>open</basic>

<contact>sip:userA@domain.com</contact>

<note>online</note></status>

</tuple>

</presence>
```

2. The response received by user A is given as follows:

```
recv=SIP/2.0 200 OK
Via: SIP/2.0/WS df7jal23ls0d.invalid;rport=44802;
received=122.160.87.159;
branch=z9hG4bKhGVaEAS182b5fsIlWufL8n6NiTbbDk6z
From: "userA"<sip:userA@domain.com>;tag=gr4hcygvktExiuzDinch
To: "userA"<sip:userA@domain.com>;tag=0b8837ea7699295b1c5e8783be06
64de-8631
Call-ID: ce1e656e-fbb4-12a5-95dc-392ed1fe9519
CSeq: 23378 PUBLISH
Expires: 90
Content-Length: 0
SIP-ETag: a.1400155961.23214.7102.0
Server: kamailio (4.1.1 (x86_64/linux))
```

3. The SUBSCRIBE request sent by user B to user A is as follows:

```
SEND: SUBSCRIBE sip:userA@domain.com SIP/2.0
Via: SIP/2.0/WS df7jal23ls0d.invalid;
branch=z9hG4bKcWtcVpdwKyFKNvtZZIb7rPCdXh4Vrq2v;rport
From: "userB"<sip:userB@domain.com>;tag=L6ITng8FhPuHaTGLK7r9
To: <sip:userA@domain.com>
Contact: "userB"<sip:userB@df7jal23ls0d.invalid;
rtcweb-breaker=yes;click2call=no;transport=ws>;
+g.oma.sip-im;+sip.ice;language="en,fr"
Call-ID: 407695ab-b463-22e6-ed93-3a360dd30a51
CSeq: 28878 SUBSCRIBE
Expires: 100
Content-Length: 0
Max-Forwards: 70
Event: presence
Accept: application/pidf+xml
User-Agent: IM-client/OMA1.0 sipML5-v1.2013.08.10B
Organization: DOMAIN
```

4. The SUBSCRIBE response that user B sends as a response to user A is as follows:

```
recv=SIP/2.0 202 OK
Via: SIP/2.0/WS df7jal23ls0d.invalid;rport=49920;
received=122.160.87.159;
branch=z9hG4bKx3GwtZNLXL9qkqWNCF52RS9PNundiBgM
```

```
From: "userB"<sip:userB@domain.com>;tag=L6ITng8FhPuHaTGLK7r9

To: <sip:userA@domain.com>;
tag=0b8837ea7699295b1c5e8783be0664de-fb4e

Contact: <sip:172.23.100.47:5060;transport=ws>

Call-ID: 407695ab-b463-22e6-ed93-3a360dd30a51

CSeq: 28879 SUBSCRIBE

Expires: 100

Content-Length: 0

Server: kamailio (4.1.1 (x86_64/linux))
```

5. The NOTIFY request sent by user A to notify user B is as follows:

```
recv=NOTIFY sip:userB@122.160.87.159:49920;rtcweb-breaker=yes;clic
k2call=no;transport=ws SIP/2.0

Via: SIP/2.0/WS 192.66.36.206:443;branch=z9hG4bKbe5c.d63f742200000
0000000000000000000000.0

From: <sip:userA@domain.com>;tag=0b8837ea7699295b1c5e8783be0664de-
fb4e

To: <sip:userB@domain.com>;tag=L6ITng8FhPuHaTGLK7r9

Contact: <sip:172.23.100.47:5060;transport=tcp>

Call-ID: 407695ab-b463-22e6-ed93-3a360dd30a51

CSeq: 25 NOTIFY

Content-Type: application/pidf+xml

Content-Length: 217

User-Agent: kamailio (4.1.1 (x86_64/linux))

Max-Forwards: 70

Event: presence

Subscription-State: active;expires=100


<?xml version="1.0" encoding="UTF-8"?>

<presence xmlns="urn:ietf:params:xml:ns:pidf">

<tuple id="a">

<status>

<basic>open</basic>

<contact>sip:userA@domain.com</contact>

<note>online</note></status>

</tuple>

</presence>
```

6. The NOTIFY response sent by user A to user B is as follows:

```
SEND: SIP/2.0 200 OK

Via: SIP/2.0/WS 192.66.36.206:443;branch=z9hG4bKbe5c.d63f742200000
0000000000000000000000.0

From: <sip:userA@domain.com>;tag=0b8837ea7699295b1c5e8783be0664de-
fb4e

To: <sip:userB@domain.com>;tag=L6ITng8FhPuHaTGLK7r9

Contact: <sip:userB@df7jal231s0d.invalid;transport=ws>

Call-ID: 407695ab-b463-22e6-ed93-3a360dd30a51

CSeq: 25 NOTIFY

Content-Length: 0

NOTIFY content = <?xml version="1.0" encoding="UTF-8"?>

<presence xmlns="urn:ietf:params:xml:ns:pidf">

<tuple id="a">

<status>

<basic>open</basic>

<contact>sip:userA@domain.com</contact>

<note>online</note></status>

</tuple>

</presence>
```

The SIP service discussed so far has covered audio/video call, registration, Presence, and instant message services. We have seen the sequence of SIP request and response messages in the preceding call-flow diagram and also analyzed the traces. These SIP services are very basic in nature and provide simple communication scenarios between two SIP or WebRTC endpoints. We are now ready to focus on more detailed services within the developer-defined call-control logic described in the next section.

Services in the Application Server

With every communication client, there are a set of basic features that need to be supported to make the client user friendly. Normally, it is taken for granted that these features will come along with any kind of communication software or hardware that the end users purchase. These include call hold/resume, call transfer/forward, call screening, call ignore, mute, redial, and so on. We can integrate these either in the frontend logic, which is written in JSP/HTML, or towards the SIP Application Layer, which is written in the form of JAIN-SLEE or SIP Servlets.

An Application Server is used to introduce call-control logic in a normal call-flow scenario. The following diagram depicts the role of Application Server, managing the call-control logic as well as components such as Registrar and Proxy Servers:

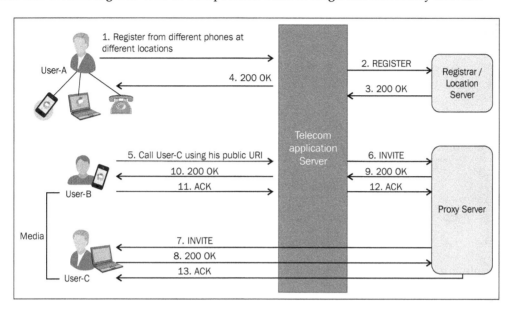

A SIP request that is sent from a SIP or WebRTC agent makes its way to the SCSCF after passing through PCSCF. At SCSCF, it is sent to the Application Server to process the call-control logic and proceed with the call accordingly. An application defines the actions that need to be taken upon particular events. For example, to find out if the caller is blocked by the user, the SIP Server will reply to the INVITE SIP request with the CANCEL request to the caller. The developers might also redirect the blocked call to an audio file, stating that the user has been blocked. Many other call-control services such as call forwarding and call transfer can also be programmed as SIP applications to be deployed on the Application Server.

In this particular section, we will throw light on the following services:

- Simple back-to-back user agent
- Call screening
- Call hold/resume
- Call logs

Back-to-back user agent

In the most basic setup of the WebRTC SIP IMS architecture, there arises two scenarios.

The first is when a server acts like a proxy agent. In this case, the call request is just forwarded to the destination end by the server without any modifications. The server acts like a mute tunnel to link the two sides in a communication channel. It can be seen in the first section of this chapter, making audio/video call via a server with SIP WebSockets support.

The second case is when the server acts like a **Back-to-Back User Agent (B2BUA)**. Unlike a proxy agent, which maintains only transactions, the B2BUA agent maintains the call state of all the SIP events.

 B2BUA is the way in which many VoIP elements such as SBCs and PBXs (Asterisk or FreeSWITCH) work. Though it is not a service itself, it has been introduced to depict the default behavior of call control by the Application Server.

The following diagram shows the SIP call flow mediated by the B2BUA deployed on the Telecom Application Server:

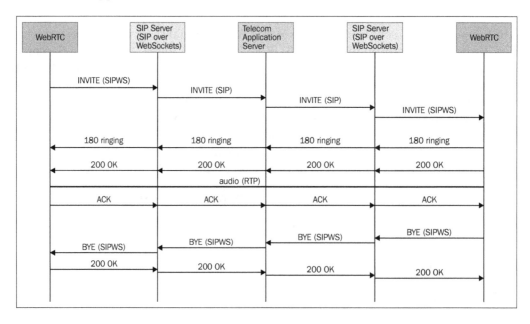

The preceding figure depicts how the Server participates in call setup, processing, and termination by maintaining a separate call log on each side, that is, between the caller and the SIP Server and between the SIP Server and the receiver. As a result of this, the B2BUA agents are generally used to perform special operations such as failover control, topology hiding, protocol interworking, and transaction with database to fetch the screened users list. B2BUA are relevant to services that entail media processing too.

Call screening

To block unwanted callers, the user might activate the call-screening service. As part of this service, the user defines a list of SIP URIs that are barred from making calls to them. This was a basic call-screening use case; however, it might also be applied with special provisions and filters. We will look into the basic call-screening process first.

Basic call screening

Let's assume that there are two users, user A and user B. A typical call screening application will block the SIP URI of user A, while they are trying to contact user B, based on preset values. In real time, when user A calls user B, the SIP request reaches the core network logic and then matches the SIP URI of user A with the blocked SIP URI list. If a match is found, the call is cancelled; otherwise, the call is continued as normal to user B. The following diagram shows the SIP call flow for a call-screening application:

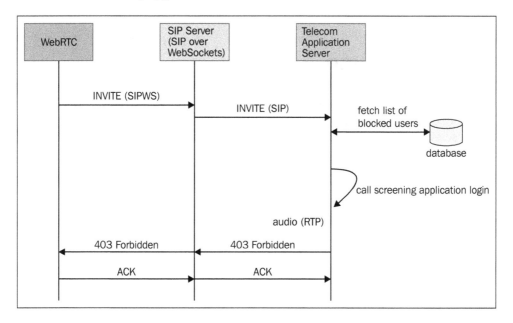

The preceding diagram denotes the case when a caller 's SIP URI is found matching the entries in the screened user's list of receivers. In such a case, the caller is responded to with an error message.

Enhanced call screening

The requirement for a more accurate call-control logic in screening applications is a primary concern for telecom service providers due to the following reasons:

- When a call is screened midway, the air interface of the Telecom Service Provider is still made use of, and then the call is dropped. It is a direct revenue loss after the usage of precious air interface. In order to generate some revenue inputs even from blocked/screened calls, a failed call should still be connected to supplementary services such as voicemails and IVR announcements and asked to leave a message so that the services that can be billed are invoked.

- To provide for a better user experience even with failed/screened calls and boost user engagement, a media playback of interactive responding services is required, instead of error messages and abrupt termination of calls.

- To enable the user to exercise more control over their incoming calls, we should give them a detailed provisioning system to enter day-time preferences and gray/white/black listed users.

- To provide the subscriber with the option to link their calendar with their call-control service so that all calls that are made during an important activity scheduled through their calendar, such as a business meeting, get screened.

Call hold/resume

It is a simple requirement to be able to put an ongoing call on hold and resume it after a period of time. During an ongoing call, that is, during the course of SRTP or RTP, the media is continuously flowing between the endpoints; however, during a call hold session, the media flow is temporarily put on hold. This prevents media exchange for the period until the user resumes it.

The following call flow depicts the call-hold and call-resume operations between two WebRTC clients:

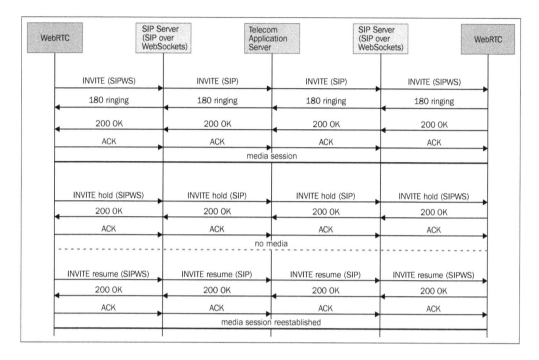

The working principle of call hold and resume lies in the correct usage and understanding of the INVITE SIP message .We use the process of sending the RE-INVITE SIP message to determine when to put the call on hold and a RE-INVITE message again to determine when to resume the flow.

Call forwarding

Call forwarding is a useful service to connect the call to a second party when the concerned party is not available to answer the call. A real-time use case is that of a boss forwarding all the incoming calls to his assistant. Call forwarding can be of two variants:

- Unconditional
- On unavailable (busy/no answer)

Unconditional call forwarding

In this scenario, all the incoming calls are transferred to a third party on an unconditional basis. The following diagram shows the SIP call flow for unconditional call forwarding:

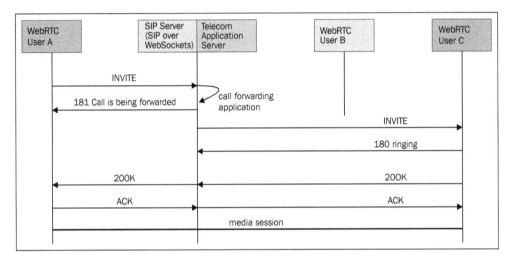

The enhanced logic can also be specified in the application that will be deployed on the application server. A user might switch on the call-forwarding service for a period of time or for specific people. These values are fed into the system using a provisioning system, which can be IVR based or web based.

Call forwarding when the user is unavailable

For instances where the call is to be forwarded on specific error responses such as **486 Busy Here** and **487 Request Timeout** (that is, the call is not answered), the SIP Server connects the call to a second party. The logic for this application, along with identities of the primary and secondary party who want to use the call-forwarding service, must be deployed on the application server.

The following diagram shows the SIP call flow for call forwarding in case of user unavailability:

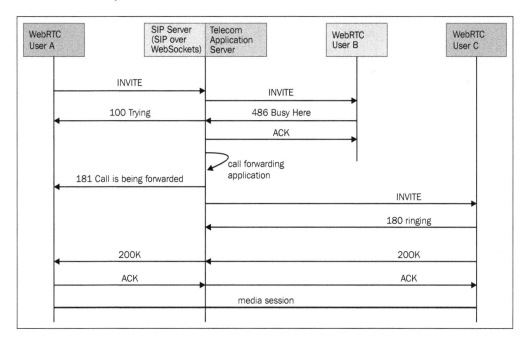

Call transfer

An ongoing call can be transferred from one user to another while a session is in progress or even before a call is received. There might arise two variations to call transfer, which takes place using the REFER SIP request and the Refer-To header; they are transfer attended and transfer unattended.

Attended call transfer

In this scenario, the user, who we assume is the transfer originator, puts the called party on hold and establishes a call with the transfer target to alert them to the impending transfer. The user then places the target on hold and then proceeds with the transfer using an escaped Replace header field instead of the Refer-To header.

The following figure depicts the attended call transfer from user B to user A:

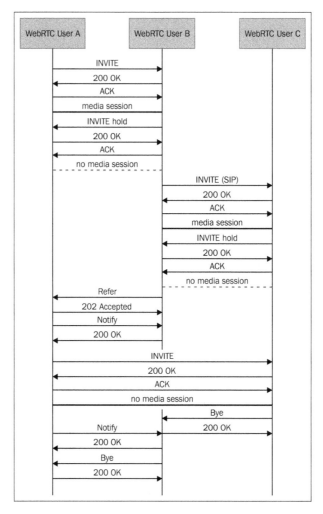

In this scenario, the first handshake between A and B creates a new RTP session and then puts it in a hold state. The second handshake between B and C creates a new RTP session and puts it in a hold state too. Then, user B passes the credentials of C to A using the REFER message, and A establishes a new RTP session with C. Thereafter, C closes the session with B, and A notifies B about the new session with C. Then, B closes the session with A.

Now, user A and user C are in a session successfully. Despite the BYE message sent by user C, the dialog still exists until the subscription created by the REFER message has terminated.

Unattended call transfer

In case of an unattended call-transfer scenario, the user provides the contact URI of the target (the SIPURI or PSTN number) to the receiver. The receiver attempts to establish a session using that contact and reports the results of this attempt.

The following diagram depicts a call flow for call transfer in an unattended manner:

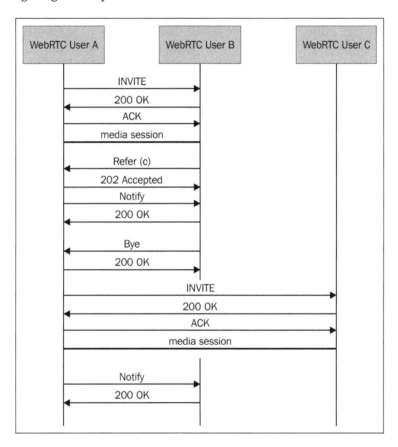

This scenario bears a substantial difference from the attended call transfer where parties were preinformed about the call transfer. However, this is not the case here. In this case, the call transfer takes place without putting any party on hold. Just like in the previous case, here too, user A calls user B initially. Thereafter, B refers C to A, and users B and A disconnect. Now, A is connected to C, which also replaces the session. In this example, the `Replaces` header field is inserted into the `Refer-To` URI to achieve unattended call transfer from B to C.

Generation of call log for tracking

Recording the call logs is a necessity for user overview and auditing purposes alike. Call logs are stored with a unique transaction ID, timestamp, caller, receiver, and duration of call.

We will look into the working principle behind generating call logs from the Application Server program. To facilitate storing details about calls made and received, the Application Server must refer to an external database entity. For every incoming call, the Application Server either initiates a temporary counter till the end of a call and then writes the values to the database or writes the values to the database in the beginning itself and updates them once the call is terminated. To adopt the latter approach, refer to the call-flow logic depicted in the following diagram:

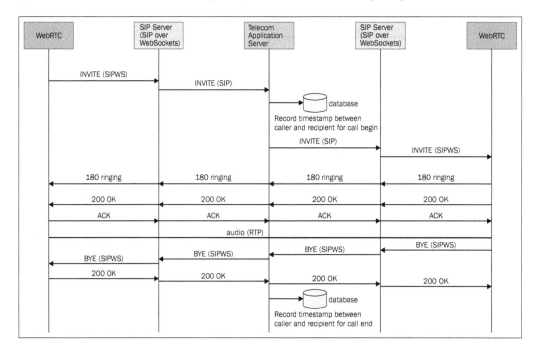

Media Server-based features

Media Servers are used for the purpose of transcoding media streams; for example, in case of WebRTC, it converts audio/video from the WebRTC standard to other codecs understandable by legacy agents.

Media-related operations such as audio/video recording, playback, announcement, and conferencing are handled via the Media Server. Few of the advanced use cases such as Music on Hold, IVR, Video on Demand, and others are also configured through the Media Server logic. Importantly, the Media Server also provides for **Media Resource Function (MRF)**, which processes real-time audio and video media streams and forms a crucial part of the IMS architecture.

Announcement

To play a simple announcement through the Media Server, the establishment of a SIP session is requested. Similarly, record and playback operations, on part of the Media Server, require the establishment of a SIP session, just as in case of a call.

The call flow for media announcement is depicted in the following diagram. It is derived from *Basic Network Media Services with SIP* in *RFC 4240*.

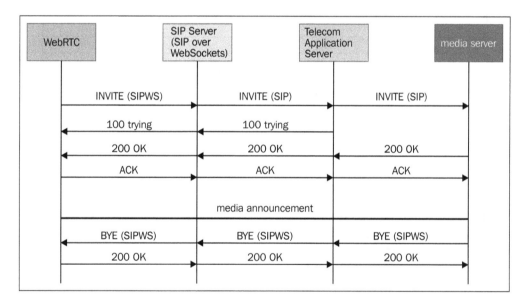

Media relay

Once the SIP signals have been transmitted successfully, a communication session is established between the two WebRTC endpoints. By default, the media flows in a peer-to-peer fashion. However, to enable the media services such as transcoding and recording text to speech, the media must not flow peer to peer. Instead, the transmission should take place through a relay agent. We can use an RTP proxy linked to a Media Server for this purpose.

An RTP Proxy can function in one of the following two modes based on configuration:

- **Basic proxying mode**: In this mode, it does not alter the media stream transmission

- **Functional mode**: In this mode, the media parameters are altered to get the best configuration

The following diagram shows the SIP call flow for media relay:

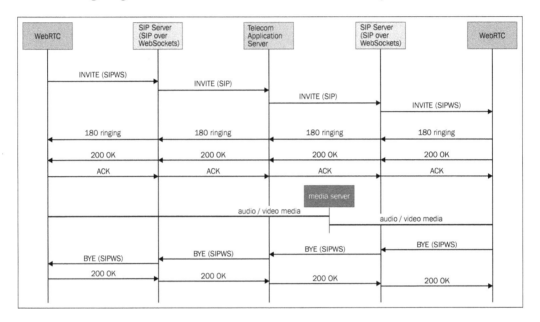

The preceding diagram depicts a media relay operation through an RTP engine inside a Media Server. The other signaling operations such as SIP Requests for INVITE, ACK, BYE, and SIP Responses for 200 OK and 180 ringing messages are unaffected.

Voicemail

Voicemail enables a user to deliver a recorded voice message to another user. Usually, this service is hit in the event of a receiver not answering the call and callers getting automatically redirected to voicemail. The voicemail application records an audio message that is delivered to the receiver through their mailbox.

A diagrammatic description of voicemail components in the WebRTC setup is shown in the following diagram:

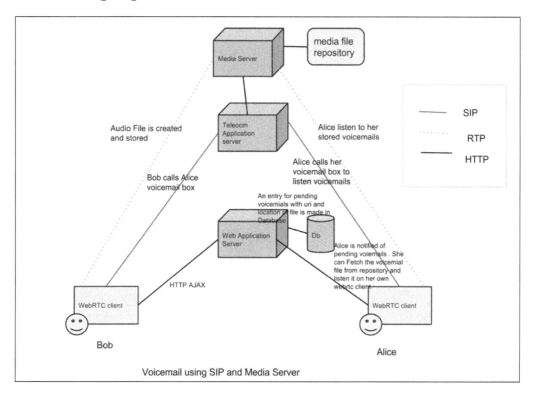

Voicemail using SIP and Media Server

The summarized working principle of voicemail is based on the call recording and playback component of Media Server, which is sometimes also referred to as the Voicemail Server.

The Application Server hosts a SIP Servlet (`RecorderServlet`) that functions as a terminal. It handles an incoming call from **Bob**; the Application Server connects it to a Voicemail Server, which hosts a VXML or MSML script. The Media Server establishes an RTP session and records voice data as an audio file in the AVI format. **Alice** receives the recorded voice mail file, which can be played by a SIP phone, WebRTC client, or PSTN telephone.

Music on Hold

When a call is put on hold, the sender and receiver receive a music playback to avoid a mute line; this service is called **Music on Hold**.

Music on Hold is established with the help of the Media Server. In a more detailed manner, when an existing SIP session is put on hold, the SIP Application Server connects the parties to the Media Server, which establishes a media session with the user and plays back an audio file. The working principle behind Music on Hold is the transfer of call from one party to the Media Server. This allows for music playback till the call is transferred back to the original communicating party.

Interactive Voice Response

An IVR is a prompt-like audio message that is played to convey information to the user. IVR is a prerecorded message that is played on the occurrence of some event. Consider the following table for some events and the IVR associated with them:

Event	IVR samples
When the recipient of a call is on another line	User is busy. Please try after some time.
On occasion of joining a conference	• You are the first member in the conference • Member X has joined the conference • Member Y has left the conference
For announcements	• Your balance is too low for the call • You are not allowed to call this number
For the main menu	• Press 1 to enable call screening service • Press2 to enable call forwarding service • Press 3 to go back to the main menu

As an IVR is a prerecorded message of a text-to-speech file, it is stored and configured with the Media Server. When a user event that requires an IVR to be played occurs, the SIP Application Server sends an invite to the Media Server that established a media session with the user and plays back the audio.

Conferencing

Conference connects multiparty audio and/or video call such that everyone has access to the ongoing media. All the members of the conference call can simultaneously participate in the call.

Multipart communication

The working principle of multiparty audio/video call conferencing is based on the playback ability of the Media Server. The following diagram depicts conferencing between multiple parties:

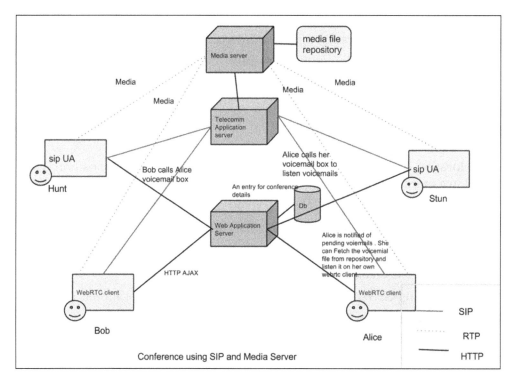

Conference using SIP and Media Server

For a dedicated conferencing app, services such as group chat, file sharing, private chat, and desktop sharing are of prime importance. WebRTC and Media Server alone cannot provide all the capabilities required to build a team conference application. The various ways of implementing a WebRTC-based conference will be discussed in *Chapter 10, Other WebRTC Use Cases*

Features of a web application

As WebRTC is more popular as a web-hosted service, it makes a lot of sense to take advantage of its web nature and utilize its full potential as a web application. The features discussed here are particular for WebRTC clients only and not applicable to usual SIP agents such as hard phones, desktop-based soft clients, and others. These features include OAuth, Geolocation, RESTful web services to fetch information such as news and weather updates, integration with social networking accounts, as well as importing contacts, sending web mails, and so on.

In this section, we will discuss the following features:

- Geolocation
- OAuth for authentication against third-party servers
- Importing contacts from other accounts
- Message to mail

Geolocation

The Geolocation API by W3C provides a method to locate the user's position. This is useful in a number of ways, ranging from providing a user with location-specific information/advertisement/search results to providing route navigation.

There are primarily four ways in which Geolocation is fetched from a computer:

- **IP Geolocation**: Using this, each IP block corresponds roughly to a geographical area, which often results in false positives.
- **GPS**: Using GPS satellites, maximum accuracy of user location is obtained.
- **Wi-Fi Positioning**: Using Wi-Fi networks and routers, especially in urban areas (using Skyhook Wireless), user location is obtained.
- **Cell Tower Triangulation**: This is based on the cellular signals that the user gets from towers. This is mostly useful for mobile devices that have built-in cellular radios.

We make use of IP Geolocation to track down the user's current location and share the same whenever required. For example, consider the following code to fetch the current position of the browser:

```
If (navigator.geolocation)
  navigator.geolocation.getCurrentPosition(showPosition);
```

The list of parameters that can be fetched from the Geolocation API embedded in a browser are as follows:

- Latitude: 28.459497
- Longitude: 77.02663799999999
- Accuracy: 25000
- Altitude: Null
- Altitude accuracy: Null
- Heading: Null
- Speed: Null

 Note that these are arbitrary values.

Geolocation is a powerful feature for any application. In the context of WebRTC clients, developers can use Geolocation to place the user's contact from the phonebook on a map as per their obtained longitudes and latitudes. The Geolocation database maintains user groups divided into different geographies as per their current location. This can be used for many interesting use cases such as targeted advertisements, currency conversion, language-based localization, and policymaking.

In case of outdated browser or dead-slow uplink speed, the Geolocation service might be unavailable. Also, when the user has not granted explicit permission in the pop-up bar that appears to share location, the Geolocation service does not work. The following screenshot shows the browser requesting for permission to allow the usage of the computer's location:

After fetching the Geolocation coordinates, it is upto the programmer to either display it in a tabular format, store it for backend processing only, or display it on a map on a web-based GUI.

The process to obtain the Geolocation coordinates through a WebRTC client and display them on a map is outlined in the following diagram:

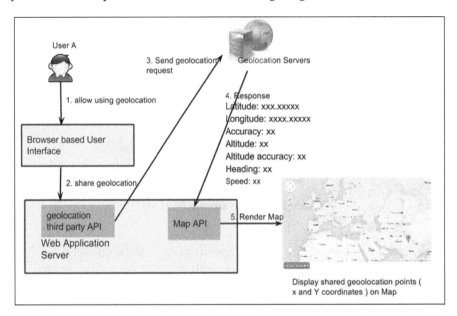

Let's briefly study the Permission, Latency, and Error Handling services in the Geolocation service. The HTML5 specification explicitly requires the user to grant permission to any web page that requests Geolocation information. Geolocation is not instantaneous. It usually takes between 1 and 20 seconds. The request for Geolocation information is an asynchronous call.

Authenticating users with OAuth

The OAuth mechanism provides a safe and easy authentication mechanism. It does away with password-based logins and introduces token-based authentication.

The working principle of OAuth with social networking sites is token-based authentication, which exists as long as the other account's session is valid. Some of the social networking accounts whose API's can be used for OAuth-based logins are as follows:

- Google
- Facebook
- Twitter
- LinkedIn

A diagram depicting the integration of OAuth API for two popular social networking platforms with the WebRTC client login is shown as follows:

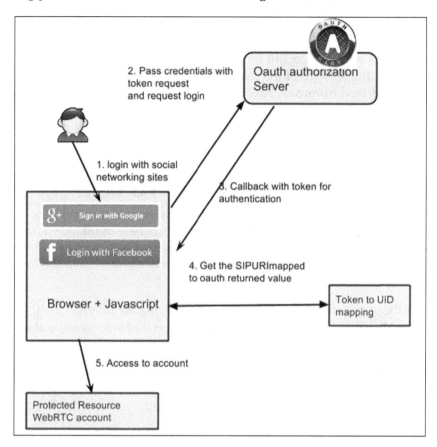

Programmers can set up a link from SIP URI to social networking ID for each account, thus maintaining an account profile for every external account linked with the WebRTC account.

Import contacts from other accounts

The phonebook holds added contact numbers and SIP URIs that the user wants for easy access. Developers can also program the WebRTC application to have the ability to merge the SIP contacts with other contacts imported from the user's social networking accounts, such as Facebook and Google+.

The working principle of this service relies on the base of linking the SIP profile ID or SIP URI with the account information imported from other platforms such as social networking or business networking sites. For example, as a user signs in with their Facebook credentials through the OAuth app, their validated username can be mapped with the SIP URI and stored in the backend database. The SIP URI is mapped to the Facebook account ID or Google account ID; when these IDs are referenced again, the SIP URI of the selected person can be fetched. This way, when a user imports a friend from, say, Facebook or Google+, the IDs from these social networking accounts are pulled in and matched with the data store for any existing mapping between SIP account holders. As an entry is found, it is added to the user's phonebook and synced with the contacts that already exist.

Advertisements in the WebRTC call

Advertisements are a good source of revenue for any service provider. They are usually shown on a section of a web page. However, in case of SIP and WebRTC, we can show or play an advertisement in the time period between after the caller makes a call and before the receiver picks it. This service is similar to the RingBack Tone Advertisement.

The logic of the application lies in the process of playing an advertisement in the call section of the WebRTC client web page, while there is a 180 Ringing status from any party. This can be achieved in two ways:

- The web application itself recognizes that there is a 100 trying or 180 ringing SIP response and displays the advertisement using the video src element of HTML5. Consider the following code:

```
<video width="500" height="450" controls>
  <source src="advertismentawalmart.mp4" type="video/mp4">
</video>
```

- The SIP Server recognizes a 100 trying or 180 ringing SIP response and connects the call to the Media Server, which plays the advertisement over RTP.

Delivering an instant message as a mail

The purpose of this feature is to send out additional messages, invites, and/or reminders to users either unavailable at that point of time or not registered with WebRTC yet.

The working principle of the mail service relies primarily on the Mail Server. The user sends a text with a target mail ID over HTTP; the web application passes this text over to the embedded SMTP client. The SMTP client authenticates itself with the SMTP server and sends the text in the message body, substituting the target mail ID in the To header. It can be configured to add a preset subject or a customizable subject as well. For example, in case user A wishes to send a WebRTC invite to user B who is not currently registered with the WebRTC client base, they can send a preset invitation to user B's mail inbox from the WebRTC client itself. The following diagram shows the mail service integrated with the WebRTC client:

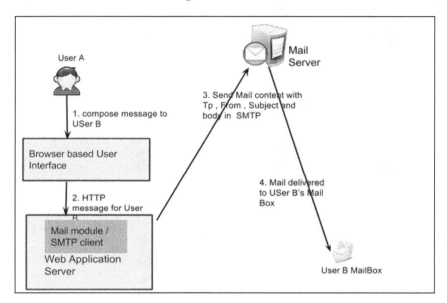

The preceding diagram shows a general SMTP message delivery sequence. By importing specific e-mail libraries in the WebRTC client application, this feature can be easily developed for the WebRTC communication tool.

The admin console

An administrator must have the privilege to view the WebRTC usage statistic in addition to framing policies and guidelines for correct use. To enable this, a developer must add an admin logic and admin console page for the administrator's accounts. The logs accumulated from calls, messages, voicemails, and so on should be shown in tabular and graphical formats. The graphical formats might include pie charts to depict call share status and bar chart to monitor the activity levels per hour. Refer to the following image that shows the charts for the admin console:

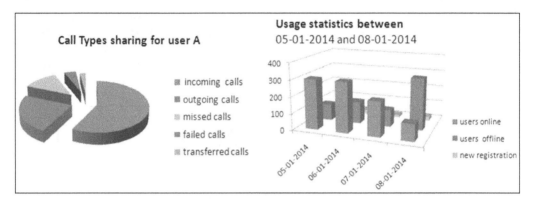

These were some suggested features that might be developed and integrated with the WebRTC project. However, the developers must exercise their own will to create more new features and integrate them with the WebRTC platform to enhance interactivity or increase productivity.

Summary

In this chapter, we discussed some features that a communication client is expected to have. It ranges from the default SIP features such as registration, call, Presence, and message to enhanced applications such as call screening, call forwarding, and call transfer. Media-related services that are basic in nature, such as media relay, announcement, voicemail, conferencing, and Music on Hold, were also described. In addition to this, the services possessed by a typical web application such as OAuth, Geolocation, admin console, and advertisements were also touched upon.

In the next chapter, we will study the process of developing a WebRTC client in the best industry-adopted frameworks, which include Struts and Spring MVC in addition to a simple JSP/Servlet web project.

7
WebRTC with Industry Standard Frameworks

In *Chapter 2, Making a Standalone WebRTC Communication Client*, we saw how to build a web page purely based on HTML, JavaScript, and CSS, that is capable of WebRTC-based SIP communication. However, to integrate WebRTC with an enterprise- or consumer-based application, it is essential that we envelop the WebRTC technology in a web-based application project. This chapter takes us through the process of actually developing the WebRTC web client application.

A service provider or the network operator hopes to benefit from WebRTC by extending it as another communication endpoint. Not only this, WebRTC also gives a new dimension to IP telephony by enabling any service provider to integrate the click-to-call service directly from his website. However, the WebRTC solution will be nonprofitable to a Telecom Service Provider if it isn't resilient, scalable, and able to integrate with the operator's already set-up infrastructure. As we know, WebRTC standards only describe media capture and streaming mechanism. To provide for signaling, we will use SIP APIs from sipML5 (refer to `https://code.google.com/p/sipml5/`). In this chapter, we will learn how to develop a web communicator project with WebRTC support.

The Multitier architecture

An efficient application is composed of multiple tiers. Tiers are used to isolate the functionality of the application between different sections. Majorly, the structure comprises three tiers:

- **Presentation Tier**: This tier deals with the GUI through which the client interacts with the application. It is usually a set of HTML elements with other frontend technologies such as JavaScript for scripting logic and CSS for design format. It will be loaded into the browser as a web page, for example, login.html, home.html, and so on.

- **Logic Tier**: The middle tier, also known as the Application Tier, is responsible for processing logic, obtaining values from the Data Tier, and delivering the results to the web engine.

- **Data Tier**: The database and repositories that hold data values and files are referred to as the Data Tier.

The following diagram shows the different layers of a Multitier architecture:

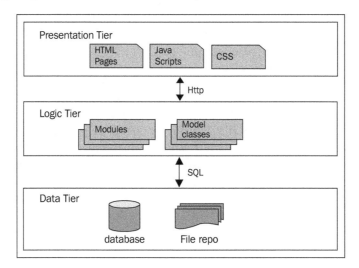

Now, we shall study the **Software Development Life Cycle (SDLC)** of a WebRTC client application in detail.

The design of a WebRTC client

A design is usually the activity planned in the first stages of SDLC; later, it's followed by development and testing (this is described later in the chapter).

Unified Modeling Diagrams (**UMLs**) aid in the design process by creating an abstract view of the system. UML diagrams can be used to do the following:

- Visually represent a system/project
- Communicate one idea or model to other parties
- Using specific tools (UML diagrams can also be used) to generate code directly

There are various kinds of modeling diagrams in UML such as Class diagram, ER diagram, Use case diagrams, and others. They give a graphical overview of the project that is about to begin. This section presents some critical design diagrams for WebRTC client web project.

The Class diagram

A Class diagram is used to visualize the overall structure of data organization in the Data Tier. The main classes used in the WebRTC client project are:

- `UserDetails`: This class contains the main field for user identification and registration, such as SIP URI, private identity, domain, display name, and password. These values are required to register a user with the SIP Registrar so that he can make use of SIP services such as call, message subscribe, and notify.

- `CallLogs`: This class is meant to record the information of every incoming, outgoing, missed, or failed call for every user in his history of transactions. The information includes caller and called SIP URI, date/time stamp, and call ID.

- `MessageLogs`: This class holds the records for all messages sent and received by the user. Similar to call logs, this class also contains member variables such as the sender and receiver SIP URI, date/time stamp, and message ID.

- `OtherAccount`: Since the WebRTC client also interacts with third-party social networking platforms and services, this table takes care of mapping between SIP URI and other account IDs. For now, it includes fields for Google, Facebook, Yahoo, and Twitter.

- `Geolocation`: The Geolocation coordinates of a user obtained through their browser's Geolocation API, Mobile phone's GPS, or by any other means is stored in this table. The values are mapped to a user's unique SIP URI for later referencing. The fields include SIP URI, latitude, longitude, date/time stamp, and so on. In this project, any user's new Geolocation values are overwritten over the existing ones.

- `Conferencing`: Since WebRTC supports a multiparty conferencing feature, this table is made to keep record of all conferences. The values include conference name, conference ID, host URI, members URI, and sequence. The host URI denotes the SIP URI of the user who is the host of the conference, and the members URI contain a list of SIP URIs of users who are guests for a conference.

- `Notification`: Any kind of notifications such as missed calls or conference call invitations are stored in this table along with date/time stamp.

- `Voicemail`: Voicemails are audio message files that are sent when a user is unavailable to receive messages or calls. This table contains links to voicemails and their associated sender's SIP URI with date/time stamp.

- `OfflineMessages`: Some messages are not delivered through the SIP Instant Message service on account of the user getting disconnected or being unavailable. Such messages can be directly sent to the user's mailbox using the SMTP gateway. The record of such messages or mails is kept in this table.

- `Phonebook`: The quick contacts or friends of users are stored in this table for easy reference. The SIP URI is used to link some values of the user details table to appear here.

- `Presence`: Online or offline status update of the user is stored in this table. The value is used to inform others about the availability or unavailability of this user.

The following screenshot shows the Hibernate mapping Class diagrams for the WebRTC web application:

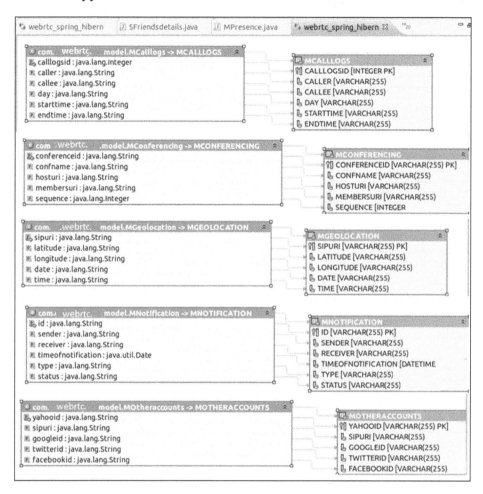

The preceding screenshot is the Hibernate mapping implemented between the classes in the WebRTC client web application project and database tables. For example, the MNotification database table and its entities point to the web project's com.webrtc. model.MNotifcations class and its member variables. Please note that it does not depict all the tables and their respective Hibernate mappings. Many classes and tables such as voicemails, user details, and offline messages are not visible.

The Entity Relationship model

The **Entity Relationship** (**ER**) model describes the relationship between various logical blocks of programs. It is a conceptual data model that views the real world as entities and relationships. For example, in a small-scale WebRTC project, the SIP URI is adopted as the primary key for uniquely identifying all other values associated with a user. A user is allowed only one unique SIP URI and they use it to log in to the WebRTC client application and register itself with the Telecom SIP Registrar. The following screenshot shows the ER diagram for the WebRTC web application:

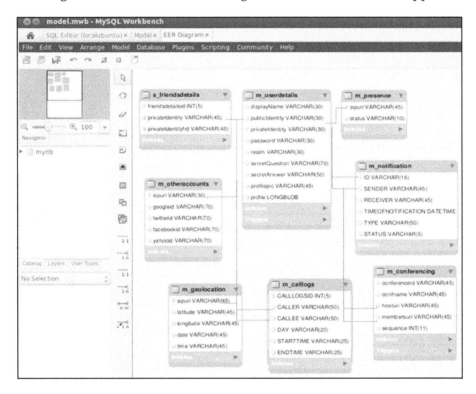

In the preceding screenshot, the field SIP URI is linked to other tables as a foreign key. An ER diagram is often used in database designing. It lets the developers quickly get started on defining the database structure in DBMS. A few shortcomings of ER modeling include no proper standards and a high level of depiction.

The environment setup

The environment setup for building a WebRTC web project is the first step in the development stage. Since our development is going to be on Java, it is essential to have the Java application development tools installed, which include:

- JDK
- Eclipse IDE
- Web application server such as JBoss/Apache Tomcat

The database set up also requires a server and client installation. Let's study all these setups one by one.

Java Runtime Environment (JRE)

In an occasion where one does not want to use a standard IDE but rather build and test Java programs with basic tools, they need to have JRE in the system. JRE is also known as **Java Virtual Machine (JVM)**. The entire **Java Development Kit (JDK)** containing the JRE can be downloaded from `http://www.oracle.com/technetwork/java/javase/downloads/index.html`.

It is noted that, though Java is platform-independent, JRE is not. Therefore, one must be cautious to download the specific JDK or JRE that is supported on a machine's operating system and bit version. Furthermore, after installation, the JAVA HOME environment variable must point to this directory.

Integrated Development Environment with Java Enterprise Edition (EE)

Integrated Development Environment (**IDE**) is used by programmers to develop Java applications. We can integrate any programming language model with WebRTC. Here, we shall be using Eclipse IDE for Java EE Developers. The following screenshot shows the Eclipse Kepler IDE for Java EE projects:

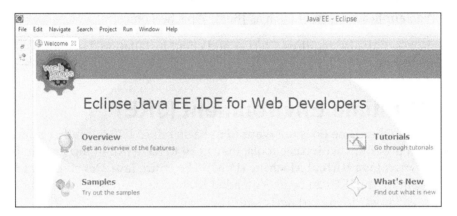

The preceding screenshot depicts a new workspace in the Eclipse Kepler IDE. It is to be noted that a standard Eclipse installation does not support Advanced or web-based capabilities by default. It is required to install **Web Tools Platform** (**WTP**) explicitly to develop web applications. More information on Eclipse WTP can be found at `https://www.eclipse.org/webtools/`.

Databases

We know that a database contains tables holding the records of user details as well as associated records from other tables using key mapping. Some simple options to choose from are PostgreSQL, Oracle, and MySQL **Database Management System** (**DBMS**). We have used MySQL 5.5 Server and MySQL Workbench to access the database. The following screenshot shows the MySQL Workbench connected to the MySQL Server instance for the WebRTC web application:

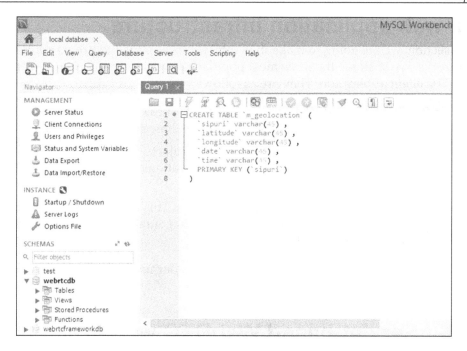

The preceding screenshot depicts a MySQL Workbench opened with a connection instance to the WebRTC database on a MySQL server. The MySQL components can be downloaded from `http://dev.mysql.com/downloads/`.

The web application server

The web application server is a container for WebRTC client application projects. We can use JBoss developed by Red Hat, or Apache Tomcat, or any other server capable of deploying a WAR file. We shall make use of Tomcat v7.0 Server for this purpose.

The web application infrastructure

In this section, we are going to make the WebRTC client suited to programming frameworks. We shall see the three most popular alternative approaches to develop a WebRTC client application. They are as follows:

- **JSP- / Servlet-based WebRTC web project**: These are small-scale applications usually employed for **Proof of Concept (POC)** building.

- **Struts- / Hibernate-based WebRTC web project**: This framework is used for more scalable and organized applications. Hibernate employs data abstraction.

- **Spring 3 MVC-based WebRTC web project**: This framework is the most preferred one for the development of rich and enterprise-grade WebRTC client application projects.

Here, we shall discuss the best framework suited to our use and applicability of WebRTC clients.

JSP- / Servlet-based WebRTC web project

In the early days of POC building, one can decide to just use the simplest of approaches for testing and verifying whether WebRTC really meets the expected performance requirements. Keeping the tight deadlines in mind, it was very obvious to proceed with whatever looked like the shortest way to a demonstrable, workable WebRTC client. A typical JSP- / Servlet-based dynamic web project is the most viable option to test the preliminary functioning of the WebRTC functions.

Some of the advantages of JSP- / Servlet-based MVC architecture for WebRTC developments are as follows:

- **Quick development**: This does not require thorough design and is ideal for small applications with light processing

- **Easy to deploy and debug**: The modules are divided into only three source folders: DAO, Model, and Controllers

Programming the JSP- / Servlet-based web project structure

The JSP- / Servlet-based application architecture has quick buildup time and doesn't require detailed design structure. However, it must be noted that it leads to complexity and becomes hard to alter once the size and number of modules begin to increase beyond a point. The components of a JSP Servlet web project are as follows:

- **Deployment descriptor**: This describes the classes, resources, and the configuration of the application and how the web server uses them to serve web requests.

- **Controller**: The Servlet acts as a controller that is responsible for processing requests and creating any beans needed by the JSP page. It also decides which requests need to be passed to which JSP page.

- **Model**: The classes here are composed of the declaration of variables and their general getters, setters, and constructors.

- **DAO**: The DAO classes are responsible for invoking the database connection object and performing **Create Read Update Delete** (**CRUD**) operations on the records stored in the database. The **Java Database Connectivity** (**JDBC**) technology is employed in this simple example.

- **View**: This comprises only the visual elements on a page. They consist of HTML and JSP pages.

The overall architecture of WebRTC web project POC, based on JSP- / Servlet-based design, is depicted in the following diagram:

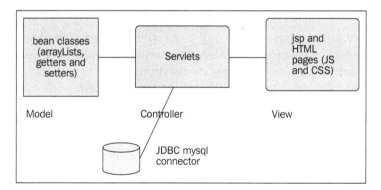

The development of modules

There are only a handful project components for JSP- / Servlet-based web project development. All of them are defined with their individual roles with no or minimal dependency on the other modules. We shall cover three prominent modules in this section:

- The User Account module

- The Communication module

- The Phonebook module

The Call module is an HTML/JSP page-driven mechanism that does not depend on Java programming. It has been provided in *Chapter 2, Making a Standalone WebRTC Communication Client*. The flow between the View and Controller classes from the process of logging in to the process of displaying the home page with user-specific data is depicted in the following diagram:

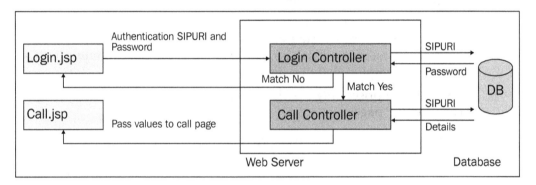

Initially, the user lands on the Login.jsp page where he is required to either register for a new account or login with his credentials. A new user must create an account so that the database is populated with his SIP entities, such as domain, display name, and private identity, and any consecutive login with the SIP URI can fetch his existing details. Once the account is created and the user has entered his credentials to login, the **Login Controller** Servlet consults the database to ascertain whether the entered username and password were correct or not. If they were incorrect, the user reaches the login page again. If the user has entered the correct username and password, then he is redirected to the Call.jsp page where he can make or receive calls.

The steps to build a JSP- / Servlet-based WebRTC application are as follows:

1. Create a dynamic web project in Eclipse; let's assume we name it `WebCommunicatorv1`.

2. Create the Controller Servlet inside the `src` folder. Make sure the Servlets are mapped in `web.xml`.

3. Create JSP pages named `call.jsp` and `login.jsp` inside the `WebContent` folder. These are the frontend bodies that bear the login and call functionality.

The User Account module

The User Account module holds the SIP entities, such as SIP private identity, public identity domain, password, and display name, that the user is registered with initially. Later, the user uses these values to login and make calls to other WebRTC users.

The logic for the login and registration processes must be programmed to enable new user registration after he has filled the registration form. The users who already have an account should be able to login with their username and password. The following code snippet is the Servlet implementation class named `loginServlet`:

```
public class loginServlet extends HttpServlet {
  public loginServlet() {
    super();
  }

  protected void doPost(HttpServletRequest request,
    HttpServletResponse response) throws ServletException,
      IOException {
  PrintWriter out = response.getWriter();
  switch (request.getParameter("processtag")){

    case("login"):
      String privateIdentity=null,sipuri=null;
      String userName = request.getParameter("userName");
      String password = request.getParameter("password");
      webrtclogin wl = new webrtclogin();
      ArrayList<registration>result=
            wl.login(userName,password,realm);

      if(result.size()!=0){
```

```
          response.sendRedirect("loginsession?name=
            "+result.get(0).getDisplayName()+"&pvt=
              "+result.get(0).getPrivateIdentity()+"&pub=
                "+result.get(0).getSipuri()+"&pass=
                  "+result.get(0).getPassword()+"&realm=
                    "+result.get(0).getRealm()+"&serverip=
                      "+serverip);
        }
        else{
          response.sendRedirect("login.jsp");
        }
        break;

    case("registration"):
      registration reg= new registration();
      reg.setDisplayName(request.getParameter("displayName"));
      reg.setsipuri(request.getParameter("sipuri"));
      reg.setPrivateIdentity(request.getParameter
        ("privateIdentity"));
      reg.setPassword(request.getParameter("password"));
      reg.setWSUri(request.getParameter("wsuri"));
      reg.setRealm(request.getParameter("realm"));
      LoginDao dao=new LoginDao();
      if(dao.register(reg)==true) {
        response.sendRedirect("http://"+serverip+":8080/
          WebRTC_presentation/addmoredetails.jsp?privateIdentity=
            "+privateIdentity+"&displayName="+displayName);
      }
      else{
        response.sendRedirect("http://"+serverip+":8080/
          WebRTC_presentation/addmoredetails.jsp");
      }
    break;

    default:
      response.sendRedirect("login.jsp");
    break;
      }
    }
  }
```

The following screenshot is the GUI representation of the Registration/Login page:

In the preceding screenshot, the top section has a registration form with input boxes for **Display Name**, **Authorization SIPURI**, **Private Identity**, **Password**, and **Domain**. The lower section has a login form that is only for registered users to login to WebRTC client using their **Authorization SIPURI** and **Password**.

The Communication module

In a WebRTC client application program, the majority of the media-related tasks are handled by the browser's WebRTC media stack and signaling through SIP stack (in our case sipML5 JavaScript library). Our responsibility is to record the logs and render the AJAX calls to SIP invite methods. It's also concerned with the display of an appropriate status message if a call is not connected. When a call is successfully established between two parties, the video window with the local and remote party's captured video as well as the captured audio must be presented on the frontend JSP page.

The following screenshot is the GUI representation of the **Call** and **Message** page:

In the preceding screenshot, the upper section is for messaging functions. It is made up of three elements: a textbox for the SIP URI of the other party in message conversion, a textbox for current messages being sent from our side, and a text area to display the most recent messages sent and received between the two parties.

The lower section is for making and receiving calls. When a user is trying to make a call or receive a call, a drop-down window appears in this section that has the local and remote party's media elements such as audio and video. Furthermore, the call can be either of two types for which two buttons are present: **Audio Call** (for audio) and **Video Call** (for video).

The Phonebook module

The Phonebook module can be used to add the SIP URI of other users for quick reference. Also, the present status of the users is indicated with a green (user online) or red (user unavailable) symbol adjacent to their SIP URI.

The following code snippet is the Servlet implementation of the `FriendListController` class for the Phonebook module:

```
public class FriendListController extends HttpServlet {
  private static final long serialVersionUID = 1L;
  public FriendListController() {
    super();
  }
```

```
protected void doGet(HttpServletRequest request,
  HttpServletResponse response) throws ServletException,
    IOException {
  String action=request.getParameter("action");
  HttpSession session=request.getSession();
  String username=(String) session.getAttribute("name");

  if(action.equalsIgnoreCase("removefriend")){
    String friendUri=request.getParameter("friendName");
    FriendListDAO.removeFriendFromList(friendUri,user);
    response.sendRedirect("phonebook.jsp");
  }

  else if (action.equalsIgnoreCase("addFriendURI")){
    String sipURI=request.getParameter("friendName");
    FriendListDAO.addFriendToList(user,sipURI,str);
    response.sendRedirect("phonebook.jsp");
  }
}
```

The following screenshot is the GUI representation of the **Phonebook** page:

The preceding screenshot depicts a **Phonebook** page that holds the contacts that the user has added to keep for future reference. There are three important elements in a phonebook interface, as follows:

- The SIP URI of the users that are added to the phonebook
- A textbox to add a new SIP URI to the phonebook
- The offline/online status of each user depicted by a red/green symbol alongside their SIP URI

The primary JAR files used are `servlet-api.jar` for Servlet and `mysql-connector-java-5.0.8-bin.jar` for MySQL connectivity. The scalability of this POC on WebRTC client depends on factors such as server CPU, server memory, bandwidth, and so on.

The following screenshot shows the Project Explorer window after the project completion of the WebRTC client POC:

The project can be run with any web server such as Tomcat, JBoss, and others. Some substantial limitations of using only JSP/Servlet pattern for a WebRTC project are:

- The properties file and the file IO systems are slow and outdated. However, in order to avoid slow disk access, properties can be defined using the environment variables.

- JavaScript-based validation can be easily overruled. They are easily subject to SQL Injection.

- Multithreading issues are not handled in the existing JSP/Servlet project. It might lead to memory leaks before the lifetime of the connection objects ends. Also, the buffer might overflow with garbage values.

Struts- / Hibernate-based WebRTC web project

The Struts framework is best suited for WebRTC client development when an agile steadfast Communication client is required. It's true that it does not offer as many plugin options as Spring, but it does meet the destined goal quickly in an organized manner.

It is usually the next phase in the transformation of an architecture from JSP- / Servlets-based MVC architecture to Struts 2.0 with Hibernate support. It is a major step ahead from the previous architecture that begins to look like a ball of entangled threads with the addition of more classes and functions. With the easy modularization approach of the Struts framework, much of the confusion and complexity is reduced.

Hibernate tools help developers by acting as code generation tools. They are used to generate Hibernate applications very fast with mapping in ORM using XMLs, dialects, annotations, and so on. Most importantly, they are database-independent. Therefore, to replace the database from MySQL to Oracle or any other DBMS, at any time, is an easy job, as Hibernate acts like a database abstraction layer between the project and the database. It also has its own table modification and query tools (**Hibernate Query Tool (HQL)**).

Apache Struts is a free, open-source, MVC framework for creating modern Java web applications. It is extensible, uses a plugin architecture, and ships with plugins to support REST, AJAX, and JSON. It helps in Web Request Validation, UI tags, and Action forms, such as extensive validation without JavaScript, and it cannot be hacked since code or URLs are not visible on the page.

Programming the Struts- / Hibernate-based web project structure

Struts uses the Model 2 architecture. The Struts Action Servlet controls the navigation flow. Struts classes, such as Action, are used to access the business logic classes named Service. When the Action Servlet receives a request from the container, it uses the request URI or path to determine what action will be used to handle the request. The Action Servlet can verify the input, retrieve information from a database, or perform data processing in the business layer. For more information, refer to `https://struts.apache.org`.

The overall architecture of the WebRTC application with the Struts framework is shown in the following diagram:

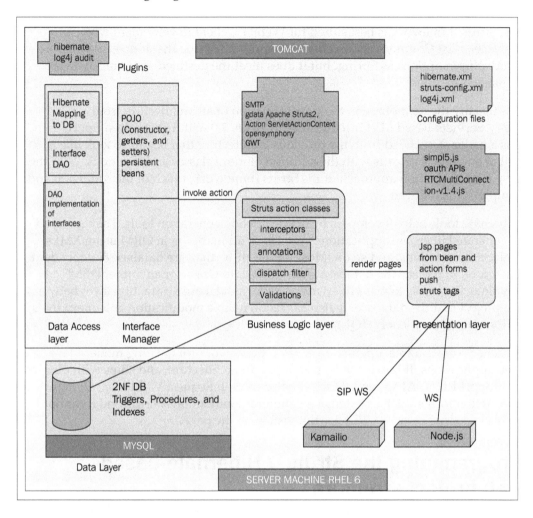

The server machine depicted in the preceding diagram is **Red Hat Enterprise Linux 6 (RHEL 6)**; however, any upgraded machine can be used in place of this. The components of **Business Logic Layer**, **Presentation Layer**, and **Data Access Layer** are differentiated. Add-on features such as SMTP for e-mail, log4j for logging, and sipML5 for SIP signaling are also depicted. The database (**MySQL** server), SIP signaling server (**Kamailio**), and WebSocket conferencing servers (**Node.js**) are shown in the lower part of the diagram.

The development of modules

Since modules for Login, Account, and Call Control have already been discussed in the previous section, *JSP- / Servlet-based WebRTC web project*, we shall cover the OtherAccount module in this part. The OtherAccount module, as the name suggests, links other/third-party accounts such as the Google account, the Facebook account, and the Yahoo account of users with his WebRTC SIP account. This will be used for extended functionality of the WebRTC application such as login using the third party, OAuth, sending e-mail from WebRTC account to offline users, importing contacts from other accounts, and so on.

The steps to build a Struts2-based WebRTC application, are listed as follows:

1. Create a dynamic web project in Eclipse. Let's assume we name it `WebRTCframework`. In the deployment descriptor (`web.xml`), define an entry for the `FilterDispatcher` class as follows:

    ```
    <display-name>WebRTCframework</display-name>
    <filter>
    <filter-name>struts2</filter-name>
    <filter-class>
       org.apache.struts2.dispatcher.ng.filter.
         StrutsPrepareAndExecuteFilter</filter-class>
    </filter>

    <filter-mapping>
    <filter-name>struts2</filter-name>
    <url-pattern>/*</url-pattern>
    </filter-mapping>

    <welcome-file-list>
    <welcome-file>login.jsp</welcome-file>
    </welcome-file-list>
    </web-app>
    ```

    The mapping of the Struts dispatcher to the `/*` pattern allows it to handle all the incoming requests. The `welcome-file` page is the first page that is displayed when a web project is hit.

2. Create a `hibernate.cfg` file to access and manage the database connection as follows:

```
<hibernate-configuration>
  <session-factory>
    <property name="hibernate.connection.driver_class">
      com.mysql.jdbc.Driver
    </property>
    <property name="hibernate.connection.url">
      jdbc:mysql://localhost:3306/webrtcframeworkdb
    </property>
    <property name="hibernate.connection.username">
      root
    </property>
    <property name="connection.password"> </property>
    <property name="connection.pool_size">5</property>
    <property name="hibernate.dialect">
      org.hibernate.dialect.MySQLDialect
    </property>
    <property name="show_sql">true</property>
    <property name="hbm2ddl.auto">update</property>

    <mapping class="com.framework.domain.User"/>
    <mapping class="com.framework.domain.Friend"/>
    <mapping class="com.framework.domain.Credentials"/>
    <mapping class="com.framework.domain.Otheraccount"/>
  </session-factory>
</hibernate-configuration>
```

3. Create an `Action` class that calls the data access functions and perform an operation.

4. Place the GUI elements on JSP pages using Struts tags. The forms should point to an action.

5. Map the actions with action classes in the Struts configuration file.

These steps summarize the building process of a generic Struts framework-based web application with Hibernate support. The detailed process of making and deploying a module on this framework with database mapping using Hibernate is provided in the upcoming section.

The OtherAccount module

The OtherAccount module is responsible for linking the SIP URI of a user to his other networking platform IDs such as the Facebook ID, the Google ID, and the Yahoo ID.

This feature helps in many service developments, such as the following:

- OAuth-based sign and ID mapping to the SIP URI
- Importing contacts from other social/professional networking sites
- Posting updates such as reminders, e-mails, and content liked to other platforms

The following are the important code snippets that are part of the OtherAccount module:

1. This is a code snippet for the JSP page in the OtherAccount module.

```
<%@taglib uri="/struts-tags" prefix="s"%>
<html>
<head>
<title>Other Accounts Page</title>
<s:head />
<style type="text/css">
@import url(style.css);
</style>
</head>
<body>
<s:form action="saveOrUpdateUser">
<s:push value="email">
  <s:textfield sipuri="sipuri" label="Sip URI" />
  <s:textfield gmail="gmail" label="Gmail" />
  <s:textfield facebook="facebook" label="Facebook" />
  <s:textfield yahoo="yahoomail" label="Yahoo Mail" />
  <s:textfield twitter="twitter" label="Twitter" />
  <s:submit />
  </s:push>
</s:form>

</body>
</html>
```

The form calls the `saveOrUpdateUser` action in the `OtheraccountAction` action class. It passes the values of the SIP URI, Google ID, Facebook ID, Yahoo ID, and Twitter ID as parameters.

2. Then you need to define the domain class to handle data exchange as follows:

```
@Entity
@Table(name="Otheraccount")
public class Otheraccount {

  private String sipuri;
  private String gmail;
  private String facebook;
  private String yahoo;
  private String twitter;

  @Id
  @Column(name="sipuri")
  public String getSipuri() {
    return sipuri;
  }
  public void setSipuri(String sipuri) {
    this.sipuri = sipuri;
  }

  @Column(name="gmail")
  public String getGmail() {
    return gmail;
  }
  public void setGmail(String gmail) {
    this.gmail = gmail;
  }

  @Column(name="facebook")
  public String getFacebook() {
    return facebook;
  }
  public void setFacebook(String facebook) {
    this.facebook = facebook;
  }

  @Column(name="yahoo")
  public String getYahoo() {
    return yahoo;
  }
  public void setYahoo(String yahoo) {
    this.yahoo = yahoo;
  }
```

```
@Column(name="twitter")
public String getTwitter() {
  return twitter;
}
public void setTwitter(String twitter) {
  this.twitter = twitter;
}
}
```

A domain class holds the variable declarations as well as the getter and setter functions for each variable.

3. The Action classes define the logic executed for user actions. The code snippet for OtheraccountAction is as follows:

```
public class OtheraccountAction extends ActionSupport
  implements ModelDriven<Otheraccount> {

// object of Otheraccount named as email
  private Otheraccount email = new Otheraccount();

// list of OtheraccountObject named as emailList
  private List<Otheraccount> emailList = new
ArrayList<Otheraccount>();

// object of OtheraccountDAO named as otheraccountDAO
  private OtheraccountDAO otheraccountDAO =
    new OtheraccountDAOImpl();
  public Otheraccount getModel(){
    return email;
  }
  public String saveOrUpdate(){
    otheraccountDAO.saveOrUpdateEmail(email);
    return SUCCESS;
  }
  public String list(){
    emailList = otheraccountDAO.listEmail();
    return SUCCESS;
  }
  public String delete(){
  HttpServletRequest request = (
    HttpServletRequest) ActionContext.getContext().get(
      ServletActionContext.HTTP_REQUEST);
  otheraccountDAO.deleteEmail(request.getParameter(
    "sipuri"));
    return SUCCESS;
```

```
}
/*  other functions */
}
```

The methods described here are `getModel()`, `saveOrUpdate()`, `list()`, `delete()`, and a few others that are not mentioned for ease of understanding.

4. This section describes the data access mechanism used in Hibernate Objects. A code snippet for `OtheraccountDAO` that is an interface for the DAO class is as follows:

```
public interface OtheraccountDAO {
  public void saveOrUpdateEmail(Otheraccount email);
  public List<Otheraccount> listEmail();
  public Otheraccount listEmailById(String sipuri);
  public void deleteEmail(String sipuri);
}
```

5. The implementation of the DAO class named `OtheraccountDAOImpl`, implementing the preceding interface, `OtheraccountDAO`, is as follows :

```
public class OtheraccountDAOImpl implements OtheraccountDAO {
  @SessionTarget
  Session session;

  @TransactionTarget
  Transaction transaction;

  /**
   * Other functions omitted please find them in the
   * attached examples with this book
   */
  @SuppressWarnings("unchecked")
  public List<Otheraccount> listEmail() {
    List<Otheraccount> courses = null;
    try {
      courses = session.createQuery("from Email").list();
    } catch (Exception e) {
      e.printStackTrace();
    }
    return courses;
  }
}
```

```
/**
 * Used to list a single object of Otheraccount by Id.
 */
public Otheraccount listEmailById(String sipuri) {
  Otheraccount email = null;
  try {
  email = (Otheraccount) session.get(Otheraccount.class,
                    sipuri);
  } catch (Exception e) {
    e.printStackTrace();
  }
  return email;
}
}
```

6. The following is the implementation of the `Strut.xml` file that is the core configuration file for the framework. It defines the mapping between the action tags and action classes.

```xml
<struts>
  <package name="default" extends="hibernate-default">

<!-- Actions mapping for other modules omitted from here,
    please find them in the examples attached with this
    book---->

<!-- otheraccount action -->
<action name="saveOrUpdateOtheraccount"
      method="saveOrUpdate"
        class="com.framework.web.OtheraccountAction">
  <result name="success" type="redirect">
    listOtheraccount
  </result>
</action>
<action name="listotheraccount"
      method="list"
        class="com.framework.web.OtheraccountAction">
  <result name="success">/otheraccount.jsp</result>
</action>
<action name="editOtheraccount"
      method="edit"
        class="com.framework.web.OtheraccountAction">
  <result name="success">/otheraccount.jsp</result>
</action>
```

```
<action name="deleteOtheraccount"
     method="delete"
      class="com.framework.web.OtheraccountAction">
  <result name="success" type="redirect">
    listOtheraccount
  </result>
</action>
</package>
</struts>
```

Like `web.xml`, `struts.xml` too should reside on the class path of the web app (such as `/WEB-INF/classes`).

The following is a screenshot of the Project Explorer window after the project completion of the WebRTC client web application using Struts Framework:

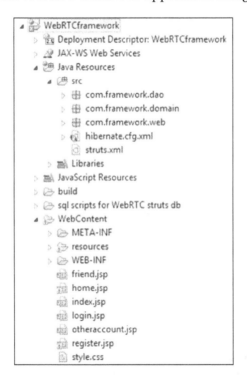

The testing phase of SDLC is explained in a later section of this chapter. For some enterprise-based applications, there exists a requirement to integrate WebRTC communication functionality in their existing Spring framework. To meet such cases, we shall also cover the development of WebRTC client on the Spring framework.

Spring 3 MVC-based WebRTC web project

Due to the robust nature of Spring and the associated plugins for database abstraction, security, handlers, and other external services, it was finally and rightly adopted as the framework to host the WebRTC Communicator web project.

Programming the Spring 3 MVC web project structure

The Spring 3 framework has considerable advancements from the previous version, Spring 2. Spring 3 is ideal for an enterprise-level application, capable of delivering efficient performance and secure control to data and application logic. Logical entities in the Spring framework are provided here with a short description:

- **Aspect Oriented Programming (AOP)**: This is used to deal with crosscutting concerns. By embedding AOP, the Spring framework modularizes the programming approach to prevent code confusion and interdependencies.

- **Object Relational Mapping (ORM)**: This deals with the mapping of objects to database tables.

- **The Spring Web module**: This is a part of the Spring web application development stack that includes Spring MVC and web services.

- **Data Access Objects (DAO)**: This is primarily for standardizing the data access work. It performs resource management by automatically acquiring and releasing database resources and exception handling by translating data-access-related exceptions to a Spring data access hierarchy.

- **Spring Context**: This builds on the beans package to add support for message sources. It also adds the ability for application objects to obtain resources using a consistent API.

- **Spring Web MVC**: This is a request-based framework such as Struts. This is the module that provides MVC implementations for the web applications.

It is important to highlight the importance of the Spring dispatcher Servlet around which the whole project is structured. The Spring web **Model-View-Controller (MVC)** framework is designed around `DispatcherServlet`. A `DispatcherServlet` Servlet dispatches requests to handlers. It may do so with configurable handler mappings, view resolution, local time zone, or even support for uploading files.

The important interfaces defined by Spring MVC, and their responsibilities, are listed as follows:

- **HandlerMapping**: This interface is used for selecting objects that handle incoming requests (handlers) based on any internal or external attribute or condition.
- **HandlerAdapter**: This interface is used for the execution of objects that handle the incoming requests.
- **Controller**: This interface comes between Model and View to manage the incoming requests and redirect to a proper response. It acts as a gate that directs the incoming information. It switches its direction by either going into Model or View.
- **View**: This interface is responsible for returning a response to the client. Some requests may go straight to View without going to the Model part; others may go through all the preceding three interfaces.
- **ViewResolver**: This interface comes into the picture when selecting a View based on a logical name for the View (optional interface).
- **HandlerInterceptor**: This interface is an interception of incoming requests comparable but not equal to Servlet filters, (its use is optional and not controlled by `DispatcherServlet`).
- **LocaleResolver**: This interface is useful for resolving and optionally saving the locale of an individual user.
- **MultipartResolver**: This interface facilitates working with file uploads by wrapping incoming requests.

The following diagram outlines the components of the Spring MVC:

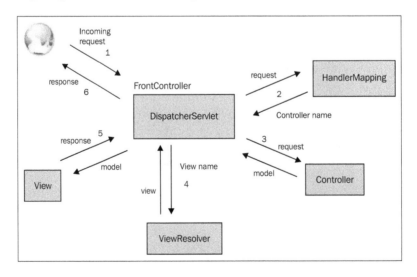

For more information on Spring features, refer to the link: `http://spring.io/`.

Out of the various features provided by the Spring 3 framework, a combination of the following was finalized for the architecture of a WebRTC client project:

- Spring 3 MVC for the middle layer
- Hibernate for database management
- Asynchronous call to Controllers using AJAX and JSON
- Spring security for Session Management
- Spring Validator for validation through dispatcher instead of JavaScript
- Annotations to map model and bean entities with the Controller

The following diagram shows the organization of code blocks, which are divided into five major segments:

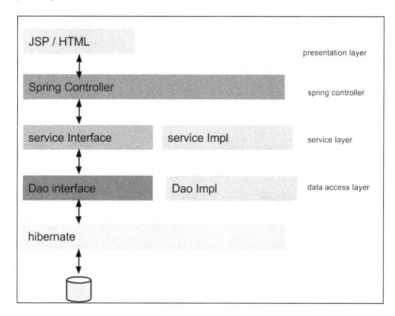

A detailed look at every segment is represented with the help of the following diagram:

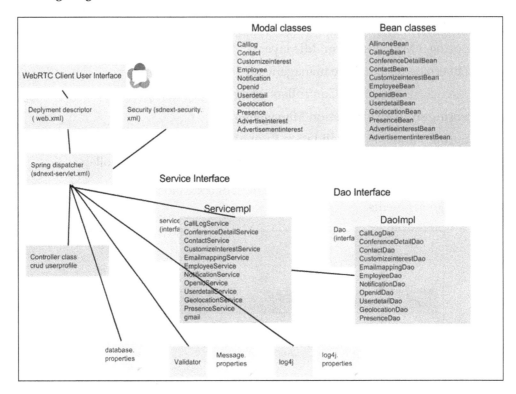

The development of modules

The modules discussed in the final Spring-based project are listed as follows:

- Admin console
- Audio / video Call, IM
- Presence
- Advertisement
- Contacts/Friends
- Conferencing
- Geolocation
- Notification

- User Profile
- Offline Messages
- Voicemail
- Call logs

The steps to build a Spring 3-based WebRTC application are follows:

1. Create a dynamic web project in Eclipse. Let's assume that we name it `WebUnifiedCommunicator`:

2. Define the resources in `web.xml` that is placed inside the project's `WebContent/WEB-INF` folder. The following code snippet depicts the Servlet name and mapping:

```
<servlet>
  <servlet-name>webrtc</servlet-name>
  <servlet-class>
```

```
      org.springframework.web.servlet.DispatcherServlet
      </servlet-class>
      <load-on-startup>1</load-on-startup>
</servlet>
<servlet-mapping>
   <servlet-name>webrtc</servlet-name>
   <url-pattern>/</url-pattern>
</servlet-mapping>
```

We can also add the error pages, shown as follows, that we want to display when abrupt terminations occur or errors are introduced by the web project.

```
<error-page>
   <error-code>404</error-code>
   <location>/WEB-INF/views/weberror.jsp?errorMsg=
      &quot;resources not found&quot;</location>
</error-page>


<error-page>
   <error-code>401</error-code>
   <location>/WEB-INF/views/weberror.jsp?errorMsg=
      &quot;resources not found&quot;</location>
</error-page>


<error-page>
   <error-code>403</error-code>
   <location>/WEB-INF/views/weberror.jsp?errorMsg=
      &quot;resources not found&quot;</location>
</error-page>


<error-page>
   <error-code>500</error-code>
   <location>/WEB-INF/views/weberror.jsp?errorMsg=
      &quot;resources not found&quot;</location>
</error-page>


<error-page>
   <error-code>503</error-code>
   <location>/WEB-INF/views/weberror.jsp?errorMsg=
      &quot;resources not found&quot;</location>
</error-page>
```

The following is the code snippet for adding a context listener:

```
<listener>
   <listener-class>
```

```
    org.springframework.web.context.ContextLoaderListener
  </listener-class>
</listener>
```

3. Set up a Hibernate properties file. It provides values of crucial property parameters such as `database.driver`, `database.url`, `database.user`, `database.password`, and `database.dialect`. These are required to successfully establish a connection between the web project and the backend database. The `hibernate.show` tag specifies whether the SQL statements on every database activity should be displayed on the console screen or not. The `hibernate.hbm2ddl.auto` automatically validates or exports the schema DDL to the database when `SessionFactory` is created. The list of possible options for this property is as follows:

   - `validate`: This option is used to validate the schema only. It makes no changes to the database.

   - `update`: This option is used to update the schema.

   - `create`: This option is used to create the schema and destroys all previous data.

   - `create-drop`: This option is used to create a fresh database on startup and drop the schema at the end of the session.

   We shall be using the `update` option in our case.

   ```
   database.driver=com.mysql.jdbc.Driver
   database.url=jdbc\:mysql\://localhost\:3306/DAVDB
   database.user=root
   database.password=
   hibernate.dialect=org.hibernate.dialect.MySQLDialect
   hibernate.show_sql=true
   hibernate.hbm2ddl.auto=update
   ```

4. Now, the `dispatcher xml` spring should be defined with the Hibernate usage inside it as follows:

   ```
   <context:property-placeholder location=
     "classpath:resources/database.properties" />

   <context:component-scan base-package="com.webrtc" />
   <context:component-scan base-package="validator" />

   <tx:annotation-driven transaction-manager=
     "hibernateTransactionManager"/>
   ```

```xml
<bean id="messageSource" class=
  "org.springframework.context.support.
    ResourceBundleMessageSource" p:basename="messages" />
<bean id="userValidator"
  class="com.webrtc.validator.UserValidator" />
<bean id="Validator"
  class="com.webrtc.validator.UserValidator" />
<bean id="LoginValidate"
  class="com.webrtc.validator.LoginValidator"/>
<bean id="jspViewResolver"
  class="org.springframework.web.servlet.view.
    InternalResourceViewResolver">
  <property name="viewClass" value=
    "org.springframework.web.servlet.view.JstlView" />
  <property name="prefix" value="/WEB-INF/views/" />
  <property name="suffix" value=".jsp" />
</bean>

<bean id="dataSource"
  class="org.springframework.jdbc.datasource.
    DriverManagerDataSource">
  <property name="driverClassName" value=
    "${database.driver}" />
  <property name="url" value="${database.url}" />
  <property name="username" value="${database.user}" />
  <property name="password" value="${database.password}" />
</bean>

<bean id="sessionFactory"
    class="org.springframework.orm.hibernate3.annotation.
      AnnotationSessionFactoryBean">
  <property name="dataSource" ref="dataSource" />
  <property name="annotatedClasses">
    <list>
      <value>com.webrtc.model.Userdetail</value>
      <value>com.webrtc.model.Geolocation</value>
      <value>com.webrtc.model.Contact</value>
      <value>com.webrtc.model.Presence</value>
      <value>com.webrtc.model.Users</value>
      <value>com.webrtc.model.User_roles</value>
    </list>
  </property>
  <property name="hibernateProperties">
  <props>
```

```
<prop key="hibernate.dialect">${hibernate.dialect}</prop>
<prop key="hibernate.show_sql">false</prop>
<prop key="hibernate.hbm2ddl.auto">
  ${hibernate.hbm2ddl.auto}
</prop>     </props>
</property>
</bean>

<bean id="hibernateTransactionManager"
  class="org.springframework.orm.hibernate3.
    HibernateTransactionManager">
  <property name="sessionFactory" ref="sessionFactory" />
</bean>
</beans>
```

5. Define the Controller logic for mapping a URL to model the View.

```
@Controller
@Scope("session")
public class MainController implements Serializable {
  private GeolocationService geolocationService;
  static Logger log = Logger.getLogger(
    MainController.class.getName());
AllinoneBean allinoneBean= new AllinoneBean();
```

6. Add the login functionality into the Controller. This is primarily a three-stage program: loading the login-related pages, adding logic to process login requests, and adding functionality for fetching the user profile details after successful login authentication in the controller.

7. Programming for any module involves the following steps:

    °   Adding the Bean classes
    °   Defining the Service logic
    °   Adding the Modal classes
    °   Defining the DAO logic
    °   Adding the HTML frontend pages

Since the previous sections have outlines for the blueprint of developing services such as login, account management, and phone book, we shall discuss the implementation of the Geolocation module with Spring MVC framework.

The Geolocation module

The Geolocation module comprises the following code snippets:

1. The Controller defines the logic for processing the URL for the Geolocation request:

```
@RequestMapping(value = "/geolocationtogether",
  method = RequestMethod.GET)
public ModelAndView geolocationtogether() {
  return new ModelAndView("geolocationtogether");
}


@RequestMapping(value = "/savegeolocation",
  method = RequestMethod.POST)
public ModelAndView saveGeolocation(@ModelAttribute(
  "command") GeolocationBean geolocationBean,
    BindingResult result) {

  Geolocation geolocation = prepareModelGeolocation(
    geolocationBean);
  geolocationService.addGeolocation(geolocation);
  return new ModelAndView("redirect:/ addgeolocation.html?
    sipuri="+geolocation.getGeosipuri());
}


@RequestMapping(value="/geolocation",
  method = RequestMethod.GET)
public ModelAndView listGeolocation() {
  Map<String, Object> model = new HashMap
    <String, Object>();
  model.put("geolocation", prepareListofBeanGeolocation(
    geolocationService.listGeolocations(
      allinoneBean.getSipuri())));
  return new ModelAndView("geolocationList", model);
}
```

2. Define the AJAX request handler for Geolocation-based requests:

```
@RequestMapping(value="/addgeolocationajax",method=
  RequestMethod.POST)

public @ResponseBody String addGeolocationAjax(
  @RequestParam("sipuri") String sipuri,
    @RequestParam("latitude") String latitude,
      @RequestParam("longitude") String longitude,
        @RequestParam("date") String date,
          @RequestParam("time") String time){
```

```
GeolocationBean bean=new GeolocationBean();
bean.setSipuri(sipuri);
bean.setLatitude(latitude);
bean.setLongitude(longitude);
bean.setDate(date);
bean.setTime(time);
Geolocation geolocation =
   prepareModelGeolocation(bean);
geolocationService.addGeolocation(geolocation);

return "Saved successfully";
}
```

3. Preparing a list of Beans for passing Geolocation objects in an array list is done using the following lines of code:

```
private Geolocation prepareModelGeolocation(
  GeolocationBean geolocationBean){
  Geolocation geolocation = new Geolocation();
  geolocation.setGeoLatitude(
      geolocationBean.getLatitude());
  geolocation.setGeoLongitude(
      geolocationBean.getLongitude());
  geolocation.setGeodate(geolocationBean.getDate());
  geolocation.setGeotime(geolocationBean.getTime());
  geolocation.setGeosipuri(geolocationBean.getSipuri());
  return geolocation;
}

private List<GeolocationBean> prepareListofBeanGeolocation(
  List<Geolocation> geolocations){

  List<GeolocationBean> beans = null;
  if(geolocations != null && !geolocations.isEmpty()){
    beans = new ArrayList<GeolocationBean>();
    GeolocationBean bean = null;
    for(Geolocation geolocation : geolocations){
      bean = new GeolocationBean();
      bean.setSipuri(geolocation.getGeosipuri());
      bean.setLatitude(geolocation.getGeoLatitude());
      bean.setLongitude(geolocation.getGeoLongitude());
      bean.setDate(geolocation.getGeodate());
      bean.setTime(geolocation.getGeotime());
      beans.add(bean);
    }
  }
  return beans;
```

```
}

private GeolocationBean prepareBeanGeolocation(
  Geolocation geolocation){

  GeolocationBean bean = new GeolocationBean();
  bean.setLatitude(geolocation.getGeoLatitude());
  bean.setLongitude(geolocation.getGeoLongitude());
  bean.setDate(geolocation.getGeodate());
  bean.setTime(geolocation.getGeotime());
  bean.setSipuri(geolocation.getGeosipuri());
  return bean;
}
```

4. Create a Bean class:

```
public class GeolocationBean {
  private String sipuri;
  private String latitude;
  private String longitude;
  private String date;
  private String time;

  /* getter and setters of the datamembers declared above */
}
```

5. Create an interface named `GeolocationService`:

```
public interface GeolocationService {
  public void addGeolocation(Geolocation geolocation);
  public List<Geolocation> listGeolocations(String sipuri);
  public Geolocation getGeolocation(String sipUri);
  public void deleteGeolocation(Geolocation geolocation);
}
```

6. The `GeolocationModel` class is provided in the following code snippet.
    It declares variables for containing the SIP URI, latitude, and longitude
    components of the coordinate, and date and time values to specify when
    the reading was recorded.

```
public class GeolocationBean {
  private String sipuri;
  private String latitude;
  private String longitude;
  private String date;
  private String time;
  /* getters and setters of above datamembers */
}
```

7. The DAO interface for the Geolocation module is given in the following code snippet:

```
public interface GeolocationDao {
    public void addGeolocation(Geolocation geolocation);
    public List<Geolocation> listGeolocations(String sipuri);
    public Geolocation getGeolocation(String sipUri);
    public void deleteGeolocation(Geolocation geolocation);
}
```

8. Develop the View component for the Geolocation service that comprises JavaScript, CSS, and HTML elements. The following screenshot shows the main page for embedding the call, phonebook, message, profile, and the Geolocation views:

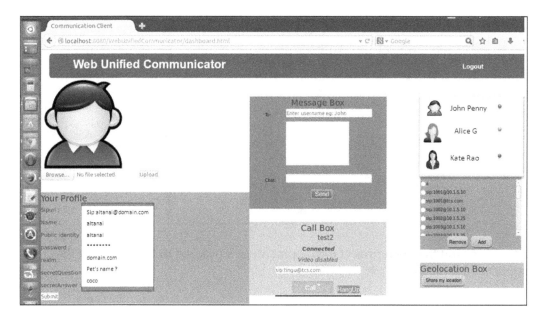

The following screenshot shows the Project Explorer window after the project completion of the WebRTC client web application using the Spring Framework. It shows the structure of the `WebUnifiedCommunicator` project based on Spring:

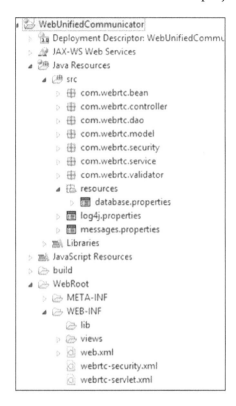

After POC and the main project development, let's proceed to the testing of the application built so far.

Testing

Just as testing marks the beginning of SDLC, testing is the milestone for project competition. By now, we should have an efficient WebRTC web project capable of video/audio calls, messaging, Geolocation, and so on. It is time to test the functionality and search for bugs that might have crept in to the code.

Testing the signal flow

Wireshark is a good tool to monitor all of the traffic flow between connected machines. We can test the packets sent and received, and generate flow diagrams to visualize the call flow between parties, end points, as well as the server. The following screenshot shows the Wireshark tool analyzing signal traces:

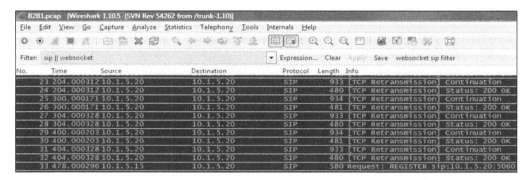

To filter the packets captured by Wireshark as per our need, filter it using `sip||websocket` as shown in the preceding screenshot.

Test cases for WebRTC client validation

Test cases are used for validation and verification of the end product. The test cases in the following table are to gauge the correct working of the WebRTC client in known situations. Of course the development/testing team will add more test cases to these already-existing ones to debug all errors that are or might occur in this project.

Test No.	Feature tested	Test description	Precondition	Test steps	Expected results
WebRTC_1	User Authorization	Initial check for a valid user		• The **Username** field is left empty • Click on the **Submit** button	Alert: Username field should not be left empty
WebRTC_2	User Authorization	Initial check for a valid user		• Enter **Username** • The **Password** field is left empty • Click on the **Submit** button	Alert: Please enter a password

Test No.	Feature tested	Test description	Precondition	Test steps	Expected results
WebRTC_3	User Authorization	Initial check for a valid user		• Enter an invalid username or password • Click on the submit button	Alert: The username or password you entered is incorrect
WebRTC_4	User Authorization	Initial check for a valid user		• Enter valid **Username** and **Password** • Click on the **Submit** button	Successful login
WebRTC_5	VIDEO Calling	Check the status of A (the calling party)	A is not logged in	• Enter **SIPURI** of B • Click on the **Call** button	The call button is disabled
WebRTC_6	VIDEO Calling	Check for validation in the SIP address field	A is logged in	• Leave the **SIPURI** field empty • Click on the **Call** button	The call button is disabled
WebRTC_7	VIDEO Calling	Check the status of B (the calling party)	• A is logged in • B is not logged in	• Enters **SIPURI** of B • Click on the **Call** button	• The call progresses • The call declines due to the absence of B
WebRTC_8	VIDEO Calling	Check for unanswered calls	• A is logged in • B is logged in	• A enters the **SIPURI** of B • A clicks on the **Call** button • B does not answer the call	An appropriate notification is received by A for status of the call as unanswered
WebRTC_9	VIDEO Calling	Check for call cancellation by the remote party	• A is logged in • B is logged in	• A enters the **SIPURI** of B • A clicks on the **Call** button • B cancels the call	An appropriate notification is received by A for the status of the call as cancelled.

Test No.	Feature tested	Test description	Precondition	Test steps	Expected results
WebRTC_10	VIDEO Calling	Check for call establishment	• A is logged in • B is logged in	• Enter the **SIPURI** of B • Press the **Call** button	• The call progresses • Remote ringing • The call is established between A and B with a message: In a call
WebRTC_11	VIDEO Calling	Check for simultaneous calls	• A is logged in • B is logged in • C is an authorized party • A and B are engaged in a call	C calls either A or B while they are in a call	The call attempt by C is declined, leaving a message that the "user is busy"
WebRTC_11	VIDEO Calling	Check for call on hold	• A is logged in • B is logged in • A and B are engaged in a call	• A puts B on hold while they are in a call • A retrieves the call	The call goes on hold and resumes as soon as A retrieves it
WebRTC_12	VIDEO Calling	Check for call termination	• A is logged in • B is logged in • The call has been established	Press the **Hang up** button	The call is terminated
WebRTC_13	Instant Messaging	Check the status of the sending party A	A is not logged in	• A clicks on the instant messaging link on the **Services** page • A enters the account name of the remote party and tries to enter a message in the message box	The message box is disabled

Test No.	Feature tested	Test description	Precondition	Test steps	Expected results
WebRTC_14	Instant Messaging	Check the status of the sending party A	A is logged in	• A clicks on the instant messaging link on the **Services** page • A enters the account name of the remote party and tries to enter a message in the message box	A is able to type the message
WebRTC_15	Instant Messaging	Check whether the message receiver, B, is an authorized user or not	• A is logged in • B is an unauthorized user	• A clicks on the instant messaging link on the services page • A enters the account name of the remote party and enters a message in the message box • A clicks on the Facebook link to send the message to the account's Facebook page	Alert: Enter an authorized account name
WebRTC_16	Instant Messaging	Success check: Message being sent by A to the Facebook account of B	• A is logged in • B is an authorized user	• A clicks on the instant messaging link on the **Services** page • A enters the Facebook account name of B and enters a message in the message box • A clicks the Facebook link to send the message	The message is successfully transferred to the Facebook account of B

Test No.	Feature tested	Test description	Precondition	Test steps	Expected results
WebRTC_17	Instant Messaging	Success check: Message being sent by A to the Gmail account of B	• A is logged in • B is an authorized user	• A clicks on the instant messaging link on the **Services** page • A enters the Gmail account name of B and enters a message in the message box • A clicks on the Gmail link to send the message	The message is successfully transferred to the Gmail account of B

Summary

This chapter was all about enveloping the WebRTC client application in frameworks that are standard and enterprise-accepted. The path from POC building to a fail-proof WebRTC client application was portrayed in this chapter. The chapter includes code snippets and step-by-step processes to develop WebRTC JSP- /Servlet-based projects, Struts- and Hibernate-based projects, and Spring framework-based projects. The various stages of SDLC were elaborated in the context of the WebRTC Client application. These included design with UML, development on Java EE, and testing use cases.

In the next chapter, we shall encounter more features that are part of a rich communication suite of services.

8
WebRTC and Rich Communication Services

Two decades ago, when mobile phones had just begun to become vital for everyone, the telecom service providers were using only basic call services to generate revenue. In a few years from then, the masses became used to the old voice calls, and the need for more service over mobile was stirred up. Then began the era of **Short Message Service (SMS)** followed by **Multimedia Message Service (MMS)**, which involved interaction with text and multimedia files. The wheel of innovation again spun in a few years. This time it led to the merging of the existing telecom services with the IP world as well as convergence between desktop computers and mobile devices as communication end points. This resulted in enhanced services such as video calls; live streaming; and syncing of messages, logs, and contacts between different call agents registered with a user. However, this also led to some issues such as handling multiple clients, services, identities, and numbers. The need of the hour now is innovation in the old format of services and the availability of a more enriching experience, for example, the possibility of being able to transfer files and share pictures, location information, voicemail, texts, and emoticons, all under one roof on one screen. The aim is towards a single identity-based, guided communication technique that is unified for all services, has centralized data management, and indicates the capabilities of other contacts in your phonebook too. This is where **Rich Communication Services (RCS)** comes into picture. The RCS initiative meets these hurdles and ambitions with international standards to smoothen out the scattered services.

In the previous chapters, we saw the process of setting up a basic WebRTC communication front. This chapter marks the transition from a normal communication client built on any protocol support with any arbitrary set of services to a standardized all-IP-based communication client that possesses rich communication features.

Rich Communication Services

The RCS is a concept of IP telephony that involves standardized architecture and a uniform set of services supported by all vendors. By profiling the existing services and setting up the defined, expected behavior from the creation of any future service, RCS aims to do away with the vendor dependency and proprietary implementations found today. The specifications are described in detail by the **Global System for Mobile Communications Association** (**GSMA**) at `http://www.gsma.com/ network2020/rcs/specs-and-product-docs/`.

A joint effort by leading telecom industry players, RCS is proving to be the cornerstone in lending network and vendor-agnostic shape to services, and also rendering them simple to upgrade and enhance since there is no vendor lock-in on proprietary protocols.

Developers today strive to build a communication platform that supports GSMA RCS 1.0/2.0/RCS-e and also refines the message-service network based on converging the traditional and new message services from the Internet, such as e-mails and updates on social networking sites and blogs.

Position and adoption of RCS

Active since 2012, RCS initially swept over Europe. It has been enhanced and made into an enterprise software package to reach the critical masses. Downloadable clients are also in market for closed environments. **Communication Service Providers** (**CSPs**) can use RCS to support IMS as a service-delivery platform and also consider offering software suites as cloud or hosted services to enterprise consumers.

Factors that drive an RCS adoption are the device's availability and the strong requirement of a standardized, open, and extensible ecosystem. Devices were initially the main factor that blocked the RCS adoption. However, all major manufacturers have announced RCS support in their handsets. Today, RCS is supported on mobile platforms such as Android, iOS, RIM, Symbian and so on; however, some CSPs might provide their own open source stack to device manufacturers. GSMA is ensuring interoperability by an extensive and continuous testing process. The growth of RCS is expected to ramp up quickly with the support of majority of OEMs in Asia, Europe and America.

Business impact of RCS

The last couple of years have seen users drifting away from some traditional telecom services such as SMS and embracing the services offered by online service providers or **Over the Top (OTT)** players. Similar trends have been observed in voice segments as well with the upcoming online audio/video call services. With this fast decline in the usage of traditional telecom services, there is a threat of loss of revenue and user loyalty to a telecom service provider. Therefore, it is now the right time to enhance the set of services that already exist and add new, exciting ones.

RCS is the way to attain a better user experience with innovative new services, but what does it have in store for CSPs and enterprises? The answer is RCS provides methods to monetize these new services while keeping the cost and timescales short. CSPs need a clear business case in relation to capitalization, besides protecting and increasing the subscriber base.

CSPs that launch RCS need to ensure quality and services better than OTT players such as Skype; they also need to ensure a high-level experience in mobile video. With proper **Quality of Service (QoS)** in place, CSPs can test out price points and find potential new revenue streams.

QoS is defined as the overall performance of a telephony or computer network, particularly the performance seen by the users of the network.

Technology impact

GSMA has stated that RCS is the gateway to innovation. An operator can use their network infrastructure that is already set up, to support the RCS cause. The elements of Ubiquity, global interoperability, QoS assurance, and security and privacy management are essentially the game changers with respect to OTTs. The following points state the positive aspects of using RCS:

- RCS will change the end-user behavior. It will help standardize the capabilities of devices for rich communication. It will also help ensure interoperability between fixed and mobile networks and between client devices from many different vendors. RCS will give an edge to CSPs only if they perform better than their competitors (that is, OTT).

- Carrier investments in IMS are better protected with RCS. RCS uses IMS to handle the underlying network features such as authenticating and charging for services. IMS defines the key interoperability requirements between RCS features, including Presence, location-based services, and connection through HSS between the network and user device.

Rich Communication Services enhanced (RCS-e)

RCS-e is defined by RCS 1.2.2 specifications. Refer to `http://www.gsma.com/network2020/wp-content/uploads/2012/03/rcs-e_advanced_comms_specification_v1_2_2_approved.pdf` for more information. RCS-e looks into the following areas of WebRTC:

- Discovery and activation
- Group chat
- Integrated messaging
- File transfer
- Geolocation push
- One-to-one chat
- IP voice call
- IP video call
- Multidevice support

Joyn

GSMA has said that Joyn is a consumer-facing brand that identifies and promotes RCS services. If RCS is the service design and implementation done by the operator, then Joyn is the visual interface implementation of the capabilities done by the device manufacturer. It is the native adoption of RCS capabilities in a device. Joyn specifications were written in order to ensure the interoperability of services across various platforms. This, in turn, prevents vendor lock-in through proprietary or over customized implementation of RCS. Like RCS, JOYN too is backed by GSMA. The GSMA RCS IOT Joyn Blackbird Implementation Guidelines Version 1.3 is the latest one now.

The RCS configuration process

The first time a user makes use of an RCS device, it is configured by the network provider. If the process is successful, the device receives the correct configuration XML, including the validity period of the associated RCS configuration parameters. If the device has no issues, that is, the device receives no errors during the registration process, then the device refrains from contacting the server again until the validity period has expired.

This process could require several retries until the provisioning in IMS is successfully performed. For those devices that have not successfully completed the configuration process, any RCS-specific UX available on the device remains disabled (known as the vanilla behavior) until a valid RCS configuration is successfully received and processed.

The use of another device's PS connection (for example, a Wi-Fi-to-cellular PS router) might lead to an incorrect identification of the requesting device. Therefore, this request can only be sent reliably by clients that are aware that any PS connection in the path towards the RCS configuration server is provided by themselves. When this initial request is performed over a non-PS access network, the RCS configuration server is unable to successfully identify/verify the identity of the requester (that is, RADIUS or header enrichment is no longer an option). In this case, the RCS configuration server will reply with an HTTP **511 Network Authentication Required** error response. This response will trigger the RCS client to start the SMS-based configuration mechanism.

RCS specifications

We will start by learning some mandatory RCS features that will help us achieve the goal of building a WebRTC client with RCS compliance. The following standardized services are a part of the 5.1 specifications of RCS:

- Capability discovery with the help of SIP OPTIONS message, or Presence, that involves precall capability discovery, in-call/in-session capability discovery, and multi-device handling
- Social Presence – the phonebook and location features are part of it
- Standalone messaging, that is, both one-to-one chat and group chat (the messaging-processing session management and multidevice scenarios are mentioned in the test case specification v3.0.)
- File transfer using HTTP/**Message Session Relay Protocol (MSRP)**
- IP voice call and video call
- Network Address Book and blacklist
- User availability through **XML Configuration Access Protocol (XCAP)**
- Notification service through REST

We will cover majority of these features one by one in this section, keeping WebRTC client as the end user tool.

Service discovery by an RCS-enabled device

A mobile network that offers RCS services to its subscriber base should be able to detect when a user connects to the network for the first time with an RCS-capable device. Upon detecting a user connection, two processes are triggered to be executed:

- **Service provisioning**: This is the process where the relevant configuration is performed on the network elements to make the RCS services available to the user (for example, provisioning an account on the IMS core and relevant application servers). In addition to this autoprovisioning on first usage, the service might be provisioned in advance by the service provider.

- **Client configuration**: This is the process where the network provides the client with its configuration. A user can only initiate the use of RCS services once their client is configured and the corresponding subscriber (uniquely identified by the relevant IMS URI, that is, a tel URI and/or a SIP URI) is provisioned by the RCS service provider to access the RCS services.

Both processes should be performed automatically (for example, when a subscriber first turns on their RCS-capable devices and connects with their Service Provider). The autoprovisioning and configuration processes for a WebRTC client is initiated by a REGISTER SIP request. The following diagram shows the WebRTC RCS client registering with the RCS server in the IMS Core environment:

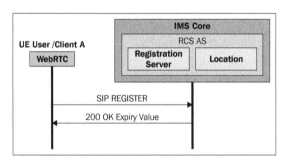

The preceding setup gives the end user the impression that the RCS services are working out of the box and minimizes any operational impacts to Service Providers. An alternative way is to use an HTTP-based configuration, but this is not discussed here for simplification purposes.

User capability exchange

The user must be able to avail the RCS/RCS-e services with other users, and in order to do so, they must know if the other party is RCS capable or not. It is for this reason that the device must send out periodic signals to check and confirm whether the contacts in the phonebook are RCS capable.

On confirmation, the user can make a rich call to that contact. The SIP request used to achieve this is called OPTION. The following diagram shows the user capability exchange for WebRTC clients via the RCS server in the IMS Core environment:

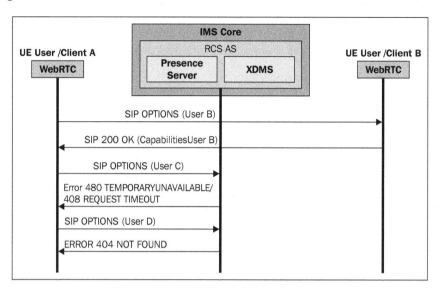

The preceding call-flow diagram used the OPTIONS message mechanism. We are assuming that user B is REGISTERED, user C is NOT REGISTERED, and user D is not an RCS user.

Chats with multimedia sharing

A rich messaging agent is expected to enable a large variety of messaging options, including chat, emoticons, location sharing, and file sharing. There must be support for the open standard protocol frameworks and a provision of one-to-one conversations and group interactions such as private chat, group chat, private file sharing, group file sharing, and others.

MSRP, which is a protocol for messaging sessions, does message encoding very similar to SIP and HTTP. Then, there is MSRP SIP and SDP to negotiate the parameters of the communication.

Messaging sessions require explicit setup and teardown. They do the following:

- Use SDP to describe sessions (where *m* means message) and SDP Offer/Answer to convey parameters
- Exchange dynamic transport addresses for communications (MSRP URLs)

- Negotiate supported message formats
- Use the SEND method to convey messages
- Might request confirmation from the remote side (on success and/or failure)
- Support for chunking of large messages (2 KB chunks)
- Use the REPORT method to provide confirmations

MSRP has two modes of operation:

- Direct communication between peers (simple case)
- Communication via relays (NATs, firewalls, policies, and so on)

As we have WebRTC platform network nodes in between peers, we will discuss the second mode of operation, that is, communication via relays.

The one-to-one text chat over MSRP

A one-to-one text chat is an MSRP data exchange inside an SIP session. The user enters in one-to-one IM and sends a message. The IM server can decide whether to stay in the MSRP media path (to store message history, for example) or let the MSRP session be established end to end. Once an IM session is established, it will remain active until one of the peers leave the IM or the inactivity timer triggers. The following diagram depicts a one-to-one chat session between two WebRTC clients:

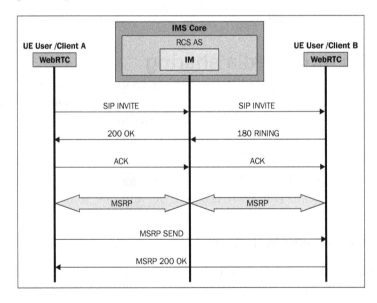

The user might leave the IM/chat window in the background, which means that the session is still active and can return afterwards.

File transfer over MSRP

File transfer goes to the background and it can be tracked in the notification area. However, note that if it is started from a chat window, the transfer information is presented on screen. The following diagram shows an MSRP file transferred from WebRTC clients via the RCS Server in the IMS Core environment:

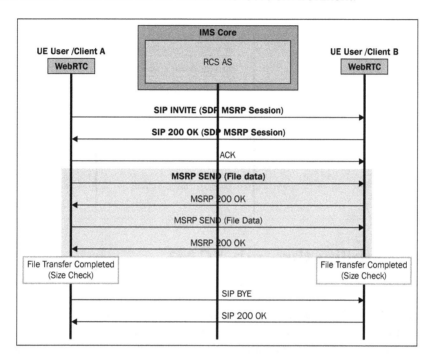

Group chat in a conference session

The group chat involves multiparty session management and delivers the text messages to users in the same way as in a two-party message. To initiate a group chat, the user enters the IM application and chooses to start a new chat. The list of RCS users is displayed and the user gets to choose one or more contacts. When a contact is selected, the OPTIONS exchange takes place to verify whether they are available for chat. This sets the request URI to the conference factory URI for the IM service in the home network of the IM user, and adds all of the invited users to the **Multi-Purpose Internet Mail Extensions (MIME)** resource list body.

The following diagram shows a group chat among WebRTC clients via the RCS Server in the IMS Core environment:

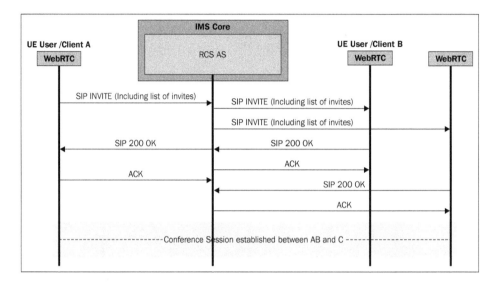

User availability through XCAP

XCAP allows a client to read, write, and edit the application's configuration data stored on a server in the XML format. It's an Application Layer protocol and maps the XML elements to HTTP URIs so that they can be accessed via HTTP requests. It can be implemented to indicate user availability on chat rooms in a WebRTC platform. We can also use XCAP for authentication, to share a file by checking the file extension through the XML file. The following diagram depicts user availability through XCAP:

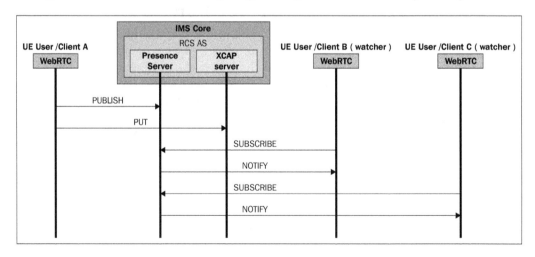

The preceding call flow diagram describes how the WebRTC client can implement the PUBLISH, SUBSCRIBE, and NOTIFY methods along with XCAP to create the feature of **User Availability Indication** in the phonebook.

REST-based notifications

Representational State Transfer (REST) is mostly applied to web services. HTTP-based RESTful APIs have POST, PUT, GET, HEAD, OPTIONS, and DELETE methods. Even though REST is not directly applicable in the case of WebRTC platform building, it can be used for third-party service integration such as weather notification, reminders, alarms, and so on. The following diagram shows the REST-based notifications:

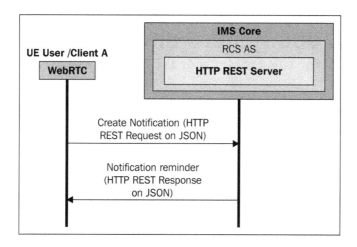

The preceding figure depicts a REST-based notification service for a WebRTC client. Before creating any REST service, we first have to identify the different resources in the application and map the actions performed over them to the HTTP methods and addresses, for example, create notifications and get reminders. Then, a media type is decided to carry data such as JSON, XML, or others. After this, the referenced resources can be fetched along with the HTTP methods.

Interoperability and interworking

The scope of interoperability not only pertains to a network but to a device as well. This is ensured by a strict adherence to **Interoperability Testing (IoT)**. A communication device/software prepares a test matrix after successful IoT and assigns self-accreditation to RCS.

In conclusion, we can configure the WebRTC platform architecture and make it RCS compliant by collaborating with GSMA RCS-accredited vendors to extend the RCS functionality in order to cover the following features/components:

- RCS Application Server, a single platform that supports both OTT and RCS apps

- RCS Joyn GSMA-accredited stack complying with all the expected standards

- Seamless integration with the underlying media engine, supporting all major codecs such as H323, H324, G-711, VP8, Opus, and others

- Adding enriched services such as enhanced phonebook, messaging, and so on, as described in the preceding sections

The RCS ecosystem and WebRTC

RCS is all about an agreed set of standards and protocols based on IMS. This section of the chapter defines the integration of RCS features into a WebRTC client. RCS defines two types of clients:

- **RCS embedded client**: This is the client that is provided as part of the handset implementation, and it is fully integrated with the native applications (address book, gallery/file browser application, calling application, and so on). Consequently, the RCS client will represent its identity, and the **International Mobile Station Equipment Identity** (**IMEI**) will be used in an SIP instance during registration.

- **RCS downloadable client**: This is a client that might be preinstalled or that has to be downloaded by the user. However, it is not part of the device's base software (that is, it has no access to internal **Application Programming Interfaces** (**APIs**) and advanced **Operating System** (**OS**) functionalities). The level of integration with the native applications is limited to the possibilities permitted by the corresponding mobile OS or the OS platform API.

In the context of WebRTC web-based communication client, we will see scenarios where SIP is RCS-capable, and the WebRTC application accesses the RCS functions through a web interface.

The following diagram shows the RCS WebRTC client that is interoperable with all call agents:

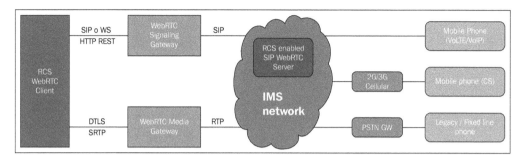

Any RCS or non-RCS enabled client, such as an SIP phone, desktop phone, PSTN agent, or a mobile phone, should be able to call an RCS WebRTC client. However, the RCS capability of end users is queried, and the services will be invoked according to each client's specifications. For example, the file transfer icon on the WebRTC RCS client will be dimmed or inactive for a PSTN phone, as the capabilities do not match.

RCS services in WebRTC

The array of services readily deployable in the WebRTC platform and complying with the RCS feature set are mentioned in this section.

User profile

RCS outlines the user's status and capabilities and service of sharing the current user's status. It includes the depiction of whether the user is online to take calls or is offline and unavailable. It has a customized status message by the user, such as **Away from desktop** or **Holidaying at home**. It also bears information about the devices that the user is currently using, for example, Android phones, Linux desktops, Nexus tablets, and so on. Information on whether the user has the ability to take video calls and play multimedia files is also displayed.

The following screenshot shows the prototype of a WebRTC profile-management service:

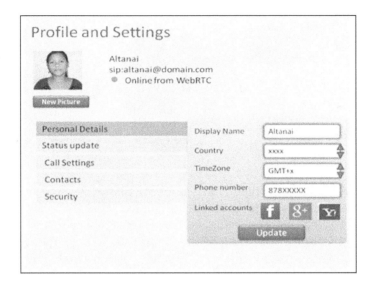

A user might also set or update their network's black and white lists. Blacklisted users are always screened from calling, while users in the white list are always given priority in calls, to the extent that their calls are connected even if the user has activated **Do Not Disturb (DND)**. The following screenshot shows the prototype of the WebRTC call-setting provisioning interface:

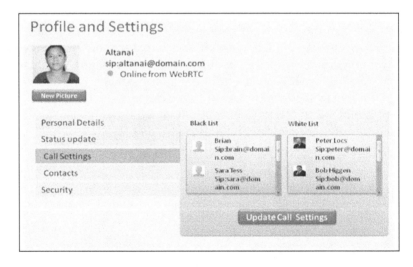

The preceding diagram shows other options in the **Profile and Settings** page too. These are covered in the subsequent sections.

Integration with social networks

Social Presence signifies the ability to link a WebRTC SIP account with an account user on other social networking sites such as Google, Facebook, Yahoo, and others. The capabilities derived from this feature are many, such as:

- Signing in without a password but using tokens. OAuth allows an application to access restricted contents (such as Facebook or Google user information). To sign in without a password, the OpenID protocol is used.

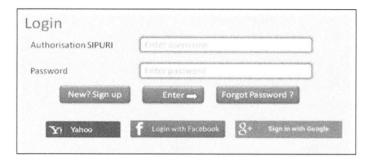

- Posting updates to other networking sites
- Import contacts from other platforms:

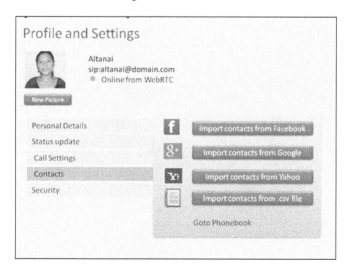

- Importing the profile status and/or picture from other sites
- Continuing a conversion even when the user signs out of WebRTC by sending messages/ mails over other platforms

The enhanced phonebook

An enhanced phonebook, also referred to as the **Network Address Book**, is synced with the user's account everywhere. It involves sharing user capabilities such as the ability to make a video call, codecs support, and others. It also helps in service discovery by mentioning the SIP URI accounts that are listed to be updated for their statuses. Rich phonebook also describes the sharing of the Presence status of a user's contacts, such as available or not available. The design of the phonebook should be such that it updates itself regularly with the status of the contacts.

Refer to the following screenshot to see a prototype of the phonebook for the WebRTC client, which shows the following information:

- A contact's latest profile picture or default picture in case no picture is available
- Links to their social networking accounts
- Timestamp of the last-accessed hour
- Presence (offline/online) and/or customized status text
- RCS capabilities support such as file sharing, video/audio call, video/audio/ text message, and others

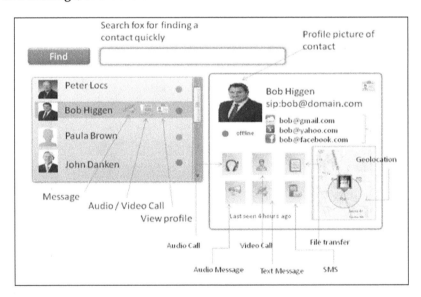

In terms of functionality, the phonebook should have a built-in way of handling click-to-call audio/video and click-to-message SMS/IM commands. The backup and synchronization of contacts across all of the user's devices should happen transparently to the user.

User capabilities and Presence

The WebRTC client must update the Presence and capabilities of contacts in the phonebook so that the user knows what services to invoke for which contacts. The following screenshot shows a contact with the RCS-e capabilities:

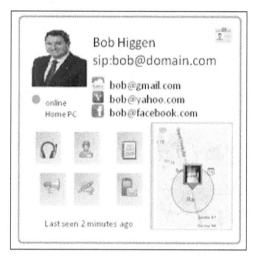

Capabilities and Presence in profile of a RCS user

The following screen shot prototype shows the contact as online to take calls but doesn't support the RCS-e capabilities. This might be the case when a subscriber has registered via an SIP phone. For example, the contact is not capable of receiving file transfers. Therefore, the file transfer icon is dimmed and nonclickable in this case.

Capabilities and Presence in profile of a non-RCS user

Unified messaging box

The message box should have the option of various message delivery options such as SMS, MMS, e-mail, IM, voice message, video message, and fax message. The idea is to combine the legacy and futuristic messaging services under one umbrella. It must aggregate the message from various servers and put them into a single view. Hence, it should have control buttons for:

- File browser
- Media gallery
- Camera application
- Desktop sharing

Some features of a messaging client, which are obviously expected, are also mentioned here. These options are a must-have:

- Forwarding a message
- Copying a message
- Sharing a chat
- Replying to a message

The prototype of the one-to-one messaging WebRTC page is shown as follows:

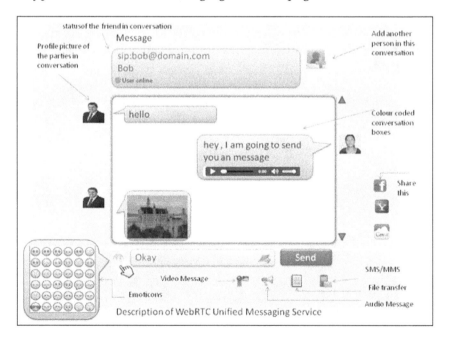

Description of WebRTC Unified Messaging Service

With these standards, a messaging solution must also allow users to share emoticons (symbols that depict emotions) to make the chat less mundane and more interactive. The prototype of the **Group Messaging** WebRTC page is shown as follows.

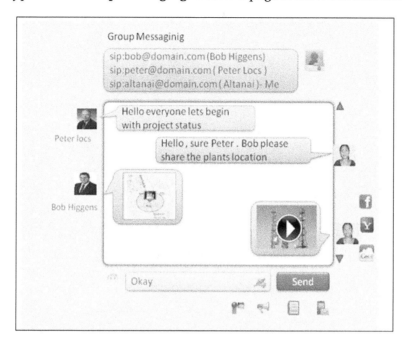

Message history

The message logs must also be backed up and synchronized like phonebook entries. The media shared between parties during the message session must also be stored and linked to the context to understand when and why it was shared.

Rich calls

The rich call service enables calls enriched with multimedia content sharing. RCS supports multiple call options and the ability to invoke rich services such as desktop sharing, file sharing, HD Call support, and others.

The following screenshot is a prototype of how an RCS-enabled WebRTC audio call page should look:

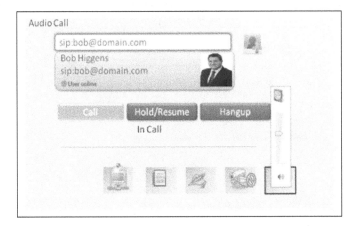

It is worth noting that the audio call screen depicts the essential operations a user can perform from their WebRTC client. This includes desktop sharing (the first icon on the tray from the left-hand side). The following screenshot is a prototype of how an RCS-enabled WebRTC video call page should look:

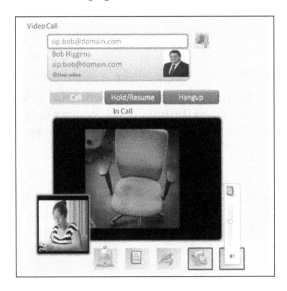

The following screenshot is a prototype of the feature of desktop sharing during a call:

Sharing remote desktop view during a Call

Call logs

The WebRTC client/server setup must synchronize with the network node of the call operator to provide a uniform view of all calls made or received until now. It must also bear the timestamp for the start and end of every call, in addition to the caller's and receiver's details.

The following screenshot shows a prototype of the **Call Logs** web page with quick links displayed on any selected entry:

The **Call Logs** page must bear quick links such as click-to-call, voicemail, messaging, or view profile links to any entry mentioned there, the same way a phonebook has.

Message history

Just as the **Call Logs** page displays the call history of the user with a timestamp, the **Message History** page is regarding the message interaction of user. The following screenshot displays the text messages received by the user in a tabular layout:

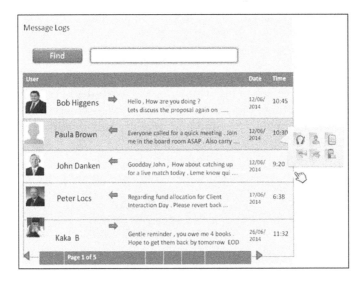

Clicking on any one of the entries opens the full message window with all the messages displayed. Just like the Call Logs page, the **Message Logs** page also bears a quick link pop-up box to let the user reply with text/audio/video or just call the other party back.

Multiparty conferencing

A multiparty conferencing session is similar in nature to a normal video call. However, the difference lies in the fact that video call between two parties does not require media mixing activities on part of the Media Server. Multiparty conferencing does require this and also the spacing for multiple windows needs to be made available on the current window frame as and when the users join. The following screenshot shows the prototype of conferencing among four users on a WebRTC client:

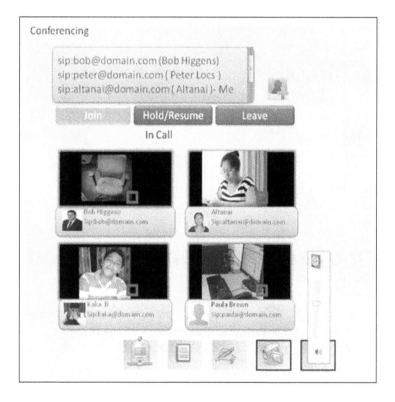

The visual representations provided in this section give a neat idea of planning a WebRTC communication interface coupled with RCS features.

WebRTC architecture with RCS modules

As the SIP server is replaced with an RCS-capable SIP server, the modules for MSRP Relay, Presence Server, Location Server, and Messaging Server become of acute importance. The following diagram depicts an overall deployment diagram for RCS-capable WebRTC communication platforms:

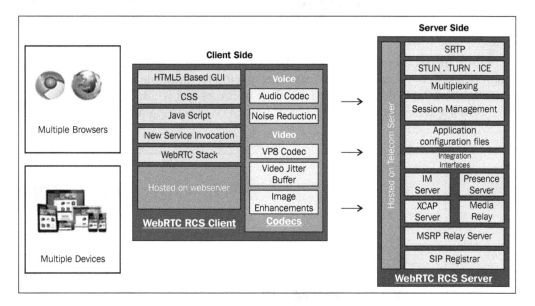

Note that this is a highly capable RCS deployment scenario, and it is okay if not all nodes depicted in the diagram are present in an RCS client server environment.

Telecom operator's benefit derived from RCS

The billing and charging models with the RCS service are multidimensional in nature. The following diagram depicts some aspects of the revenue generation model derived from an RCS-capable WebRTC communication platform aimed towards **Business to Business (B2B)**:

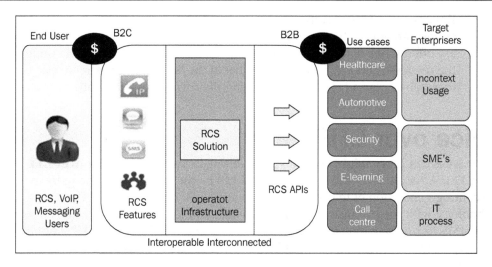

The following charging models are primarily for the Service Provider's benefit, as they discuss the monetization aspects of an RCS-enabled communication:

- **Subscription-based model**: This model allows full RCS usage after a monthly payment. This is a flat-pricing model. It adds RCS features on top of a user's existing service plan. After the expiry of the subscription period, the user is reverted to the old service plan.

- **Service bundled model**: In service bundling, the user's existing service plan is completely replaced with the RCS service plan. The performance is better than the subscription-based model, and no separate billing is required to handle subscriptions.

- **Loyalty model**: This model can be offered to specific sections of users or premium users. Here, the RCS service set is customized to meet the requirements of a set of users such as Enterprise users, the healthcare industry, and the manufacturing industry. Such filtered targeting is done after a thorough analysis of communication trends in that industry segment.

- **RCS-enabled Applications**: In this scenario, the service provider exposes RCS APIs to the developer community. This encourages the developers to make their own applications using the APIs that hook into the telecom service provider's network infrastructure and data. The interests of the service provider lies in the fact that such applications indirectly result in revenue generation either through services or through the generation of chargeable events such as calls, messages, data fetching, and others (for example, the RCS API for rich messaging for online doctor consultation application).

- **Revenue through advertisements**: Revenue generation through advertisements is the current industry trend. In this scenario, the RCS services are offered free of cost, but an advertisement is displayed or played along with the rendered service (for example, a bar at the bottom of the screen space to message or play advertisements during the ringing tone in a call).

Voice over LTE

While we are at it, we might as well study a thing or two about **Voice over LTE** (**VOLTE**). After all, RCS and VOLTE are said to be the major game changers in the coming generation of telecommunication. VOLTE is an all-IP mobile-access technology with the promise of high bandwidth and low latency. VOLTE is a subset of the IMS technology that is discussed time and again in the book. LTE is not just a concept anymore with commercial LTE network setups at many places and huge investments. There already is mass interest in VOLTE from telecom operators, equipment manufacturers, and even GSMA.

Combination of WebRTC, VOLTE, and RCS

This combo has the potential to completely revolutionize the way we see communication today. It provides the environment for innovative service creation while adhering to open standards. An architectural depiction of these technologies working together is shown in the following diagram:

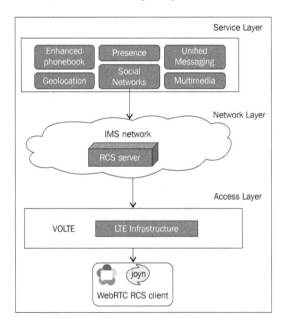

Why is it important for CSPs? The combo of WebRTC, VOLTE, and RCS will enrich the user experience in ways that OTT players can never match, for example, preinstalled software in the phone, greater quality standards and reliability. More so, not only is it aligned to the BYOD trend that is catching up pretty fast, but also results in the **Capital Expenditure** (**CAPEX**) reduction.

Summary

This chapter talked all about the evolving technology standards in the telecom domain and their usage in the context of WebRTC. We provided insight into RCS and its feature implementation in the WebRTC web client, such as enriched call experience, converged phonebook, unified messaging, and service discovery, among others. We also discussed the RCS-enabled SIP Server for the WebRTC client.

In addition to this, we briefed on JOYN, which is a standard to embed RCS features in an end user device. We also shed some light on VOLTE, which is an access-layer technology for faster speed in the IMS environment.

In the upcoming chapter, the compatibility of various browsers, SIP softphone, and mobile applications to WebRTC standards will be gauged. We will also discuss the methods to bridge the gaps in enabling communication between WebRTC browsers and SIP devices.

9
Native SIP Application and Interaction with WebRTC Clients

With the passage of time, better standards for mobile phone networks emerged that which were much faster than their predecessors. This led to the widespread adoption of VoIP protocols to communicate between different kinds of devices over wireless networks. As WebRTC is meant to be used not only over a LAN but also over mobile data packet networks, it is crucial for all the functionality, performance, and interoperability scenarios to be ascertained. WebRTC is intended to be a homogeneous technology for every browser; however, there are marginal differences between the browser types/versions for devices and **operating systems (OSs)**. Intercommunicating between a native SIP client and WebRTC is also a challenge, considering the format of Media codecs and signaling used. While native SIP phones use SRTP or RTP for media, G.7xx, AMR-xx, Speex, GSM audio codecs, and H.263 and H.264 video codecs, WebRTC offers SRTP as a video codec for media flow, G.711 and Opus as audio codecs, and VP8 and H.264 AVC as video codecs.

In *Chapter 4, WebRTC Integration with Intelligent Network*, we discussed how to extend WebRTC client calls to handheld mobile phones such as smart phones that have 2G (UMTS), 3G, and 4G (LTE devices). In *Chapter 5, WebRTC Integration with PSTN*, we came across the WebRTC network configuration to support public-switched landline phones. While *Chapter 8, WebRTC and Rich Communication Services*, was all about upgrading the standard communication services to RCS, this chapter takes us through the support and interoperability of the WebRTC platform with other kinds of devices and SIP software. We will take into consideration popular desktop-based softphones, mobile applications, and widely used browsers to depict WebRTC's scope of usage. Some browsers that are popular and occupy a good market share but are not interoperable with standard WebRTC calls as yet are also taken into consideration. Furthermore, the use of the Flash plugin is also discussed.

The W3C WebRTC and IETF RTCWeb working groups are busy defining standards for web-based real-time communication to use the power of the Web without plugins for audio/video calls. However, many browsers that occupy a major chunk of the market have not adopted WebRTC as yet or are not interoperable with the standard WebRTC functions. The challenges in the interoperability of WebRTC with phone applications pertain not just to signaling but also to media standards. Let's categorize the SIP phones into four groups.

Category 1	This consists of SIP phones that work on SIP signaling and have traditional codecs support, that is, video codecs, such as H.263, H.263, and so on, and audio codecs, such as G.711
Category 2	This consists of SIP phones that work with SIP but have codec supports via Opus and VP8, just as WebRTC does
Category 3	This consists of SIP phones with SIP over WebSockets but that do not support codecs supported by WebRTC
Category 4	This consists of SIP phones that support SIP over WebSockets for signaling and also support WebRTC-supported codecs such as Opus and VP8

In category 4, the SIP phones that support SIP over WebSockets for signaling and also support WebRTC supported codecs do not require any additional setup, as they are already WebRTC-compliant.

For the phones in categories 1 and 2, we need to set up a WebSocket gateway that converts signaling from SIP over WebSockets to traditional SIP signaling. However, we observe that, even though the SIP signal flows between two endpoints and calls can be made, as soon as these calls are picked, there is an abrupt termination. This is caused due to media incompatibility between the end points. It is for this reason that, for the phones in categories 1 and 3, we must configure a Media Server to support all the audio/video codecs that our endpoints might use. It should be able to interconvert between standard WebRTC and traditional codecs.

While running a WebRTC application on a browser, challenges arise due to the fact that all browsers do not yet support WebRTC functionality. What can a developer do when the particular browser is not WebRTC supported? A developer can:

- Refrain from showing communication options (WebRTC components) if the website is opened from a non-WebRTC-supported browser

- Restrict access of non-WebRTC-supported browsers to the website

- Build a backward plugin, for example, using Flash

We will take a deep dive into the extent to which WebRTC can be used by itself, the temporary solutions using Flash-based SIP, and interoperability from other platform-specific native SIP applications in the upcoming sections. Let's first divide the test cases for WebRTC client functioning across various operating systems. It will be followed by browsers and software supported by the particular OS.

Support for WebRTC in various operating systems

We will cover all the major SIP-based endpoints to establish their compliance/ noncompliance with a WebRTC client. We will look at native browser support for a WebRTC client and SIP softphones capable of interacting with a WebRTC client for the following desktop operating systems:

- Windows OS for computer

- Linux OS for computer

- Mac OS for computer

We will also analyze the support for WebRTC communication from mobile phone operating systems. For this purpose, we will chiefly analyze the following three OSs for mobile platforms:

- Android OS for mobiles/tablets
- Windows OS for mobiles
- iOS for mobiles/tablets

Let's first divide the test cases for WebRTC client functioning across various OSs. It will be followed by browsers and software supported by the particular OS.

Windows OS

Windows OS is the most widely used operating system in the world, occupying more than half the market. The following pie chart shows the percentage of usage of this OS in the common public space; refer to `http://www.netmarketshare.com/operating-system-market-share.aspx`:

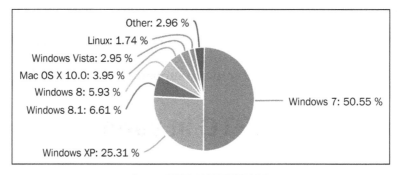

Source: NETMARKETSHARE

It is, hence, of acute importance to establish the reach of WebRTC support and interoperability to various SIP endpoints over the Windows OS. The WebRTC communication solution has been tried and tested in four major Windows versions, namely, Windows XP, Windows Vista, Windows 7, and Windows 8. The performances of these are primarily the same, which is an absolute compliance, using standard WebRTC-compliant browsers of latest versions.

Native browser support for WebRTC clients

This section takes a deep dive into WebRTC compliance with major web browsers on the Windows OS.

Chrome browser support for WebRTC clients

Chrome hosts many different versions, in addition to stable builds such as the Dev and Beta channels. It is worth pointing out that while Google Chrome is essentially closed-sourced, the Chromium project, which is the base of Chrome, is open source (refer to `http://www.chromium.org/`). Google Chrome is the stable build for public use. Above Version 25, the Google Chrome browser supports WebRTC without changing the flag settings. The latest version of Google Chrome, currently Version 36, now supports these functions by default. The following diagram is the screenshot of WebRTC running from a Windows 7 Chrome browser:

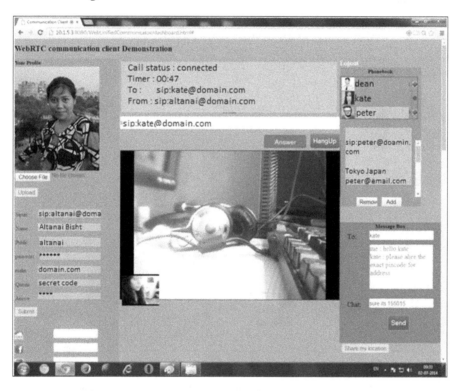

Chrome Dev and Beta channels are majorly for the purpose of testing and reporting for bugs before launching a public release. Google provides official Canary builds for Windows and Mac too; unlike the other channels (Beta and Dev), Canary's side-by-side feature allows builds to be installed without overwriting a regular Chrome build. It is a developer's playground to install plugins, switch between flags, and test and try out extensions for a web product without affecting the stable Chrome. Chrome Canary is shown to support smooth WebRTC audio calls, but it does not support video calls without proper settings. For old Chrome browser versions as well, we need to ascertain that they support PeerConnection functions by taking a look at the flags.

The preceding screenshot shows WebRTC running from a Windows 7 Canary browser. It is favorable if the users have updated versions of Google Chrome to use WebRTC.

Mozilla browser support for WebRTC clients

Mozilla Firefox also shows compliance to WebRTC ranging from audio/video calls, messaging, Geolocation, and so on. The following screenshot shows WebRTC running from a Windows 7 Firefox browser:

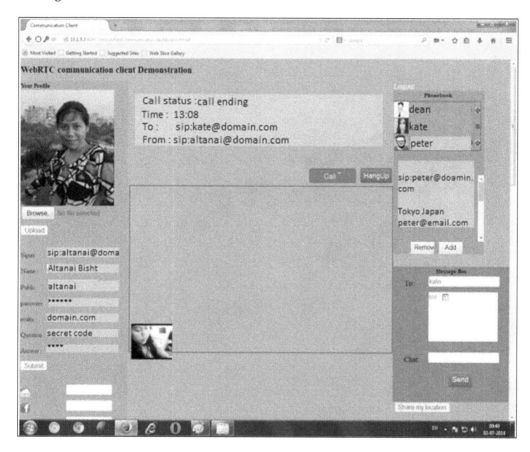

Mozilla also releases its builds in many versions, mainly, Beta, Aurora and Nightly.

The Nightly version is the one under heavy development. It was least stable and secure and was the first to come with WebRTC support in late 2012. The Nightly release is aimed at performing first tests of new features and should only be used by experienced users/testers. The latest Nightly builds also support the WebRTC function by default. The following screenshot shows WebRTC running on a Windows 7 Nightly browser:

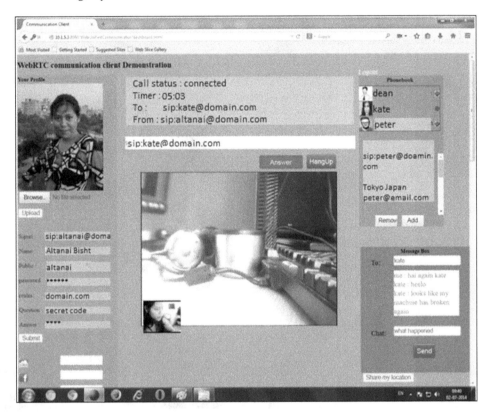

Firefox Beta (as of 16 May, 2013) and Chrome 25 and later are interoperable but currently require a small degree of adaptation on the part of the calling site. For more information, visit `http://www.webrtc.org/interop`.

Opera browser support for WebRTC clients

It is interesting to note that Opera too has joined the league of WebRTC since early 2014. The following screenshot shows WebRTC running from a Windows 7 Opera browser:

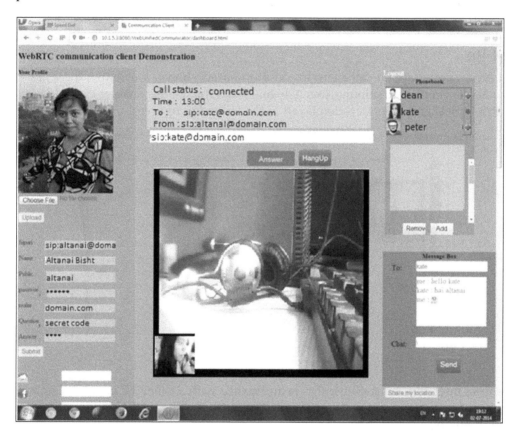

The preceding screenshot shows that it renders seamless intercommunication with other WebRTC web clients for both audio and video calls. After the study on WebRTC capable-browsers, let's proceed to the SIP softphones that are majorly used for VoIP calls from the Windows operating system.

SIP softphones capable of interacting with WebRTC clients

There are many SIP-based call applications in the market for Windows OS, both in the free and paid spheres. We will discuss some popular ones here to show WebRTC's interoperability.

X-Lite

X-Lite is a very popular call agent for desktop-based phones. Currently, there are two X-Lite versions in popular use: new and old. First, let us consider the old version with a typical gray interface, displayed in the following figure:

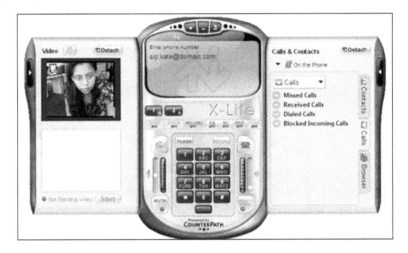

It shows intercommunication only via audio calls with a WebRTC client. X-Lite with a newer Lite version and with more codec support also shows the same compatibility with WebRTC.

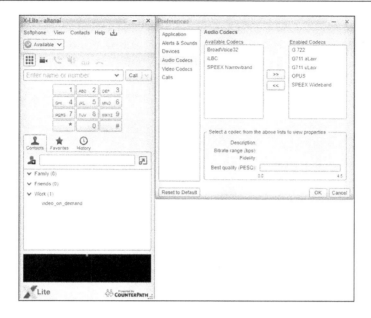

Codec support by the X-Lite Lite version (new) is displayed in the preceding figure.

Zoiper

Zoiper is a third-party SIP phone that is supported by all major OS platforms.

The preceding screenshot displays its interworking with a WebRTC client registered via a common SIP server.

Boghe

Boghe is an RCS-enriched SIP softphone; it shows compatibility not only with WebRTC-based audio and video communication but also with Instant Messaging, Presence, MSRP file transfer, and so on. The UI for Boghe IMS / RCS SIP softphone on Windows OS is displayed in the following figure:

The SIP softphone, Boghe IMS/RCS client

The RCS capabilities of a Boghe SIP softphone can be used after specific modules such as XCAP, Presence, and MSRP are deployed on the WebRTC SIP server. To read more about the RCS features, refer to *Chapter 8, WebRTC and Rich Communication Services*.

WebRTC unsupported browsers interacting with WebRTC clients

Internet Explorer (IE) is the default browser for any Windows user. However, as standard WebRTC functions are not supported by IE, there is a prominent requirement to use a plugin that can perform the job of media capture and streaming using the SIP protocol. The `webrtc4all` plugin aimed to achieve the end goal but was unable to realize it. The `webrtc4all` plugin is an extension meant to support WebRTC's PeerConnection JavaScript API in all browsers on the Windows OS, including IE9+. It was part of sipML5 solution. The source code of the `webrtc4all` plugin can be found at `https://code.google.com/p/webrtc4all/`.

The Temasys plugin also brings support for WebRTC to desktop versions of Safari and IE. These plugins can be downloaded from https://temasys.atlassian.net/wiki/display/TWPP/WebRTC+Plugins.

The intercommunication between a non-WebRTC-capable and a WebRTC- or SIP-based end point can be realized by the Flash plugin, which accesses the webcam and microphone of the user and uses SIP for signaling. A good example of this is the sip.js project, which uses the Flash network to make intercommunication between non-WebRTC browsers such as IE and WebRTC browsers such as Google Chrome a reality. A live demo can be found at http://theintencity.com/sip-js/phone.html?network_type=Flash.

A screenshot of the Phone app is shown as follows. It is registered with the SIP server, receiving incoming calls from a WebRTC client and requesting permission to access user media through Adobe Flash.

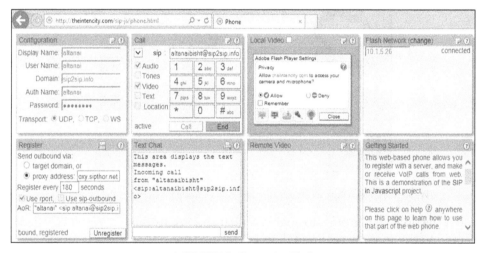

A SIP-JS Web client using Flash

 Note that media flow difficulties might arise, resulting in abrupt call hang or termination after ringing, but this is solvable using the Media Server.

Linux OS

Linux OS has a rich variety of flavors and each flavor has a different purpose. The WebRTC communication client must be supported by a majority of flavors of Linux to aid the Linux users' community. Some noteworthy OS candidates are SUSE, Red Hat, Ubuntu, Fedora, and CentOS.

Native browser support for WebRTC clients

This section explains WebRTC compliance with major web browsers on Linux-based OSs.

Chrome browser support for WebRTC clients

Chrome on the Linux operating system supports WebRTC functionality without any hassles just as in the Windows operating system. The popups to allow a web page to capture media from the microphone and camera, Geolocation, and so on are also similarly displayed.

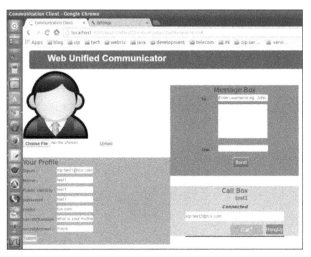

WebRTC functionality and traces displayed in a Chrome browser in the Linux OS

For older versions of Chrome, to enable screen sharing through a WebRTC client, we should verify that the required flags of Chrome are set. This can be achieved by typing `chrome://flags` in the address bar of the Chrome browser and verifying that the required flags are all set.

Flags set for WebRTC functionality screen share

The flag, described as follows, must be enabled for screen sharing to work on WebRTC:

Enable screen capture support in getUserMedia(). Mac, Windows, Linux, Chrome OS

Allow web pages to request access to the screen contents via the getUserMedia() API. #enable-usermedia-screen-capture"

Mozilla browser support for WebRTC clients

Mozilla Firefox on a Linux operating system supports WebRTC functionality. The Firefox Nightly Linux operating system also supports WebRTC functionality. Note that, since 2014, Mozilla Firefox (current version 29 for Ubuntu Canonical) shows full support to WebRTC.

The preceding screenshot shows a WebRTC client functioning from a Mozilla browser in real time.

Opera browser support for WebRTC clients

Opera for Linux does not support WebRTC functionality as yet. However, in the light of the fact that Opera for Windows has WebRTC compliance, we might soon see Opera Linux with the same capabilities as well.

SIP softphones capable of interacting with WebRTC clients

There are many Linux-based SIP clients in use. We will consider a few of these to establish WebRTC interoperability with a desktop-based SIP softphone on Linux. However, due to interface limitations, advanced features such as Presence, Notify, and file sharing are not supported.

Kapanga

Kapanga (through the Wine Windows compatibility software) is compatible with WebRTC clients for communication. The following screenshot shows Kapanga:

Note that Windows-to-Linux compatibility software such as Wine can run other SIP software meant for Windows OS in Linux OS too.

Linphone

Linphone's open source SIP Phone is available on mobile and desktop environments. It renders good results while communicating with WebRTC clients. There are marginal differences between Linphone features for various operating systems' mobile phones and desktops; however, the base libraries remain the same. The audio codecs generally supported are G711, Speex, G722, AMR-WB (G722.2), GSM 6.10, AMR-NB, iLBC, SILK, G729, and Opus. The video codecs are H.263, H.264, MPEG-4, and VP8.

The preceding screenshot shows Linphone communicating with a WebRTC client. Linphone also offers the web plugin, the demo of which can be found at `http://web.linphone.org/`.

Yate

Yate is another SIP softphone capable of interoperability with WebRTC and easily downloadable from the Linux Software Center. A screenshot of the Yate phone connecting with the WebRTC SIP server is displayed here:

SFL

An SFL phone is yet another SIP softphone capable of interoperability with WebRTC. A screenshot of the SFL phone with supported codecs is displayed in the following screenshot:

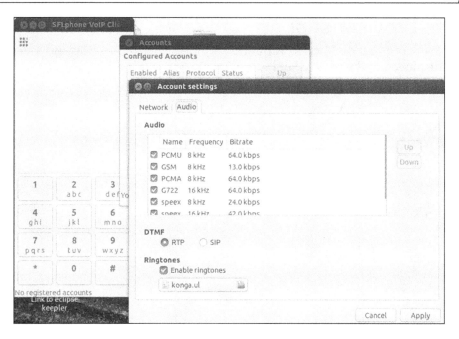

Many other SIP phone applications are present to verify the interoperable status of WebRTC.

Mac OS

The Macintosh desktop OS gives a perfect response when using a WebRTC-supported browser such as the Chrome browser for audio/video call, presence, Geolocation, and instant messaging. However, some well-known and useful browsers such as Safari do not have WebRTC compliance as yet and pose a serious limitation to the usage of WebRTC interoperability. To tackle this, there is a temporary solution of using the Flash plugin, which allows for media capture and streaming with the SIP server, that can then be connected to WebRTC-based endpoints. A good and working example of a Flash-based SIP client is available at `http://theintencity.com/sip-js/phone.html`.

Native browser support for WebRTC clients

The Chrome browser on Mac OS supports WebRTC calls, both audio and video. This is displayed in the screenshot here:

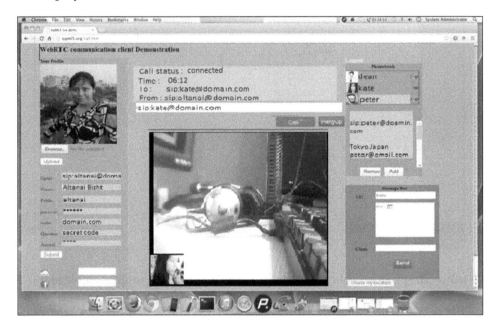

The Mozilla browser on Mac OS supports WebRTC calls, both audio and video. This is displayed in the screenshot here:

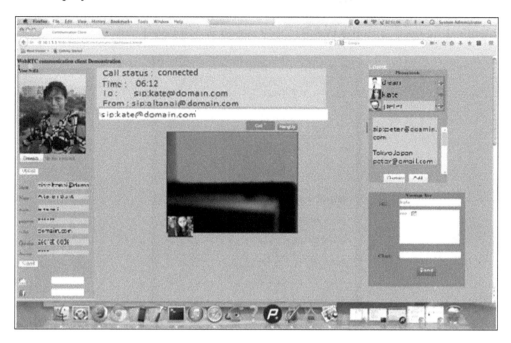

After discussing the browser-based WebRTC accessibility options, let's now consider the existing SIP solution that should be able to interoperate with the WebRTC endpoints.

SIP softphones capable of interacting with WebRTC clients

Mac OS can interoperate with WebRTC using many of its native-build SIP softphones such as Linphone 3CX, Jitsi, and Zoiper. They deliver WebRTC interoperability when traversed via the media server for transcoding.

iDoubs

The iDoubs SIP client is also an open source SIP phone that bears RCS capabilities. A screenshot of the iDoubs SIP client running on Mac Version 10.6 Mountain Lion, authenticating itself with the WebRTC SIP server is displayed here:

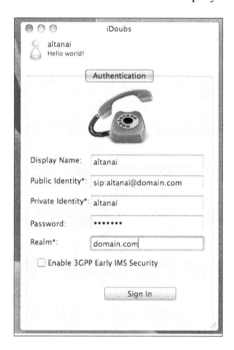

Note that iDoubs is an RCS-rich communication client from Dubango, and its source code is free for native application building for the Mac and iOS operating systems. Also, the WebRTC-favorable codecs such as PCMA, PCMU, and VP8 are supported. For more information, refer to https://code.google.com/p/idoubs/wiki/UserGuide.

Jitsi

Jitsi is a multiplatform open source SIP softphone. It runs on Mac OS as well. Jitsi supports RTP, Secure RTP, and ZRTP for encrypted media transmission. The audio codecs supported are Opus, SILK, G.722, Speex, iLBC, G.711 (PCMU and PCMA), and G.729. For video it can support H.264, H.263, and VP8. The royalty codecs need purchased licenses, of course.

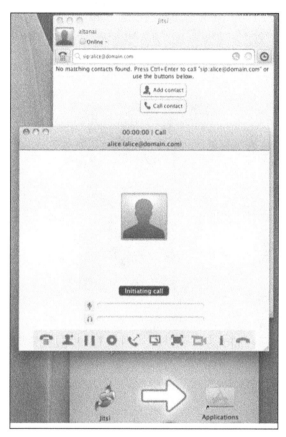

The Jitsi SIP client calling a SIP user from Mac OS

The preceding screenshot depicts a Jitsi softphone in the process of making a call. It is worth noting that besides SIP, the Jitsi softphone also supports the XMPP protocol and can send instant messages to MSN, Yahoo, and ICQ/AIM. Jitsi can be downloaded from `https://github.com/jitsi/jitsi`.

WebRTC unsupported browsers interacting with WebRTC client

The Safari browser on Mac OS has not yet come up with support for WebRTC media APIs, but the Flash plugin support enables us to make a web client capable of interoperability with WebRTC clients, also discussed in the *WebRTC unsupported browsers interacting with WebRTC clients* section. The following screenshot uses a customized version of SIP-JS open source code, used to communicate with WebRTC users. It shows the WebRTC functionalities and traces displayed on a Safari browser running through the Flash network:

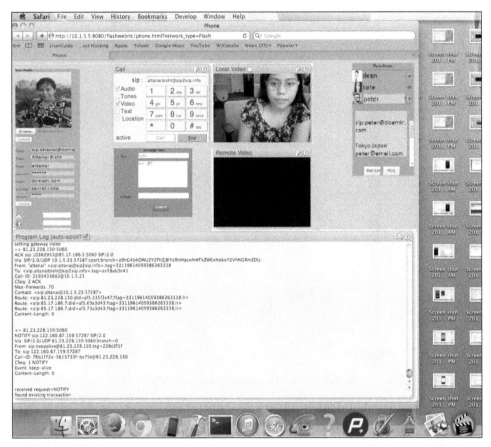

WebRTC functionality and traces displayed on a Safari browser running through the Flash network

It is to be noted that, while Safari on Mac supports the Flash plugin, the iOS tablet and iOS phone do not support Flash. The WebRTC accessibility options in the iOS tablet and iOS phone will be discussed under the *iPhone/iPad IP applications interacting with WebRTC clients* section later in the chapter.

Android OS for mobiles

Android for mobiles such as Samsung, Micromax, and Karbon and for Android tablets, such as Nexus, has been thoroughly tested for WebRTC adherence, as interoperability between mobile browsers and desktop browsers is critical for the growth and acceptance of WebRTC.

Native browser support for WebRTC clients

Android phones' and tablets' mobile Chrome browsers support WebRTC. The screenshot depicting the Chrome mobile browser seeking user's permission to access the camera and microphone is seen here:

WebRTC functionality from an Android phone's Chrome browser

A Screenshot depicting the Nexus Android tablet engaged in WebRTC communication through the Chrome browser is displayed here:

WebRTC functionality from an Android tablet's Chrome browser

Mozilla on Android tablet and phone also shows seamless support with WebRTC. The following screenshot shows the WebRTC web client in action from the Mozilla mobile browser, making a call to another WebRTC client.

While the mobile browsers for Chrome and Mozilla show full support for WebRTC, the Opera browser on Android *does not* support WebRTC yet.

Android phone's/tablet's SIP applications capable of interacting with WebRTC clients

In the process of determining the interoperability status of a WebRTC application, some popular SIP-based Android applications that run on both Android tablet and Android phone were tested. The following are some popular SIP apps that can be considered in this respect:

- **SIPdroid**: This is an open source Android-based SIP application. It shows audio compatibility with a WebRTC client as long as the Media Server plays the role of transcoding. SIPdroid in action is displayed in the following screenshot:

- **Linphone**: As mentioned earlier for other OSs, this is a popular SIP call agent application for Android OS as well. An audio call between a WebRTC web client and Linphone application that traverses through the Media Server is a successful scenario, while a video call faces some difficulties in delivering the remote video even though the WebRTC client user is able to view both remote and local videos.

The preceding screenshot of an Android mobile phone depicts an ongoing audio call with a WebRTC client.

Developing a lightweight Android SIP application

To demonstrate WebRTC interoperability (Presence, audio/video call, message) with a native Android client, it is a good option to develop a lightweight Android SIP application and customize it for your company's requirements, such as logo, theme, and so on. This also enables added services to the WebRTC client, such as Geolocation, visual voicemail, phonebook, and call-control options, to be set from an Android application as well.

An overview of the steps to build a customized SIP application in Android is as follows:

1. Get the development environment, which is an ADT bundle for the OS, in use from `http://developer.android.com/sdk/index.html`.

2. Import the sample application provided under samples to get a hang of the development process.

3. One can import an open source SIP phone or develop one's own from scratch. In case you choose option two, take care of the SIP stack and codecs to handle the signaling and media traversal from the device.

4. Deploy and run the SIP phone on a simulator/physical Android phone to register with the SIP server and make calls.

5. One can also add additional views for features such as importing contacts into a WebRTC-synced phonebook from an Android phonebook.

As the GPS on a phone achieves Geolocation with greater precision than the HTML-based Geolocation, it is a good idea to implement Geolocation using GPS on a phone.

For more information on Android native support for SIP, refer to `http://developer.android.com/guide/topics/connectivity/SIP.html`.

Windows OS for mobiles

Unlike the Windows desktop OS, Windows mobile shows no support for WebRTC communication features from its native browsers. This can be directly tested by opening the SIPML5 demo page directly from the Windows mobile phone.

We can see that the **Login** button is disabled. This is because the webpage did not find WebRTC support in this browser. We can use a native windows phone SIP application such as Zoiper to interact with the WebRTC web client. We also have the option of developing our own SIP-based Windows 8.1 phone application, which provides a better compliance with WebRTC than the third-party software.

Apple iPhone

Unlike the iOS Mac OS, the iPhone shows no support for WebRTC communication features from its mobile Chrome browser. As iPhone is a widely used device, it is expected that soon some means for intercommunication between the iOS phone and WebRTC users will be established. Developers have the option to advertise the use of the existing native SIP applications in store, to set up media transcoding support in the WebRTC infrastructure, or develop a new one that already embeds the WebRTC-supported codecs. Let's study this in detail in the next section.

iPhone/iPad IP applications interacting with WebRTC clients

For intercommunication between WebRTC and iPhone, we can use some native iPhone-specific SIP applications. Linphone is a viable option. Tested for functionality through the FreeSWITCH Media Server, a Linphone application is able to take audio calls without any trouble from an iPhone. A Screenshot of Linphone successfully registered with the SIP server and ready to make calls is displayed in the following figure:

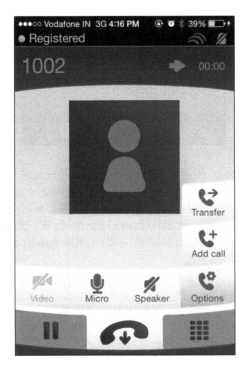

The iOS tablet also shows interoperability with the WebRTC client through Linphone's native application. The media server takes care of codec exchange on the network side.

The preceding screenshot is that of a Linphone SIP client on an iPad. This can be downloaded from the iTunes store at `https://itunes.apple.com/in/app/ linphone/id360065638?mt=8`.

Developing an iPhone SIP application

Similar to the native SIP application development for Android, to demonstrate WebRTC interoperability with an iOS device, the iOS developer team also has the option to build a native iOS application using Xcode. The advantages of doing so are personalized appearance; enhanced functioning; RCS support; and the addition of many WebRTC client-specific services, such as profile management, phonebook, and others.

An overview of the steps to build a customized SIP application in an iOS is as follows:

1. Get the Xcode development environment on Mac.

2. Build an application with the SIP stack and codecs to handle the background functionality of calling and media flow.

3. Provide a user interface for user interaction such as call, phonebook, and authentication.

4. Run and test the application on an iPhone/iPad simulator.

 Run the application on a real iPhone after obtaining the developer's license. For more information on iOS app development, refer `https://developer.apple.com/devcenter/ios/index.action`.

Summary

In this chapter, we saw the various means and resources to enable the adoption of WebRTC communication technology by the masses. This was achieved through the analysis and study of WebRTC-capable browsers such as Chrome, Mozilla, and Opera. This chapter also uncovered the technique to enable other noncompatible browsers, such as IE on Windows and Safari on Mac, to communicate with WebRTC clients using the Flash plugin till the time they do come with native support for WebRTC APIs. In addition to this, we also saw many desktop-based native SIP clients and mobile platform-based SIP applications that are able to receive and make calls to the WebRTC web client. *Chapter 10, Other WebRTC Use Cases*, is an interesting look at the use of the WebRTC technology in various trades such as online marketing and consultation. The chapter also shows how WebRTC can play a pivotal role in delivering communication features in gaming and educational sites.

10
Other WebRTC Use Cases

Creative minds can use WebRTC for other purposes besides just communication. Games, real-time marketing, and targeted advertising services can be built over WebRTC too. In this chapter, we shall discuss more of such applications, keeping in mind the role played by WebRTC.

We begin with a simple **Team Communicator** application with WebRTC and progress to make it a customized Communicator for specific enterprise segments, such as branches and back-office communications; for **Customer Relationship Management (CRM)** systems; and for network and operations tools. We will cover the use of WebRTC in the HR management tool as a separate section, since it involves keeping employees' records and recruiting new candidates. New ways of social networking are the burning need of the hour as users find themselves devoting a large share of their time to get in touch with their family and friends over social networking platforms. Thus, the book also explores the applicability of the WebRTC communication engine for social networking platforms.

How retail services that involve e-commerce and customer care can benefit from WebRTC in a big way will be explained in this chapter. The next section describes WebRTC's implementation in fun- and entertainment-based use cases such as online multiparty games, streaming music, **Video on Demand (VoD)**, sharing an ongoing movie via multipoint conferencing, interacting through group chat or conferencing while watching a live broadcast of a match, and so on. This section describes how there is plenty of room for more creativity and innovation with WebRTC. The chapter ends with how WebRTC is applied to education by connecting classrooms across the geographies.

The purpose of this chapter is to inspire the reader to think of varied ways to apply WebRTC applications, not necessarily plain communication, that can be beneficial. The true potential of WebRTC is realized when it's integrated with the foundation of the signaling protocol. Since the existing WebRTC standards do not provide a fixed signaling protocol, it is up to the integrator to use any means of signaling they find best suited to the work environment.

Unified Communicator

The easiest and the most likely application of WebRTC is building a unified Communicator and target enterprises. WebRTC can easily fit into the role of a Team Communicator by virtue of its simplicity. A WebRTC communication endpoint is purely a web-based application that does not require the user to install any additional plugin or set it up before making calls. To get connected to their teams, users only need to be logged in to their WebRTC SIP accounts through a browser. This way, the team can share files, text-chat, conference, share screens, make audio/video calls, or simply know each other's device capability and presence status.

Team Communicator

The WebRTC communication client is essentially a browser-based phone having features such as audio/video calling, Instant Messaging, and file sharing. The WebRTC-based software is a web-based SIP phone using HTML5 and JavaScript. It can interact with another web phone or softphone with the help of a middleware proxy server that acts as a convertor between SIP over WebSocket and SIP over TCP/UDP. Features expected from a standard Communicator are audio/video calls, instant messages, conference calls, file sharing, contact book, and user presence.

Some sample screenshots of a unified Communicator for team communications are shown on the following pages:

The following screenshot depicts a typical home screen with an ongoing call in a web-based unified team Communicator client. It has frames for phonebook, profile, calls, the call history page, and so on.

The following screenshot depicts a multiconference session between team members. Such a scenario is possible while brainstorming ideas with people from different locations.

Since WebRTC does not require a special plugin or any installation process for participating in a call, such calls can be taken from any computer that supports the latest version of Chrome, Mozilla Firefox, or the Opera browser in any computer or mobile device.

The following screenshot depicts the use of the screen-sharing feature of WebRTC to share the Eclipse **Integrated Development Environment** (IDE) screen with the team manager to show the actual coding in progress.

Code review through screen sharing in a WebRTC-based inter team communication tool

Since this use case is only aimed at intercommunication between team members in an office and does not necessarily need a telecom operator's network, it is feasible to use a simple signaling mechanism such as plain WebSocket signaling through a signaling server; for example, Node.js. You can find the detailed description in *Chapter 1, Running WebRTC with and without SIP*.

This way, WebRTC's communication technologies can help build a unified Communicator for team communication. Further, we shall see how other collaborative applications such as Geolocation, voicemail, and **Internet Protocol television** (**IPTV**) can also be integrated with the WebRTC communication platform.

Customized Communicator for specific enterprise segments

A SIP WebRTC solution is intrinsically only a web technology with browser support. It is possible to integrate WebRTC-based communication services into almost any kind of online web project. WebRTC can serve as a communication medium between branches and back to the **Network Operation Center** (**NOC**) that involves large groups of people spread across different geographies, or for **Business to Business** (**B2B**) communication needs.

For an enterprise, WebRTC can serve as a communication technology over LAN to help users to communicate within an office without having to set up any specialized software and hardware except for the web server and the signaling server. This will greatly reduce expenditure to third-party call agents or service providers as all the communication is taking place over an IP network. Enterprise communications would be transformed from a fixed point-to-point architecture to an integrated, multidevice, mobile architecture. WebRTC calls at the employees' desks can be preceded with a screen display of call-related information with the ability to selectively answer or not answer the call.

Branches and back office communications

In this section, by back office system processes, the task of generating an order, provisioning, shipping, invoicing, and applying the payment are implied. These processes are essential to help run an organization itself. Generally, these processes are heavyweight and involve a lot of tracking and record keeping.

These activities can be broadly classified into three groups:

- **Enterprise Resource Planning (ERP)**: This is used to streamline internal business processes and operations. It involves the backend processes such as product planning, development, manufacturing processes, finance, accounting, and so on.

- **Supply Chain Management (SCM)**: This is used for maintaining logistics with external partners. It involves activities such as order tracking, inventory control, product distribution, transportation, and so on. The Communicators within the SCM domain include suppliers, manufacturers, distributors, and partners.

- **Field Force Management (FFM)**: This is used to keep employees organized and coordinated for better output. The Communicators involve technicians, ground engineers, transporters, and so on.

Besides automation, for the preceding software, communication plays a key role in determining the success for each activity. In the existing system, the modes of communication are restricted to e-mails and phone calls with PSTN calls, SMSes, and faxes also in some cases. It's a difficult task to assimilate information from various sources, maintain histories of calls and e-mails, check the progress of these calls and e-mails, and so on. The following diagram shows the existing interaction between various players in an organization's operation:

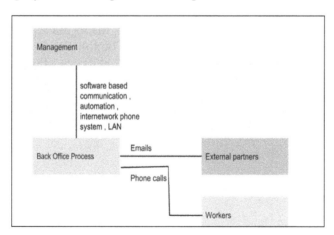

WebRTC can bridge the gaps of communication barriers between various parties, and also provide the one-stop solution to handle all interactions. Needless to say, this saves a lot of investment in time, software, and hardware to keep the parties well communicated. The following diagram shows the WebRTC-based interaction between various players in an organization's operations:

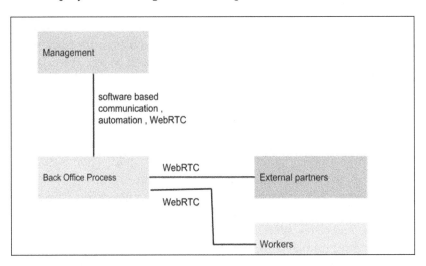

By implementing the PSTN and GSM gateways, a WebRTC client can even reach out to laborers and on-the-move workers for coordination. Also, with the provided Geolocation and Presence capabilities, the location and availability status of employees can also be tracked real-time. The following screenshot shows WebRTC and Geolocation services as part of the **Work Force Management (WFM)** and depicts how contacts are located on the map using Geolocation API's of browsers and the GPS of phones.

Using this WebRTC client, the manager may call or send an instant message to a technician based on his proximity to the specific area as depicted from the map:

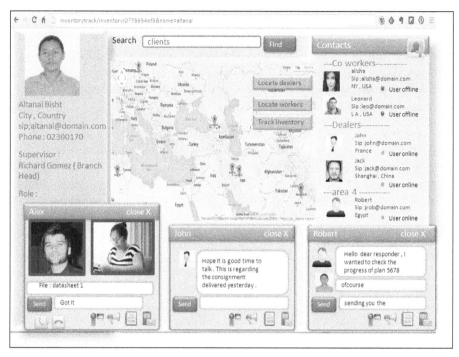

WebRTC and Geolocation services as part of Work Force Management

The Customer Relationship Management system

The CRM system involves customer-facing interactions such as order capture, configuration, pricing, and order query. While ERP is used for internal communication, CRMs facilitates collaboration between customers. CRMs are used more like a sales-and-marketing tool to stay in contact with current clients, track opportunities, and create new business opportunities with leads, such as Salesforce, BPMOnline, and so on. As evident from the description, a CRM solution mostly requires an engaging interface. With WebRTC, the user engagement levels can reach new heights as members can directly connect with each other in a call without navigating away from the CRM page or using their physical mobile devices to make calls. This is in contrast to the existing system of writing mails to each other and awaiting replies.

The life cycle of transforming a lead to closing deals spans several systems, including CRM, ERP, and SCM, and involves a number of roles, including call center agents, shipping clerks, order process analysts, and managers. Communication via e-mail or phone may take several minutes or days to complete. Also, such processes require an approval and oversight from higher management from time to time. This is where WebRTC comes in. The Sales and Marketing life cycle, combined with rich communication features, can accelerate the growth for a business organization as call history, purchases, documents exchanged, and everything else can be done at one place without relying on external service providers.

A sample screenshot of the CRM system designed using WebRTC as the communication medium between various parties is shown as follows. It demonstrates a typical home page for a CRM client and shows the tabs for **Work History**, planned **Work items**, **Contacts**, and various other data available. Also, it shows the profile pictures of people who are marked as important:

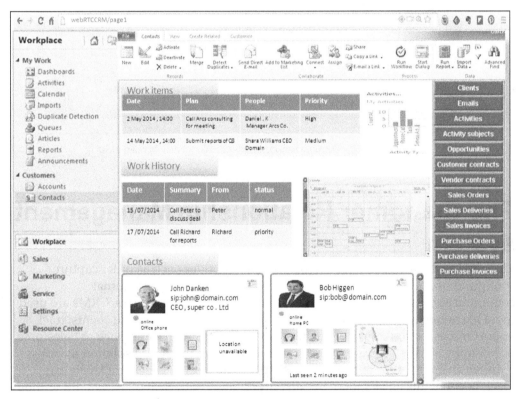

The home page of a web-based CRM solution

The following screenshot shows a presentation shared between multiple users over the WebRTC CRM solution. In addition to viewing a current ongoing presentation, users may also send files or engage in a group or private chat. The files shared with each party are stacked in the drawer area. The drawer area refers to the **Shared Items** window that is present at the bottom panel of the following screen:

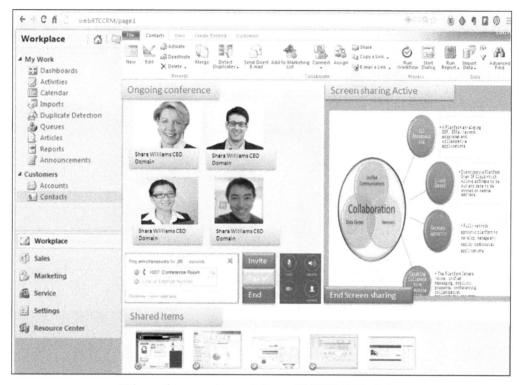

Video conference and presentation on WebRTC CRM solution

Note that a CRM system is independent of the OS or browser version but WebRTC is not. A list of WebRTC-supported devices and interoperable endpoints is given in *Chapter 9, Native SIP Application and Interaction with WebRTC Clients*. Besides this, it is also possible to connect to GSM- or UMTS-based mobile users via WebRTC. So, with some additional setup, a CRM system designed with WebRTC can have absolute phone integration.

The following screenshot shows how a mobile user is also able to participate in a conference session using their mobile browser on WebRTC.

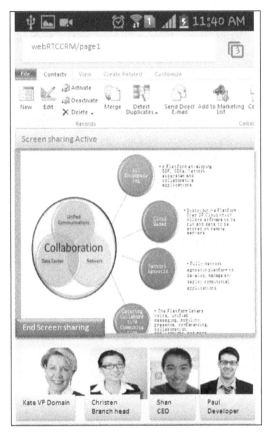

Video conference and presentation on WebRTC CRM solution from a mobile browser

The following figure gives an overall architecture for the deployment and integration of WebRTC-enabled communication with a CRM setup. The services such as reporting tools, handling workflow, and scheduling, are part of services under the **Business Layer**. The interaction with third-party servers is handled via web services. The outbound and inbound call handling is handled via WebRTC from the online CRM's browser-based customer interface.

Additionally, the Presence feature of SIP provides an indication of when a user is reachable to respond to calls. In a situation when the user is not reachable, the logic to redirect the call to his voice box is defined in the SIP server. The integration of advanced SIP services such as **Virtual Private Network** (**VPN**) and call routing are provided by the SIP Application Server; media services such as IVR, **Dual Tone Multi Frequency** (**DTMF**), and transcoding are provided by the Media Server.

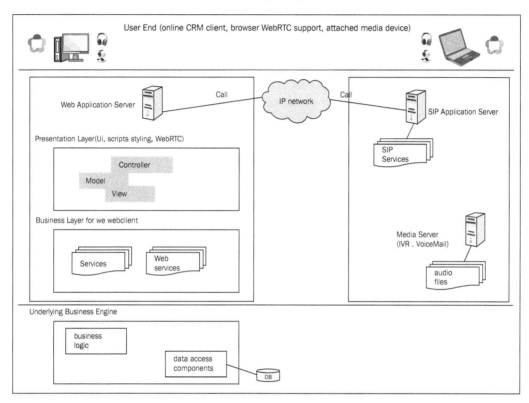

There are various roles and responsibilities of a CRM besides the ones mentioned in this section. Since the subject at hand is to make the CRM screen capable of making instant calls, the WebRTC-related points are highlighted. The implementation and design of other features, such as offline access, tickets, escalations, incentives, quotes, expense management, and automation, are left to the developers and integrators of the CRM application.

This way, WebRTC's communication technologies can help build a unified Communicator that is aligned to the goals of both the operator and the enterprises. In fact, the Communicator use cases described earlier demonstrate the potential to build a value chain that can bring financial and commercial benefits, operational savings, and process streamlining to the vertical industry segments involved. WebRTC can also play a pivotal role in creating new market business opportunities for the operator, service provider, web application management firm/enterprise, and so on.

Network Operation Center

NOC is the main entity that is responsible for emitting control over the enterprise network, which can be a computer system or a telephone system. WebRTC technology provides the opportunity to merge the real-time communication ability with in-context usage and benefit to the NOC functionality. The NOC admin can view the Presence status of users to determine their availability and call them as they are logged into their WebRTC accounts from their systems. As a user reports a fault or raises a ticket to resolve a problem on his system, the NOC representative can get in touch with directly and them instantaneously. The following screenshot depicts an NOC admin's control screen with tabs for **Hardware**, **Software**, and **Network**. The admin is also authorized to monitor traffic and exercise control over the system behavior remotely. Of course the screen-sharing feature of WebRTC is very valuable for this use case.

Every NOC personnel have their own ID for signing into the WebRTC portal with privileged access. The users on the other hand sign in to their office portals with their IDs that are also callable. The NOC admin will get a list of issues or matters in their inbox and they can contact the concerned user from the web portal itself.

The human resource management tool

An HR personnel must be able to manage various user groups and should be immediately reachable in case of concerns. In addition to this, an HR personnel also must primarily manage two things, that is, communicate with candidates for an opening post directly from the job portal, and for interviewing and recruiting the candidates. Hence, such a system requires database management for user skills and provisions for immediate audio/video communication if the user is online.

Communicating with candidates for an open post directly from the job portal

A recruitment-based WebRTC client allows an HR personnel to make direct audio/video calls in context with the available requirements. A WebRTC client allows sharing the skill set and profiles to the concerned person seamlessly during a call. Thus, it's applicable to be used as an HR management tool. A simple call can be directed to any particular HR or the manager as per the associate profile. HR personnel, managers, and associates have their own login credentials, using which they can track a particular department. The record of requirements for any particular project and skills can be maintained for HR personnel and managers. The user's profile preview from the contact book too should contain a brief summary of their skill set and work history. By enabling high definition video calls, the interaction between the recruiter and the candidate will become lifelike. The following screenshot gives a good representation of this use case.

The skill set of the user is displayed alongside the user's call window for easy reference while talking to a client on their expertise and work experience.

A sample project for a WebRTC-based HR communication system is provided along with the book. In this proposed WebRTC-based interviewing and recruitment system, the applicants for a job are sent a notification for a scheduled series of interviews through the WebRTC message service. The file sharing service of WebRTC enables a candidate to send in their resumé without employing the traditional e-mail service. The WebRTC audio/video call facility enables both parties, the recruiter and the applicant, to engage in an interview session. In case the application requires technical testing or problem solving, the screen-sharing capability of the WebRTC agent enables the recruiter to see the applicant typing in the code and executing it for output in their own machine.

Social networking – targeting consumers

WebRTC develops user interaction by providing a simpler, quicker, and hassle-free medium of interconnecting two call parties. With the power of web-based social networking, WebRTC will bring about a massive wave of change in the way people socialize over the Web.

Social networking platforms

With WebRTC, we may build a standalone social networking platform or a common platform to let users link their social networking profile and interact over WebRTC communication technologies. The array of features begins right from the process of signing up/logging in through the token-based OAuth mechanism. Further, integrating the friend list by importing friends from other accounts, finding new people through friend suggestions, and search options are part of the solution. The following screenshot shows the flow of how to access social networking solutions and make WebRTC calls:

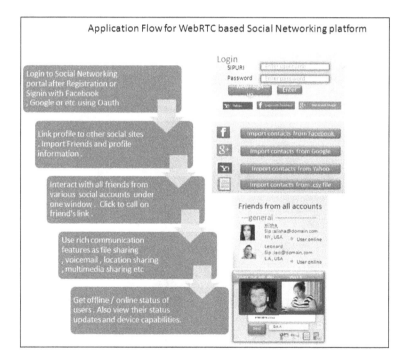

A WebRTC-based social networking platform is realized by giving an interactive outlook and an array of interactive services, such as sharing pictures/videos/posts, click to call, sharing updates about life events, and others. With the advanced features of SIP, the communication choices can range from chat, group chat, audio call, video call, multiparty call, file transfer, real-time location updates, Presence and status updates, and so on. Also, the device capability through which a user accesses the WebRTC social networking client at that point of time can be exchanged; these device capability factors include the OS name, whether the camera and microphone are attached, whether the user is on an RCS-enabled client, and so on. Other features such as sharing posts and media publically can also be done over RCS-specific protocol such as MSRP as an alternate option. A timeline-based history of shared posts is a desired requirement for social engagement.

A sample view of the WebRTC-enabled communication through a social network portal is shown in the following screenshot. The mock web view shows the user's self-profile section on the extreme left, the history of shared updates from others in the middle section, and the friend list on the extreme right. It also depicts an ongoing text chat and video call with two different users over WebRTC. Likewise, many additional features can also be integrated with a WebRTC-based social networking platform:

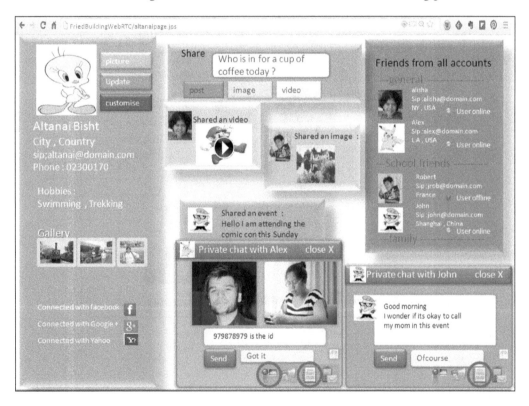

WebRTC's interaction with other social networking accounts such as Facebook, Google+ through OAuth, messages via SMTP, and inviting existing friend contacts give an upper hand to WebRTC's role in enabling the user to interact with people around the world in a text/audio/video conversation.

Dating sites with anonymous call and chat

Of late, the trend of dating sites and web matrimony platforms is on the rise. The prime requirement of users here is to interact with the other party without revealing too much of their actual identity details, such as personal mobile number, e-mail, or even their name, at the first instance. For such instances there could be an anonymous WebRTC call session between the users. Here, the user is assigned an alias URI for every session and the user's actual identity such as their telephone SIP URI is kept secret.

The screenshot of one such site is given as follows. This page is the homepage where a user can navigate through a list of persons or filter them as per their interests or location:

The following screenshot depicts an audio/video call, voicemail, or a chat option alongside the person's profile that the user has set the focus on. The embedded functionality to make calls lets the user to get connected with the other user instantly.

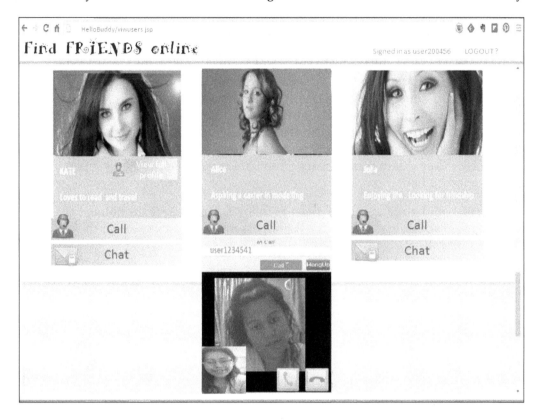

This use case has been discussed to exhibit the low-lying fruits of the WebRTC technology. It is possible to track the user by packet sniffing such as lawful interception through analyzer tools such as Wireshark and it is also possible to mask the user identity by assigning a temporary user ID and setting up 1-minute timers for every session.

Moreover, the public IP of the other party that might be visible in the SDP can also be masked by using a gateway in the middle. The service provider can come up with many ways to charge for the call, such as recharge the account through payment gateways before making calls and then charge for calls per minute or make the first minute of the call session free but require payment for the conversation session to continue.

Retail services

Retail services cover a wide spectrum of many big and small services. The act of proactive marketing from advertisements/offers to answering calls regarding the product's enquiry or complaints is all covered under retail services. This also includes various other services such as connecting users to online marketing agents after clicking on an advertisement, invoice tracking through Geolocation, and updates from the SCM system regarding the consignment delivery. WebRTC can be effectively used to fasten the process and inject transparency for the end user to get connected to all parties with the click of a button on a web page. In contrast to this, the traditional scenarios of looking up the call center toll-free number from the Web, notifying and keying it down on mobile phones, waiting for the circuit-switched call to be converted to IP-based at network, and then being able to talk to a customer care person seems long and tedious.

We shall start the discussion with the WebRTC-based Online Marketing System and end it with WebRTC integration with the existing contact centers.

WebRTC online marketing centers

Marketing through advertisements is the most common way of luring customers to buy a product. However, the goal is not reached until an order is finally placed. Enabling the journey between the user clicking on an advertisement and convincing him enough to finally click on the buy button is a tough job. Some sites employ a live chat facility to let the users express their interest or concerns regarding a particular product and others employ an old e-mail-based system to achieve the same result. WebRTC can help the process here.

A sample screenshot of an online marketing application integrated with WebRTC communication mode is shown as follows:

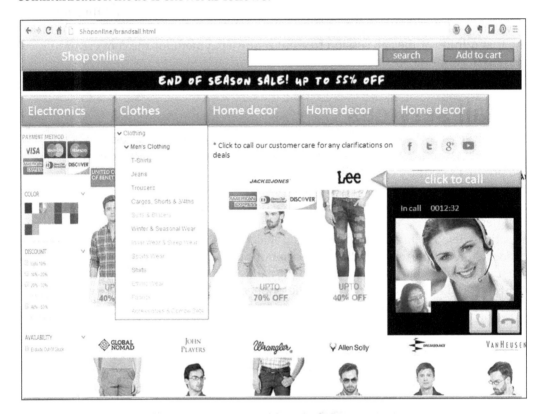

Many a times, people find it better to talk to a person, such as a shopkeeper, about a certain product before actually shelling out money for it. Also, a number of facts about a particular product are not depicted well in a picture or textual description. WebRTC blends in perfectly in such cases, which lets sellers to directly communicate with the prospective customers by further talking about a product before they buy it. This way the given proposal will not only enable marketing agents to personally introduce their product to the users, but also fetch quicker results for the users as well.

WebRTC contact centers

Call centers have come a long way from **Private Branch Exchange (PBX)** to today's virtual call centers. The modern call center infrastructure provisions maximum business process automation. The routing solution on the network side is built on an **Automatic Call Distributor (ACD)**-based and IP-based platform, supporting the receipt and intelligent routing of incoming calls. The call center agents use unified Communicator softphones.

Typically, a call center solution today should contain an ACD/multichannel routing, reporting, and analytics tool, IVR, and self-service automation through user DTMF input, outbound dialing, and multichannel recording. Over-the-top enhancements include knowledge management, Quality of Service, admin monitoring, and WFM. Often, calls to call centers are also followed by customer satisfaction surveys. The following screenshot displays a call center architecture with WebRTC end points:

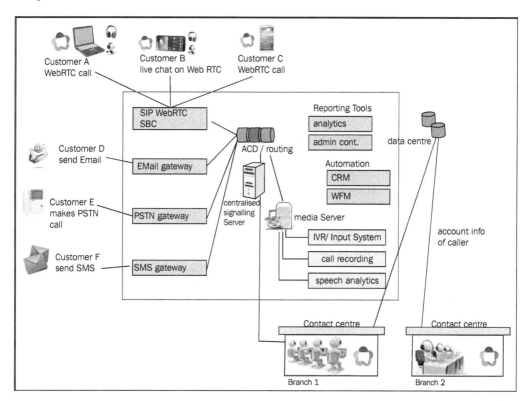

This section described the ease of processing a call from the user end to the contact center. The next sections deal with some contact center use cases that include the customer calling up customer care to fetch answers to queries.

Users contacting customer care

In the present day scenario, for an aggregated customer to address his concerns with a customer care agent, they have to first look for a toll-free number on the site, dial the number, navigate through a chain of IVR and response input, and then be connected to an agent. With the introduction of a WebRTC-based click-to-call service on the web page, a customer can save himself a lot of effort. For example, a consumer using their smartphone interacts with an airline to change a return ticket. The consumer uses WebRTC-integrated services to select an interactive chat response and engage in a live conversation with a customer support agent to obtain a new boarding pass. The experience is simple, fast, seamless, and strengthens the overall customer satisfaction. Systematic, real-time marketing, and offer management would become much more precise for customer service operations.

WebRTC enables browsers to be another end point for customer-to-call center interaction besides mobile phones, landline phones, e-mails, and live chats. In fact, WebRTC-based live interaction between a customer and a call center executive is quicker and a more sophisticated way of resolving issues, then and there with just the click of a button on the web page. WebRTC will not only provide direct IP-to-IP calls but also fosters the development of more specific call routing right from the start, a task that is currently handled by a complex IVR system and response.

For example, answers to customer queries regarding the whereabouts of a store and availability of a product. Alternatively, suppose that a user wants information on the stores selling a particular product around a user right now, and then they can just contact the call center from the web page or their phone. The customer care officials at pronto call center use the retail measurement API to find out about all stores selling the particular product near the user. After collecting the information, the call center official shares the information with the user on the same call.

WebRTC is a revolutionizing technology that enables one to call other people through a browser. With the help of gateways, it is also possible to make calls from WebRTC to a traditional mobile or telephone system and vice versa. In cases where the user is calling through a WebRTC client, his real-time location can be fetched using the HML5 Geolocation API and shared with the customer care executive so that the user doesn't explicitly have to share his location. The user end devices could be any mobile phone (3G/GSM/PSTN) for GSM calls or WebRTC-supported browsers (for example, Google Chrome, Opera, and Mozilla Firefox) for WebRTC calls. The customer care center executive is able to take calls via the WebRTC API on his web browser. The network consists of the SIP signaling server, Media Transcoder, Application Server for call queue logic, and third-party retail APIs for finding answers to user queries.

A sample component diagram using the Kamailio SIP server for SIP over WebSocket to SIP signaling, FreeSWITCH for media management, Application Server to host the web application, and third-party retail APIs for information retrieval is shown as follows. As you can see in the following diagram, there are many endpoints to reach the customer care center (more information on WebRTC to GSM network connectivity and WebRTC to legacy PSTN network connectivity has been described in *Chapter 4*, *WebRTC Integration with Intelligent Network* and *Chapter 5*, *WebRTC Integration with PSTN*, respectively). Of course a customer care center has the option to not set up the architecture itself, but rather to use the existing network of conversion services by telecom operators.

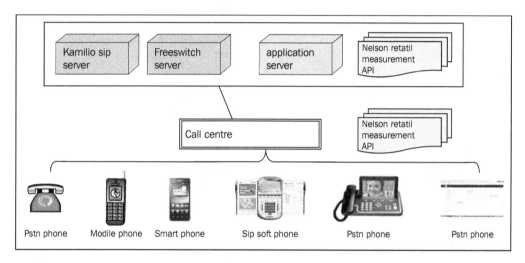

Now, we shall progress towards the application of WebRTC in nonconventional areas, such as healthcare, which is described in the next section.

Health care

As mobile technologies become more widespread, medical institutions are aiming to take patients from hospitals to their homes. Using the power of the Web, WebRTC provides the platform for such a health care portal for patients to communicate with a medical practitioner just with the click of a button on a web page, with the help of which one can also view the doctor's location, status, and availability. WebRTC allows options to share files and engage in a multiparty conference for discussion between many doctors; it can be integrated as the web component of the existing hospital management system, and much more.

Online medical consultation with the doctor

The WebRTC call functionality can be embedded into the software belonging to big hospitals dealing with multiple tasks as described earlier. However, here we shall only consider WebRTC's integration with the online HealthCare portal. Every doctor, nurse, and other officers in the hospital can have a unique call ID (SIP URI) using which they can be contacted in times of emergency. The patient can have a direct login to the WebRTC client after getting their registration ID. Since WebRTC doesn't require an installation or special equipment, patients will be able to directly call the doctor without bothering about the setup. Consulting patients and providing diagnostics in remote areas is also possible with WebRTC. Additionally, the code for recordkeeping, maintaining call histories with every patient and doctor, sending message reminders for the next call/meeting, and other hospital communications can be built and integrated with the healthcare WebRTC project. The following scenarios show how WebRTC solves communication barriers and aids in delivering services to the user:

- Users could describe symptoms to doctors and show HD videos that enable doctors to get a cursory look at surface symptoms, for example, skin ailments such as rashes, scars, and others. This enables them to get an initial assessment of the disease.

- The routine checkups or follow-ups that do not require an actual visit to the hospital can also be carried out with WebRTC that saves the patient the hurdle of commuting to the hospital personally to meet the doctor.

- If a patient has a general question, for example, on the dosage or prescription such as "Will the *XYZ* medicine cause a problem with my other dose of *ABC* pills?" These brief communications can be easily done anywhere and any time with WebRTC.

- Due to the collaborative nature of WebRTC, multiple teams of doctors from different locations can also study a case together and share views on the best treatment.

A sample architecture depicting the role of WebRTC in a doctor-patient communication, where the WebRTC communication platform integrates with an online healthcare and hospital portal, is shown in the following screenshot:

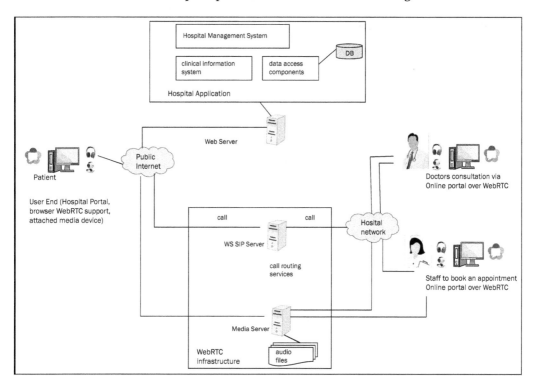

The sample screenshot of a proposed healthcare portal is shown as follows. This is the initial screen that depicts a portal for patients to find doctors online that they think can best solve their ailments. The details of doctors are categorized as per their departments and specialities, so that patients can themselves easily navigate through to find the doctor they want to be treated by.

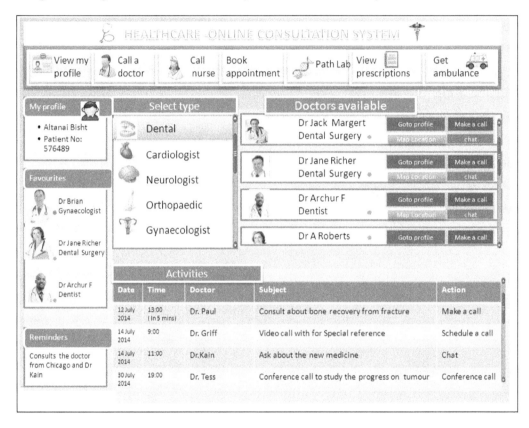

The following screenshot shows a video call in action between a patient and a doctor:

Since health is a vital subject, it is axiomatic that patients are serious about every call and would not react calmly to a long waiting music, complex IVR menu, or a machine response to their queries. It is hence necessary to build a special program logic to provide immediate human support to any of the patient concerns. However, due to workforce limitations from the hospital's end, it is not a practical solution. Meeting this challenge will be tough since the doctors do not have a direct reachable number and they cannot be present near the hospital computer/phone system all day long. By delivering the call through browsers, it can land directly on their phone, PC, or tablet. This aids in reachability.

Financial services

Financial services, which are mostly of the **Business to Consumer (B2C)** type in nature, consist of online trading, banking, insurance claims, and so on. There are many instances when a secure form of communication is required between a bank and a user. In present times, these are made using a normal GSM/UMTS phone call through mobile phones. WebRTC can simplify communication by enabling users to connect directly through their desktop, mobile, or kiosk browsers. A few relative use cases are highlighted in the following sections; these include communication between a bank agent and a customer regarding loans and offers, communication between an insurance agent and a customer regarding a refund, or communication from a distressed user at the ATM to the bank to report wrong withdrawal of money.

Communication with financial services

The concept of net banking has become very popular in the last decade as it simplifies fund transfer, checking account transactions, and going through the latest offers from the bank. Consider the situation when the user logs in to his net banking account; a financial agent connects with him over the call to assist in reviewing new loan policies and offers. This agent-to-customer communication has many advantages. An agent can discuss new benefits and policies face-to-face with the customer. This way, a user can direct his queries to the bank representative directly without the need of visiting the bank. For extra safety there are many state-of-the-art face recognition systems that can recognize a customer's identity through face and voice recognition. This goal is realized with WebRTC that enables agent-user communication to be embedded right inside the web page with many extra features. Of course end users will need to have access to a well-organized personal document repository that can be used to support faster and more precise communications with the financial enterprise,

A sample workflow that uses WebRTC to connect to a financial adviser is described in this section. In the web navigation sessions, the customer accesses the website and communicates with the customer service or specialized financial advisers on their device of choice. The web page will display a customer-specific directory that will offer all of the unique points of contact for various services such as opening a new account, applying for loans, requesting a credit card, and other such tasks. This directory would include the branch, customer service, special advisers, loan officers, insurance specialists, and so on. A click-to-call button alongside every unit/department is displayed that lets users directly call a bank representative on any matter.

A simplified customer-and-bank agent call scenario regarding opening a new bank account is shown in the following screenshot. The customer has queries between different types of account that she is able to resolve directly from the agent on the bank's website itself without having to make a call from a mobile, write chains of e-mails, or meet the agent personally.

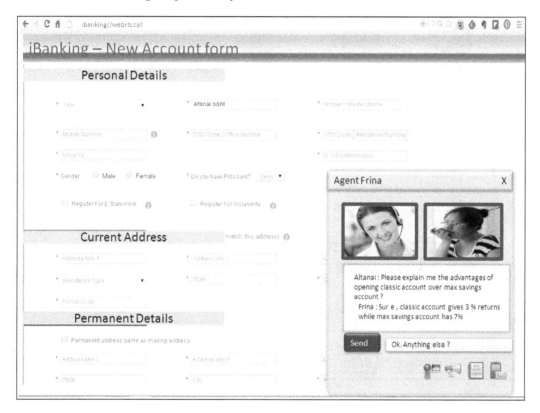

The banking software is mostly a part of **Software as a Service** (**SAAS**) with additional banking logic as required; also, a CRM system is built within it. A simple architecture representing a banking portal, core banking system, and WebRTC components in one is shown as follows:

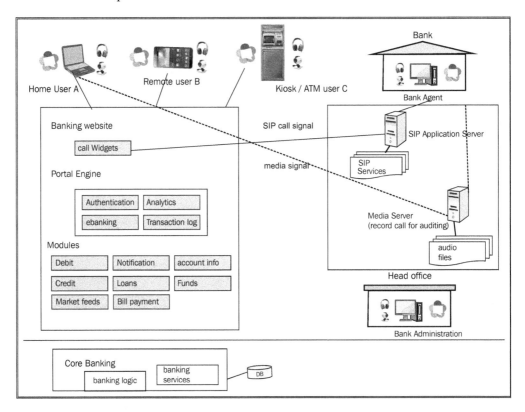

The preceding screenshot is of a very high-level view and must be further refined by adding logic to various entities such as analytics, the authorization engine, and others.

Insurance claims

The advancing digital economy allows users to invest in various short-term and long-term benefits. This may be in the form of loans, or new investment schemes such as fixed deposit, recurring deposits, or even insurance.

In present times, when a user logs in to his online insurance website, the details of the available insurance plan and other policies, schemes, and offers are displayed. Users have the option of filling up forms to apply for any scheme online or view their own insurance status.

However, the users might have instant questions and would need clarification about certain points mentioned in the terms and conditions, or might want to alter a certain clause. In the later stages, when the request for insurance funds reaches an insurance agent, the agent too would want to clarify certain things from the user before sanctioning the funds. The existing click-to-call features on banking sites are not actually click-to-call in essence. They merely ask for numbers from users to make a call on. The users' attention diverges from the content on the website to the mobile phone awaiting a call. The proposed WebRTC-enriched online insurance system aims to eliminate these communication hiccups in the existing system.

Consider an example where the information needed by an insurance company after a minor accident is rapid and there is automatic access to emergency assistance. An automotive insurance claim after an accident will be processed by the end user through the use of WebRTC, instead of using third-party services such as e-mail clients, telephonic conversations, fax, letters, and others. In the case of a car accident, there are two categories of insurance that can be obtained; health insurance and automotive insurance. The following screenshot depicts the communication links between various endpoints involved in insurance through a WebRTC-enriched online insurance system for auto motives:

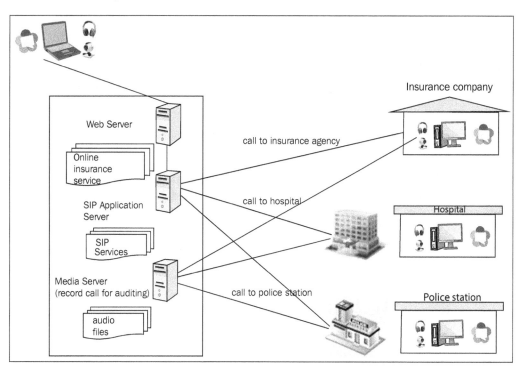

The application touch points are **insurance agency** for reporting the insurance claim; **hospital** to get the medical reports and for the verification of injuries and the amount spent on the treatment; and **police station** to report the accident and property damage of. Through WebRTC-based communication systems, the parties can engage in conference calls and finish the verification in minutes; this would otherwise take a number of days to complete. The documents could be easily exchanged between parties and the majority of the manual form-filling process could be automated through a single unified system. As mentioned earlier, the service could be standalone on a simple WebSocket signaling protocol or could be integrated with SIP for connecting with other communication endpoints such as PSTN, GSM, and others, thus meeting the open standard specifications.

Calling from the ATM

The process of reporting the loss of a credit/debit card, enquiries regarding automatic deductions from the account, or the generation of a new PIN to unlock a blocked account are often sudden and encountered while at the ATM. The process of contacting the bank and solving the problem is not only long but also complex, as the users have to first navigate through the intense IVR system and then authenticate themselves through a set of numerous questions. Also, the current system is dependent on mobile device for any communication with the bank. This is far from the ideal in terms of customer satisfaction. With WebRTC-based communication, customers can communicate with anyone within the financial services enterprise from a web browser in an ATM itself, all with the click of a button. The quality of services for handling customer concerns will improve drastically.

Remote management

Besides the obvious applications, WebRTC can play a significant role in other spheres such as security, remote device management, and gaming. Here, remote management refers to the act of monitoring or controlling the activities of connected computer systems. The WebRTC solution is for anyone who needs hassle-free remote access, including parents, technicians, engineers, IT consultants, managers, and system administrators. Users can control remote computers from WebRTC browsers on Windows, Mac, or Linux and even through mobile browsers on android. They can use calls or connect via Instant Messaging to chat, send, and receive files; get remote system information and session statistics; and work behind firewalls, proxies, and NAT.

Surveillance

The use case involving surveillance recording to be sent as a stream through WebRTC media API is a low-cost and effective solution to monitor a remote location without installing any hardware or software other than a desktop with attached camera. This section describes how WebRTC's feature-rich communication suite can be extended to security-based use cases. WebRTC allows media capture from remote devices to local devices. If automated for various intervals with media permission granted to the website beforehand, a WebRTC-enabled browser can send a call to the inspecting user's browser at that specified time. This enables the local user to get a view from the remote IP camera and microphone. The WebRTC site must be under the HTTPS protocol to achieve this. A sample view form of the Administrator web page is shown as follows. The local media captures taken from four locations are being transmitted to the surveillance web page in real time. There is a provision to sound an alarm as and when one detects an unusual activity on the screen. Also, the media captures from the surveillance locations are being recorded to be monitored at a later stage.

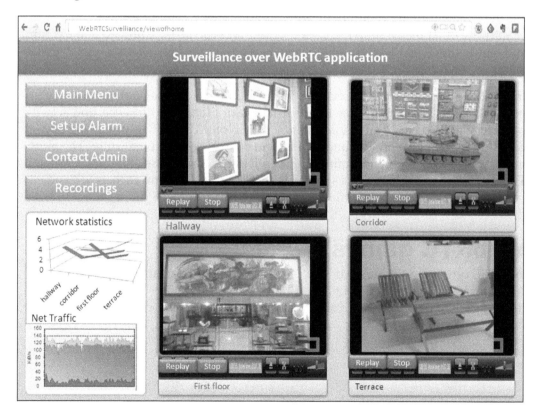

Also, there is a motion-sensor software implemented in JavaScript that triggers an event as soon as the camera detects an activity. Events such as these can be programmed to send WebRTC calls to users for their inspection. Their alarm system, thermostat, and security cameras are enabled to work together and send a WebRTC call to the owner who can access the information (audio, video, data, or images). In the future, we may see smarter WebRTC applications where every automobile and home may have a computer component containing call features. Owners or security officials should be able to track the activity around in the area just by switching on the WebRTC media stream and remotely control the operations by what they see.

Managing the connected device

An enterprise computer system (that is, desktops on various cubicles) is often managed by an admin department responsible for tracking the health of these systems, ensure that it is virus-free and has optimum network speed to connect to the Internet, and so on. Not only enterprises, but a house owner too would like to control his connected devices from one place. The desktop-sharing feature of WebRTC enables this and also lets the remote user to communicate with the admin user without using any hardware or software other than a simple browser. Consumers can achieve unified home control and monitoring. The WebRTC API that enables remote desktop sharing is provided at `https://developer.chrome.com/extensions/desktopCapture`.

Innovation in the automation section will eventually lead to devices operated by network-based intelligence. The inputs from a user's location, Presence, and activity patterns will help create an environment wherein services such as unlocking the car, turning the lights on/off, and others, will be managed automatically. The most important component in designing such services is data capture and data sharing. The WebRTC integrated with a standards signaling mechanism, such as SIP and implying the security specifications, can make both ends meet.

WebRTC games

WebRTC can play a pivotal role in fun- and entertainment-centric business. A few targeted factors from gaming and movies-based services areas that can directly benefit from WebRTC calls, Presence, and chat are described in the upcoming sections.

Two-player games

Using the power of web-based real-time communication, the gaming server allows the game players to engage in a video conference along with an ongoing game; not only can they see, but they can also hear each other's voice, which boosts interactivity. The players of a team can use WebRTC-based audio call to instruct each other for a specific command or action within a game unlike the way a live chat was employed earlier. This saves the user from diverting their attention from the game screen to chat screen as WebRTC can function in the background with the game being played on the foreground of the screen.

A sample two-party game could be any board game such as checkers, chess, and others. The following screenshot shows a two-party chess game with the WebRTC technology:

A WebRTC two-point call is a relatively simple process due to its peer-to-peer nature. However, a multiparty call involves media relay and multiple remote screen views. This is described in the upcoming section.

Multiplayer games

A sample multiparty game could either be a war game, racing game, or a strategy game such as poker. The online game played by multiple players could be coupled with WebRTC-based chat, call, and Presence services. The following screenshot represents a WebRTC SIP-based game. The users participating in the game are able to chat alongside the play area. Note that the SIP session is active for group chat till the period when the game is active.

The following screenshot represents another WebRTC-based game. The users participating in the game share their video streams with other members so that each member can view other members in real time.

After exploring WebRTC application for games, we will proceed toward applying a WebRTC communication channel and endpoint to TV-based services.

TV experience with WebRTC

WebRTC has been applied in the basic communication sector with overwhelming results. However, there the capability to stream media is not just limited to communication; it can be applied to stream multimedia content from the server as well. This section describes the application of WebRTC in IPTV, VOD, and online FM (audio from Radio stations online). All this is possible without the need to download plugins or any additional installations of third-party products. Also, with the inclusion of the <video> element in HTML5, there is no requirement for external handles to display and play the multimedia content on the web page.

Live broadcasting

The multimedia content could be directly streamed to the server right after recording from the field. An instance of the first use case could be live broadcasting of FIFA on a web page directly from the stadium. In the case of a two-way communication channel, the viewers can also stream their local camera captures with other viewers of the game in real time, and have a group chat via the WebRTC DataChannel API too.

For realizing the proposed solution, there is a requirement for a real-time encoder that records the media from the playground and sends it to the media server, which further relays it to various WebRTC viewers after transcoding to VP8 and encrypting it via DTLS/SRTP routed through NAT traversal techniques.

A sample screenshot of a live match played on WebRTC media APIs along with an interactive group chat between viewers is depicted as follows:

To draw more clarity on the process of transmitting live video feed on WebRTC, we will study the main solution components briefly. The signaling server negotiates the audio and video codecs through SDP. The media engine responsible for transcoding the streams to the requested codecs and encrypting them are brought into action. The user only needs to call the operator's SIP address through their SIP phone or WebRTC browser and get the content streamed to your client. Additionally, using WebRTC DataChannel APIs, there may be multiple user conferencing in any permutation and combination of text, audio, or video.

IPTV integration and streaming

Using the WebRTC browser page as a TV to watch the channels is as lucrative to viewers as TV channel operators. The multimedia content is streamed from a server that is connected to an IPTV content provider's network or video content repository.

IPTV refers to streaming of TV channels over IP protocol that can be viewed from smart TV's or from web-based interfaces. The content is delivered through an IPTV Server and the session exists between the user's WebRTC endpoint and SIP Server just as a normal SIP call-based session.

VoD is also a service aligned to IPTV. While the content broadcasted on the IPTV service is independent of the user's control, VoD lets the user to directly decide on what to watch now as they can request for any particular video or movie to be streamed to their account.

An architectural representation of the proposed application is shown as follows:

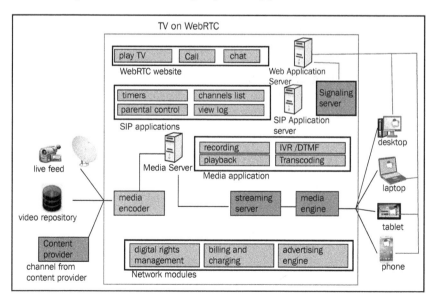

Let's go over the different components and their interaction with each other for a WebRTC SIP-based IPTV and VoD infrastructure as follows:

- **Media Source**: Media Source can either be a live feed or a video from the media repository; it can even be a live channel from the content provider.

- **WebRTC user client**: This is where the SIP stack is provided in JavaScript code and the media are exchanged via WebRTC browser APIs. The client is designed for WebRTC-compatible browsers that fit different devices such as desktops, laptops, tablets, smartphones, and others.

- **Signaling server**: A signaling server is responsible for acting as a proxy agent between the SIP infrastructure and WebRTC endpoints. It also converts the SIP over WebSocket to plain SIP, understandable by back network.

- **Media engine**: A media engine is the intermediary between the WebRTC SIP server that supports transcoding DTLS-SRTP streams to normal RTP and vice versa, and browser APIs.

- **Media transcoder**: A media transcoder role is for intercodec conversion so that a streamed video can be played over RTP to a recipient. A user should be able to watch the session not only on his WebRTC browser, but also on legacy SIP phones' software.

- **SIP Application Server**: The logic to connect media streams for applications, such as IPTV or VoD, is embedded in the SIP application that often acts as the end point for a call. The user calls up the SIP address depending on the content they want to watch. The call is made between the user and the SIP Server. Once a subscriber calls up at the IPTC service module in the SIP Application Server, the Server inspects the SDP body of the `INVITE` message to figure out the device's capability that includes a list of supported audio and video codecs, platforms, routes, ports, and so on. It uses this information to stream the video content directly from the media repository or source to the client by setting up a media path. When the call is ended, the application server needs to tear down the streaming session, release resources, and make the server ready for a new session.

Streaming movies among peers

The multimedia content could be streamed from a server that is connected to a video source. An instance of the second use case could be a group of users playing multimedia content in a synchronized way, such as five friends watching a movie streaming from a single user's desktop.

The following screenshot shows multiple users watching a movie streamed over WebRTC TV:

This is multipoint, one-to-many video conferencing in action. The first step in this process is when the client-side broadcaster sends out a single media stream to the server. The network-signaling server makes sure that the media stream is headed in the right direction, and then the network media server enables all the participants to have an open, active session. The web client can itself modify the media features such as resolution, frame rate, and bit rate. A requirement for real-time streaming services is that the media should be in multiresolution and bandwidth-adaptive streaming formats.

 Note that the issues of piracy and digital rights management are meant to be addressed separately and are not included within the context of this book.

Interfacing services

WebRTC-based communication technologies are very customizable in nature and can fit into any communication scenario. With a JavaScript-based signaling stack and a peer-to-peer media connection, WebRTC enables users to get connected like never before. Besides the many kinds of use cases mentioned in the book, there are thousands of more ideas that need the creative adoption of WebRTC to boost their efficiency such as call-to-connect Governance and e-learning with WebRTC-based classes. In this section, we shall cover WebRTC's application in e-learning (distant education through online classrooms) and e-governance (expressing concerns over a subject directly to government officials in a real-time multiconference session).

WebRTC for e-learning

This application of WebRTC is for the **Learning Management System** (**LMS**) that includes e-portfolios, online open course, smart education, and others. More students and educators are interacting online every day, but currently this is primarily using standard web page- and document-based user interfaces. The only video and audio conferencing options commonly available to educators and students today are those using proprietary systems. Each of these solutions require additional software and often a completely standalone application to be installed. The setup time to establish each of these calls is usually quite high, and some of these solutions also require a licensing fee or setup cost. Therefore, it is high time that an open standard-based, easy e-learning solution that does not require any setup software, plugin, or installation comes about. The following diagram depicts WebRTC in e-learning:

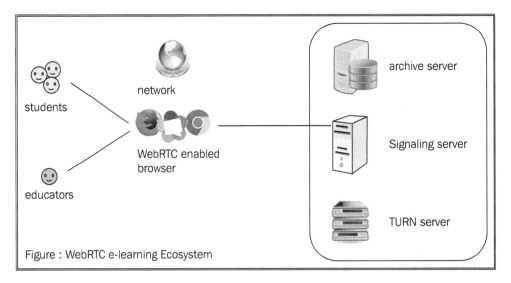

Figure : WebRTC e-learning Ecosystem

WebRTC helps to consolidate services hosted across different domains such as Presence, Instant Messaging, audio, video, and web conferencing, and to deliver an IT and educational application to the end user. This application can create a new learning platform that will allow classroom collaboration at any time with participants anywhere. The interactivity and ease of use of the interfacing service determine its adoption in use. It will help students to take up online courses, interact with professors of different universities, and communicate with foreign classrooms in an interactive and easy way.

The general architecture for this type of application or platform consists of seven key elements that work together to deliver an overall experience:

- **Educators**: This is the account for educators and takes care of the payment of fees

- **Students**: This is the account for registering for a subject course and fee submissions

- **WebRTC capable browsers**: Google Chrome and Mozilla Firefox browsers now support the draft, WebRTC 1.0

- **WebRTC e-learning application**: These platforms provide the perfect launch pad for connecting users via WebRTC

- **Signaling server**: This can be either be the SIP-based Kamailio or the non-SIP-based Node.js

- **TURN server**: This is used for media relay

- **Archive server**: This is used to store copies of the course or the education material

While introducing WebRTC into an e-learning environment, there are issues that are commonly faced, such as restrictive network policies and outdated browsers. While upgrading the browsers is in the hands of the user, the network control policies are not. An organizational network system may block ports, protocol, or sites from reaching the end user. These factors can cause problems in smooth WebRTC communication. The solution to these problems is to use a public network while making WebRTC calls or set up a NAT traversal through effective TURN/STUN server configuration.

The benefits of the ease of use and removal of barriers for setting up an audio or video call or screen-sharing session cannot be underestimated. This will drive more interpersonal interaction between educators and students, among students themselves, and even among educators themselves.

The distributed peer-to-peer nature of WebRTC can also lead to some significant network and infrastructure cost reductions.

WebRTC for e-governance

The digital revolution has raised the standards almost everywhere for information, communication, and electronics. The Government is also rapidly employing IT to upgrade its mode of communication in various countries. In the age of e-governance, it should be no surprise if the WebRTC browser's CONNECT functionality is used to reach out to any particular government official regarding the state of affairs in their designated department or area. This not only leads to more transparency in public sector information sharing, but also lets us establish our **Right to Information** (**RTI**) in a better way by directly communicating with the concerned authorities. The WebRTC platform with the gateway to the PSTN and UMTS world can play an important role in such a system as it can send information and media over IP networks to the telecom operator's network and vice-versa. So, if a party is not online over WebRTC web application, they can still take calls and join the communication.

Summary

After the digital revolution, general inhibitions about Internet technologies and insecurity around it were relieved. Now, every industry fragment, from hospitals to banks, is investing in web technologies to meet their goals while enhancing their user experience. The plugin-free communication technology is open to innovators and entrepreneurs to integrate and develop new use cases.

In this chapter, we saw how WebRTC can be used by doctors, teachers, government officers, gamers, insurance agents, and many more. We also saw how new applications, such as movie streaming, games, and others, can be built using WebRTC as the base communication technology. Due to its ease of use and extremely customizable format, it is as useful for small- and medium-sized business organizations as it is for enterprises.

The age of web communication is already here and many service providers and other OTT player companies are trying to cash in in the IP-based communication technologies by developing their own extensions, plugins, or protocols, to support it. Some are so closed that the protocols are supported only through their closed source hardware/software while others have developed their own layers over existing open source communication protocols as SIP.

In this confusion, WebRTC is a breath of fresh air for developers who are trying to build a unified communication platform that meets open standards and is backward-compatible as well as extensible for future needs.

Index

Symbols

A

B

C

D

Data Access Objects (DAO) 223
databases
  about 202
  Oracle 202
  PostgreSQL 202
DataChannel function 18
Data Tier, Multitier architecture 196
dating sites
  anonymous call 323, 324
  chat 323, 324
design, WebRTC client 197
development environment, Android OS
  URL 300
Domain Name Server (DNS) 87
Do Not Disturb (DND) 256
Dual Tone Multi Frequency (DTMF) 317

E

Eclipse WTP
  URL 202
Enterprise Resource Planning (ERP) 311
Entity Relationship (ER) model 200
environment setup, WebRTC web project
  about 201
  databases 202, 203
  IDE, with Java Enterprise Edition (EE) 202
  Java Runtime Environment (JRE) 201
  JSP- / Servlet-based WebRTC web
    project 204
  Struts- / Hibernate-based WebRTC web
    project 213
  web application infrastructure 204
  web application server 203
ER diagram, WebRTC web application 200
Evolved Node B (eNodeB) 118
existing WebRTC setup, limitations
  about 74
  firewall issues 75
  media transcoding 75
  Network Address Translation (NAT)
    issues 75

eXtensible Messaging and Presence Protocol
  (XMPP) 9

F

Field Force Management (FFM) 311
financial services
  about 334
  calling, from ATM 338
  communicating with 334, 336
  insurance claims 336-338
firewall 75
FOKUS Home Subscriber Server
  (FHoSS) 94
Forward Call Indicators (FCI) 146
FreeSWITCH Media Server
  about 99
  configuring 101, 102
  installing 99-101
FreeSWITCH media services
  using 103-108

G

Gateway GPRS Support Node (GGSN) 116
General Packet Radio Services (GPRS) 116
Geolocation class 198
Geolocation module 232-236
Geolocation, web application
  about 188-190
  Cell Tower Triangulation 188
  GPS 188
  IP Geolocation 188
  Wi-Fi positioning 188
getUserMedia 10-12
Global System for Mobile Communications
  Association (GSMA)
  URL 244
Graphical User Interface (GUI) 46

H

HandlerAdapter interface 224
HandlerInterceptor interface 224
HandlerMapping interface 224

Thank you for buying
WebRTC Integrator's Guide

About Packt Publishing

Packt, pronounced 'packed', published its first book "*Mastering phpMyAdmin for Effective MySQL Management*" in April 2004 and subsequently continued to specialize in publishing highly focused books on specific technologies and solutions.

Our books and publications share the experiences of your fellow IT professionals in adapting and customizing today's systems, applications, and frameworks. Our solution-based books give you the knowledge and power to customize the software and technologies you're using to get the job done. Packt books are more specific and less general than the IT books you have seen in the past. Our unique business model allows us to bring you more focused information, giving you more of what you need to know, and less of what you don't.

Packt is a modern, yet unique publishing company, which focuses on producing quality, cutting-edge books for communities of developers, administrators, and newbies alike. For more information, please visit our website: www.packtpub.com.

About Packt Open Source

In 2010, Packt launched two new brands, Packt Open Source and Packt Enterprise, in order to continue its focus on specialization. This book is part of the Packt Open Source brand, home to books published on software built around Open Source licenses, and offering information to anybody from advanced developers to budding web designers. The Open Source brand also runs Packt's Open Source Royalty Scheme, by which Packt gives a royalty to each Open Source project about whose software a book is sold.

Writing for Packt

We welcome all inquiries from people who are interested in authoring. Book proposals should be sent to author@packtpub.com. If your book idea is still at an early stage and you would like to discuss it first before writing a formal book proposal, contact us; one of our commissioning editors will get in touch with you.

We're not just looking for published authors; if you have strong technical skills but no writing experience, our experienced editors can help you develop a writing career, or simply get some additional reward for your expertise.

WebRTC Blueprints

ISBN: 978-1-78398-310-0   Paperback: 176 pages

Develop your very own media applications and
services using WebRTC

1. Create interactive web applications
   using WebRTC.

2. Get introduced to advanced technologies
   such as WebSocket and Erlang.

3. Develop your own secure web applications
   and services with practical projects.

Getting Started with WebRTC

ISBN: 978-1-78216-630-6   Paperback: 114 pages

Explore WebRTC for real-time peer-to-peer
communication

1. Set up video calls easily with a low bandwidth
   audio-only option using WebRTC.

2. Extend your application using real-time
   text-based chat, and collaborate easily by
   adding real-time drag-and-drop file sharing.

3. Create your own fully working WebRTC
   application in minutes.

Please check **www.PacktPub.com** for information on our titles

Microsoft Lync 2013 Unified Communications: From Telephony to Real-time Communication in the Digital Age

ISBN: 978-1-84968-506-1   Paperback: 224 pages

Complete coverage of all topics for a unified communications strategy

1. A real business case and example project showing you how you can optimize costs and improve your competitive advantage with a Unified Communications project.

2. The book combines both business and the latest relevant technical information so it is a great reference for business stakeholders, IT decision makers, and UC technical experts.

Twilio Cookbook
Second Edition

ISBN: 978-1-78355-065-4   Paperback: 334 pages

Over 70 easy-to-follow recipes, from exploring the key features of Twilio to building advanced telephony apps

1. Updated to include picture messaging, call queuing, and Twilio Client; all recommended by Twilio.

2. The only book that teaches you how to set up your own conference calling system or how to build a PBX for your company.

3. Each recipe is a carefully organized sequence of instructions to complete the task as efficiently as possible.

Please check **www.PacktPub.com** for information on our titles

www.ingramcontent.com/pod-product-compliance
Lightning Source LLC
Chambersburg PA
CBHW062048050326
40690CB00016B/3014